SPORT AND PE

A COMPLETE GUIDE TO

GCSE

SECOND EDITION

BARRY HODGSON

Hodder & Stoughton

A MEMBER OF THE HODDER HEADLINE GROUP

To my wife Jane, for her continuing support.

Every effort has been made to trace the copyright holders of material reproduced in this book. Any rights omitted from the acknowledgements here or in the text will be added for subsequent printings following notice to the publisher.

Orders: please contact Bookpoint Ltd, 39 Milton Park, Abingdon, Oxon OX14 4TD. Telephone: (44) 01235 400414, Fax: (44) 01235 400454. Lines are open from 9.00–6.00, Monday to Saturday, with a 24 hour message answering service. Email address: orders@bookpoint.co.uk

A catalogue record for this title is available from The British Library

ISBN 0 340 802944

Second edition 2001

First published 1998
Impression number   10   9   8   7   6   5   4   3   2   1
Year   2004   2003   2002   2001   2006   2005

Typeset by Pantek Arts Ltd, Maidstone, Kent.
Printed in Italy for Hodder & Stoughton Educational, a division of Hodder Headline Plc, 338 Euston Road, London NW1 3BH.

Contents

Foreword

This new edition of *Sport and PE: A Complete Guide to GCSE* has been published to coincide with the introduction of new syllabuses introduced by all examination boards for students starting on GCSE PE and Games courses in September 2001.

The book has been written making extensive use of the syllabuses and sample material produced by all examination boards. Although all the syllabuses are now available on the internet and in booklets from the examination boards, I would like to take this opportunity to thank the staff at Edexcel, Oxford and Cambridge and RSA Examinations (OCR), Assessment and Qualifications Alliance (SEG and NEAB), Welsh Joint Education Committee (WJEC), Northern Ireland Council for Curriculum Examinations and Assessment (CCEA), and the Scottish Qualifications Authority for providing me with draft information in advance of publication and their helpful responses to my requests.

The layout of the book is similar to the first edition, being divided into various sections and closely aligned to all examination syllabus in structure and content, making it suitable for all GCSE physical education and games syllabuses, both full and short courses. Throughout the book there are many practical tasks which help students consolidate their learning of theory through practical activities. Every chapter now has an extensive range of questions, which are suitable for all students, ranging from multiple choice questions, to a variety of examination type questions of graded difficulty.

The accompanying teachers' pack has revision checklists, practical worksheets for use in class and for homework, and more questions of varying difficulty enabling students of all abilities to test their knowledge and understanding of the subject.

Over 100,000 students took GCSE physical education in the 2000 examinations, and for many of these students it was their best subject, and probably their favourite subject. I hope this second edition proves useful to all those students who take GCSE PE and Games in the future, and that physical education continues to be their favourite subject. It is still mine!

Barry Hodgson

Acknowledgements

The author would like to thank the following organisations for the information they have provided:
AQA – Assessment and Qualifications Alliance; Cyd-Bwyllgor Addysg Cymru (The Welsh Joint Education
Committee); Edexcel Foundation; OCR – Oxford and Cambridge and R.S.A.; the English Sports Council; the
Central Council for Physical Recreation; Youth Sport Trust; National Coaching Foundation; Department for
Education and Employment.

The publishers would like to thank the following for permission to reproduce copyright images and
material (page numbers given):
Action Images 48, 266, 74 (bottom), 76; Bongarts 88, 109, 118, 148, 167, 200, 201, 246; Pressesports 0;
Action Plus 0 (right); Chris Barry 58 (bottom); Glyn Kirk 58 (top), 61, 70, 77, 94, 121, 145, 160, 198
(right and left), 223, 241, 249, 253; Steve Bardens 2, 91, 74 (top), (bottom); R. Francis; Neil Tingle (top),
(top and bottom); Peter Tarry 75, 206 (top); A. Fox; J. Ravilious; **AKG** John Hios; Erich Lessing; **Alan
Edwards** 1, 36, 38, 262, 263, 278, 51, 54; (both), (top), (bottom), (bottom), 55, 67, 73, 75, 76, 93 (top
and bottom), 92, 118, 119, 124, 125, 129, 168, 169, 159 (top), 179, 191 (both), 242, 245, 245, 256,
281, 288, 285; **All Sport** John Gichigi; **Associated Press** 114, 175, 204, 210, 219, 137, 240; **AVS**,
Loughborough University 0, 0; **BAGA Marketing Ltd** 581 (bottom) **BBC** 227; **British Olympic
Association** 194, 146, 158, 238; **Hulton Deutsch Collection Limited** 165, 201 (bottom), 202, 237,
239; **Hulton Getty**; **Julian L. Gothard** (GMC) 1997, 135, 265, 144; **Life File**, Andrew Ward 271; Joseph
Green 211; Barry Mayes; Xavier Catalan 254; **London Aerial Photo Library**; **Mary Evans Picture
Library** 207, 233; **Mike Dawson** 209; **National Asthma Campaign** 272; **National Coaching
Foundation** 80; **PA News** 152 (left), Rebecca Naden 211; **Raymonds press agency**, Leicester City
Football Club 155; **Science Photo Library** 37, 44, 277; **Sheffield City Council** Andy Barker 140; **Sports
Colleges** 171; **The Back-Up Trust** 188; **Youth Sport Trust** 186. New photos for the second edition
appear courtesy of Empics, Corbis and Duomo/Corbis and PA Photos.

Cover photograph by Telegraph Colour Library.

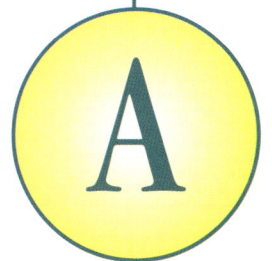

Body in Action

Skeletal System

The skeletal system is the framework of the human body. The skeletal system is made up of a range of different types of bones. The skeleton is held together by ligaments at the joints. It gives the human body its unique shape.

LEARNING OBJECTIVES

- functions of the skeletal system
- bones
- joints
- types of body movement

Functions of the skeletal system

PROTECTION

Many body parts are delicate and need to be protected from the knocks and bumps of everyday life. The most delicate part of the body is the brain, and this is surrounded by the skull. From the brain runs the spinal cord – a bundle of nerves running down the back of the body. This is enclosed by the vertebrae, which allow movement but at the same time prevent damage to the spinal cord.

The body also has many soft tissues: the heart and lungs are protected by the ribs. All of the ribs together are known as the rib cage.

SUPPORT

The skeleton gives the body its shape. Muscles are mainly attached to the bones on the outside of the body, while attached to the inside are vital organs.

MOVEMENT

The joints of the body where two or more bones come together allow movement. The types of bone and joint determine what kind of movement there can be.

BLOOD PRODUCTION

Red and white blood cells are produced in the bone marrow, which is a substance inside the larger bones of the body.

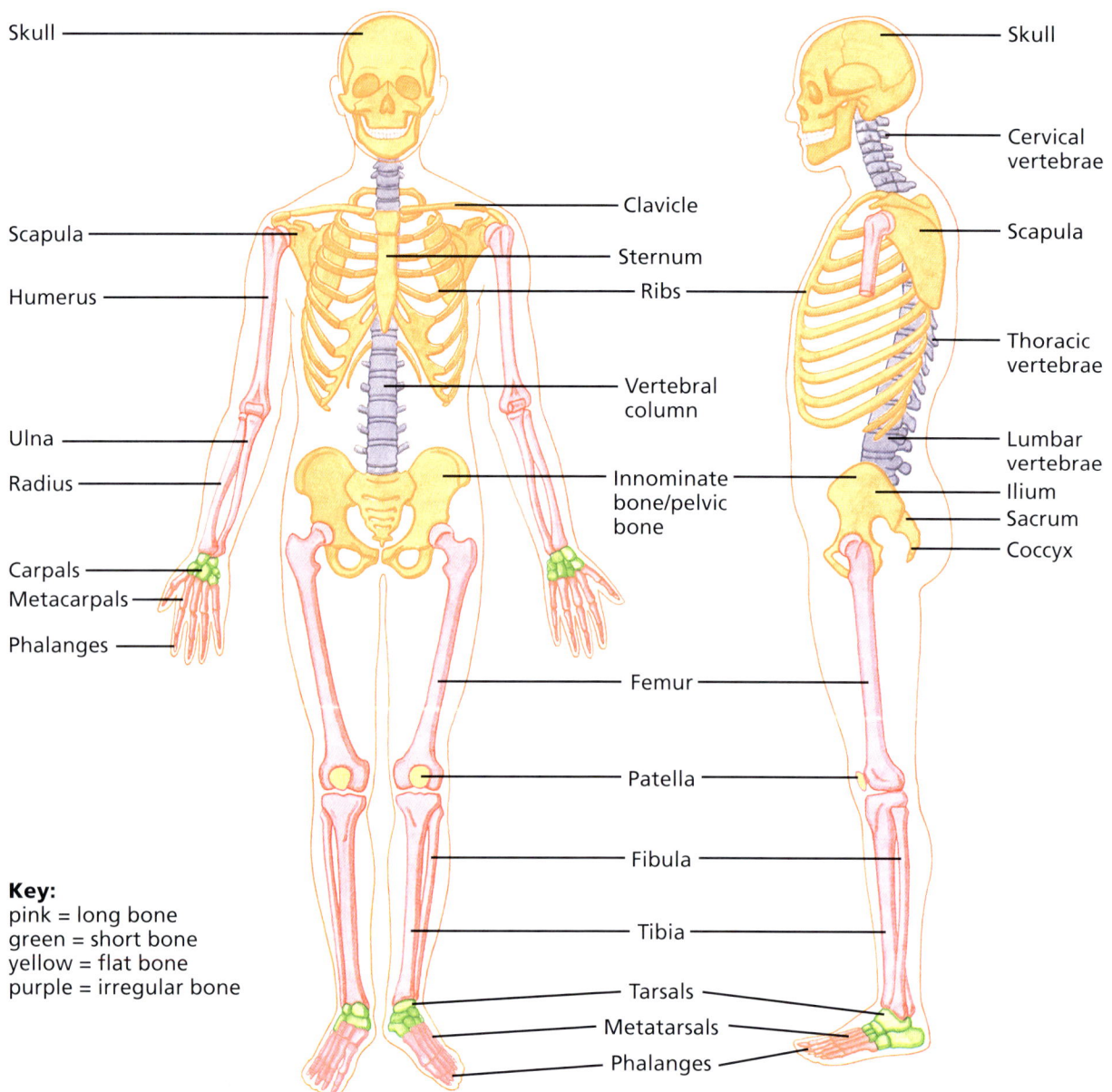

Skull

Scapula

Humerus

Ulna

Radius

Carpals
Metacarpals

Phalanges

Clavicle

Sternum

Ribs

Vertebral
column

Innominate
bone/pelvic
bone

Femur

Patella

Fibula

Tibia

Tarsals

Metatarsals

Phalanges

Skull

Cervical
vertebrae

Scapula

Thoracic
vertebrae

Lumbar
vertebrae

Ilium

Sacrum

Coccyx

Key:
pink = long bone
green = short bone
yellow = flat bone
purple = irregular bone

Front view of the skeleton

Side view of the skeleton

Bones

TYPES OF BONE

There are 206 bones in total. These are divided into four types:

- long
- short
- flat
- irregular.

Each type has a special function.

Long bones

These are the bones in legs, arms, ribs and collar bones. They are not solid bones but contain marrow in the centre. This structure enables them to be strong without being too heavy. The tibia, fibula, humerus and femur are examples of long bones.

With a partner measure the length of your femur, your radius bones and your height. With the rest of the class, decide if there is any relationship between height and the length of these bones.

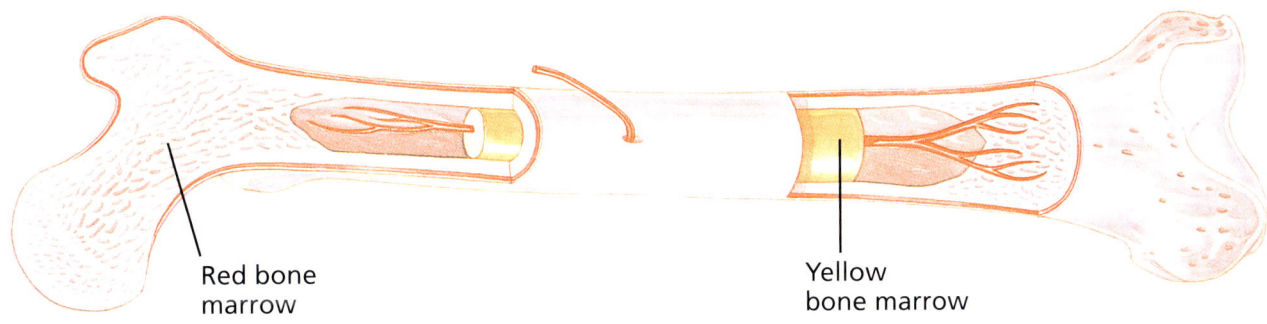

Red bone marrow

Yellow bone marrow

The femur is an example of a long bone

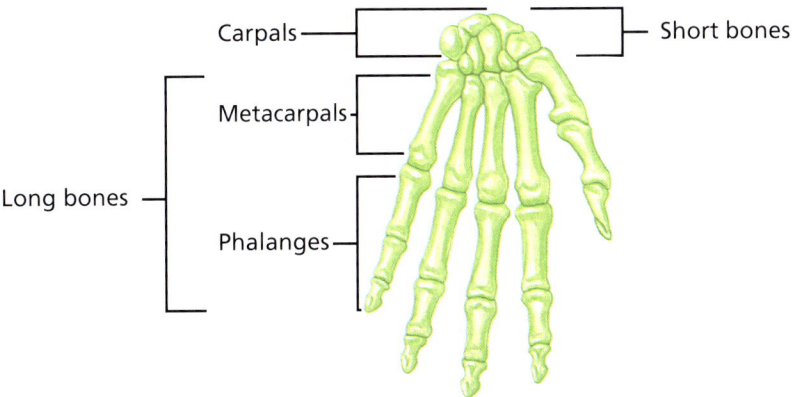

Carpals — Short bones

Metacarpals

Long bones

Phalanges

Short bones in the hand

Short bones

Found in the wrist and ankle, these are short and squat. They are spongy, with an outer layer of compact bone. This means that they are light and strong, necessary for the type of fine movement required at the wrist and ankle joints. The carpals in the wrist and tarsals in the feet are examples.

Test a partner on the main
bones in the arms and legs.

Flat bones

These are plate-like bones which form the skull. Also, the scapula and pelvis are composed of flat bone. The larger surface area is needed for protective purposes and attachment of a variety of muscles. The correct name for the skull is the cranium, which is an example of flat bone.

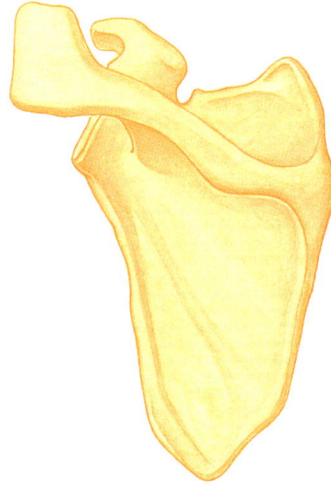

Flat bones – the scapula

Irregular bones

Vertebrae of the vertebral column and small bones in the face are classed as irregular bones. Similar to short bones, they are spongy inside with an outer layer of harder compact bone. The knee cap or patella is an example of irregular bone.

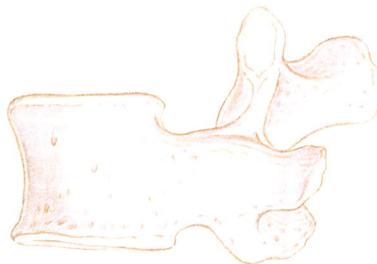

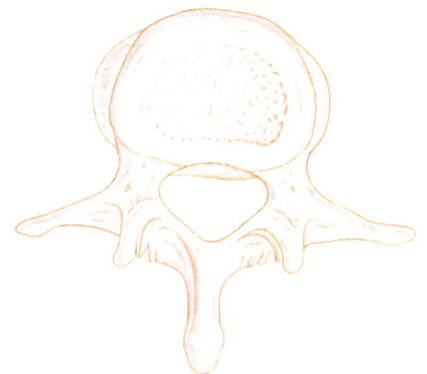

Irregular bones – the vertebrae

BONE GROWTH

Like any other part of the body, bone grows in length and thickness with time. The bones in young children are not as hard or rigid as in adults. The bone is formed from cartilage by a process known as **ossification**. With age, bones become harder and more rigid. In older people, bones can become brittle and break easily if a person has a bad fall.

There are two main parts to the skeleton:

- the **axial** – skull, rib cage and vertebral column
- the **appendicular** – shoulder and pelvic girdles, and attached limbs.

AXIAL SKELETON

Skull

This protects the brain. It consists of eight flat bones which fuse together over time.

Rib cage

This consists of 12 pairs of ribs. They join the vertebral column at the back, and at the front the sternum is the centre joint for seven pairs of ribs. Because of the way the ribs are joined, they form a type of cage around the heart and lungs, providing protection for the heart and a means of breathing (see Chapter 4).

Vertebral column

This is often referred to as the spine. It consists of 24 movable vertebrae and two groups of fused vertebrae at the lower end of the spine. The vertebral column allows considerable movement: leaning forwards and backwards and twisting movements. The vertebrae are in special groups for particular purposes.

APPENDICULAR SKELETON

Attached to the spine are the shoulder and pelvic girdles. These provide an attachment to the axial skeleton which is quite rigid, but attached to these girdles are the arms and legs which are free to move. Both of these girdles give a firm base of muscle attachment to the limbs.

See next page for a diagram of the axial and appendicular skeleton.

Feel both of the clavicles (collar bones). Do they feel the same? They might be slightly different if you have broken a collar bone in the past.

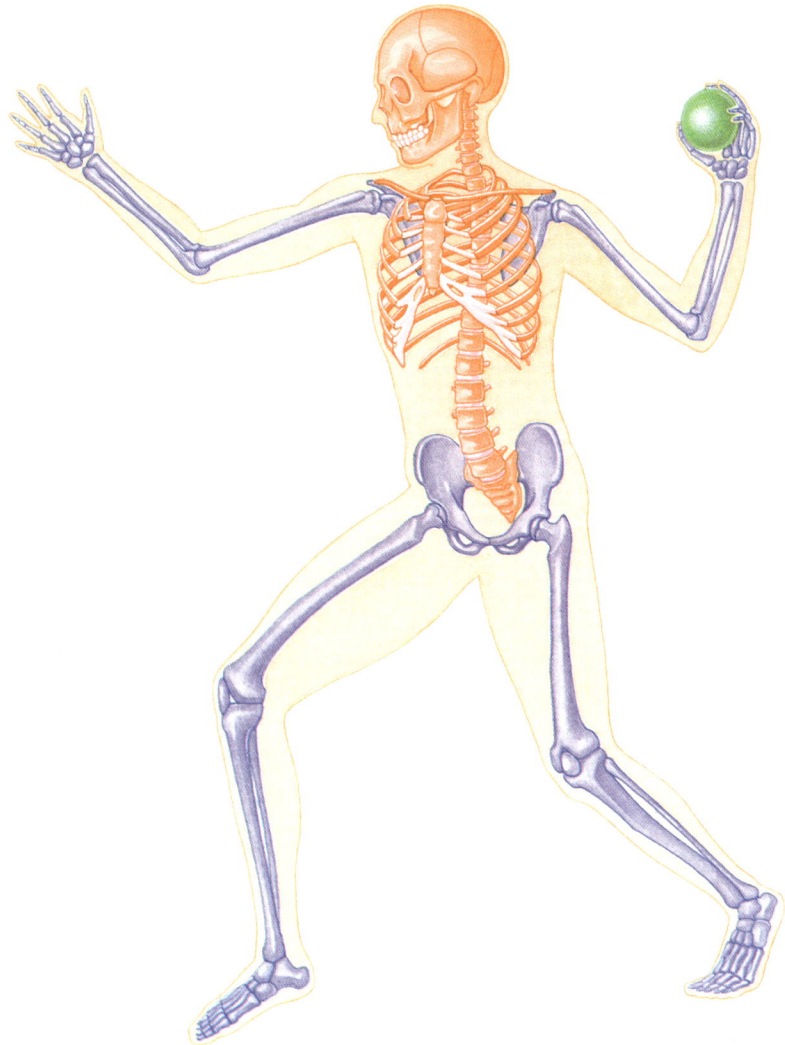

Key:
red = axial skeleton
blue = appendicular skeleton

Axial and appendicular skeleton

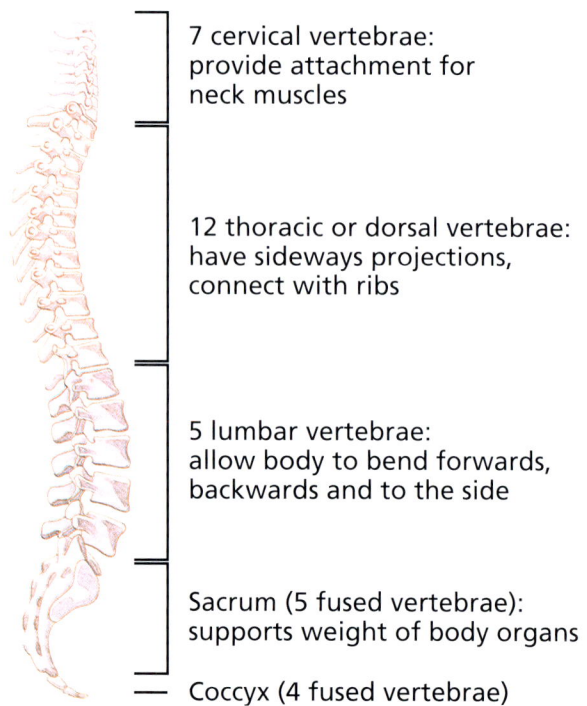

7 cervical vertebrae:
provide attachment for
neck muscles

12 thoracic or dorsal vertebrae:
have sideways projections,
connect with ribs

5 lumbar vertebrae:
allow body to bend forwards,
backwards and to the side

Sacrum (5 fused vertebrae):
supports weight of body organs

Spine

Coccyx (4 fused vertebrae)

Shoulder girdle

This is formed by the scapulus (shoulder blade) and the clavicle (collar bone):

- the shoulder girdle is attached to the vertebral column
- attached to the shoulder girdle are the arms
- the arms consist of a series of bones starting from the shoulder to the hands
- the humerus ends at the elbow joint, where the ulna and radius start
- these end at the wrist, where there are eight small bones, the carpals
- the hand has even smaller bones
- the metacarpals make up the palm, and 14 phalanges are found in the fingers.

Pelvic girdle

Because of its function to carry the body weight through the legs, it is much heavier than the shoulder girdle:

- the girdle is in two halves which are fused to the bottom of the spine at the sacrum. Attached to the pelvic girdle (hip girdle) are the legs
- the long single bone from the hip to the knee is the femur
- at the knee joint, the tibia and fibula are the bones of the lower leg
- the ankle consists of seven tarsals, five metatarsals and there are 14 phalanges in the toes.

Joints

Using both hands press gently on your sternum. Can you explain why there is some slight movement?

There are three classifications of joint:

1. **fibrous** – there is no joint cavity or movement in these joints, but the bones are held together by fibrous tissue. Examples of these are in the skull and pelvis
2. **cartilaginous** – although linked by cartilage, there is some slight movement. There is no joint cavity. Examples of these are between the vertebrae, and also between ribs and sternum
3. **synovial joints** – joints which allow movement are synovial joints, and there are many different types.

Bone   Fibrous tissue

Joint

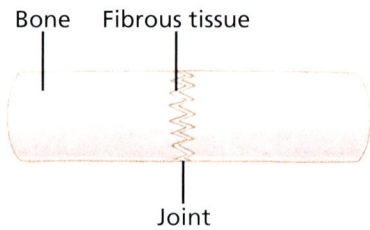

Fibrous joint

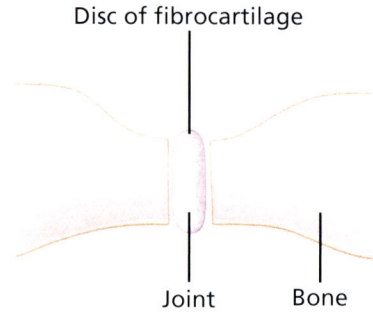

Disc of fibrocartilage

Joint   Bone

Cartilaginous joint

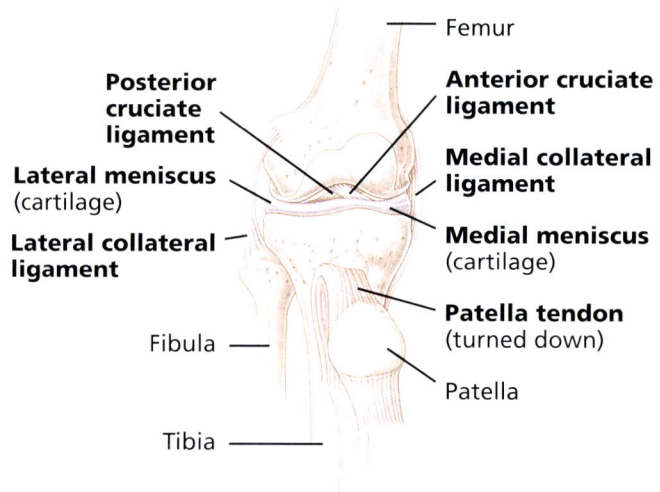

Femur

Posterior
cruciate
ligament

**Anterior cruciate
ligament**

Lateral meniscus
(cartilage)

**Medial collateral
ligament**

**Lateral collateral
ligament**

Medial meniscus
(cartilage)

Patella tendon
(turned down)

Fibula

Patella

Tibia

**Cross section of cartilage and
ligaments in the knee**

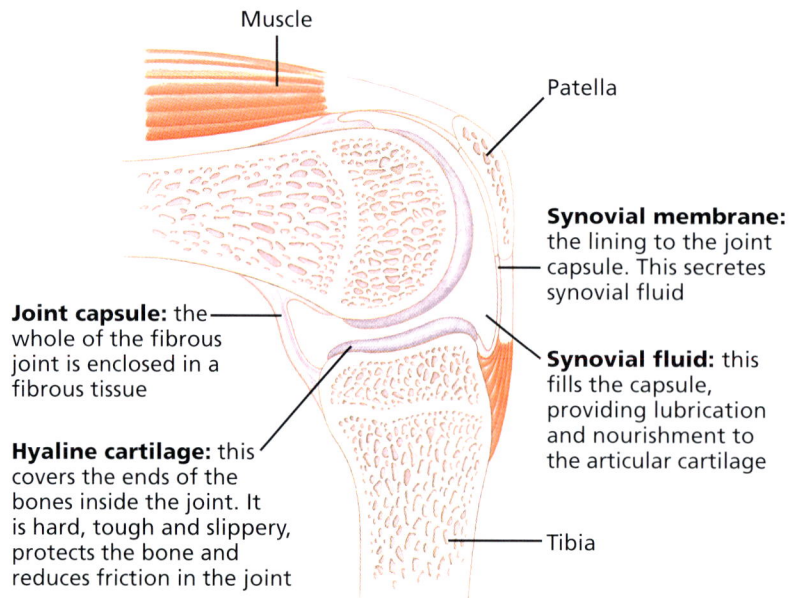

Muscle

Patella

Synovial membrane:
the lining to the joint
capsule. This secretes
synovial fluid

Joint capsule: the
whole of the fibrous
joint is enclosed in a
fibrous tissue

Synovial fluid: this
fills the capsule,
providing lubrication
and nourishment to
the articular cartilage

Hyaline cartilage: this
covers the ends of the
bones inside the joint. It
is hard, tough and slippery,
protects the bone and
reduces friction in the joint

Tibia

Synovial joint – the knee

TYPES OF SYNOVIAL JOINTS

Although synovial joints differ in shape and movement range, they all have similar characteristics.

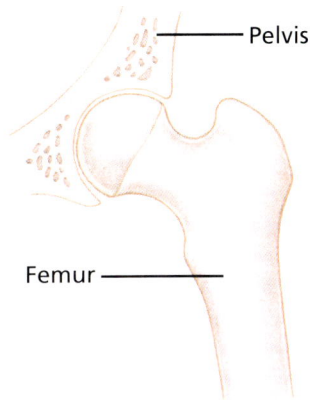

Pelvis

Femur

Humerus

Ulna

Ball and socket joint: found in the shoulder and the hip. Designed to allow a wide range of movement

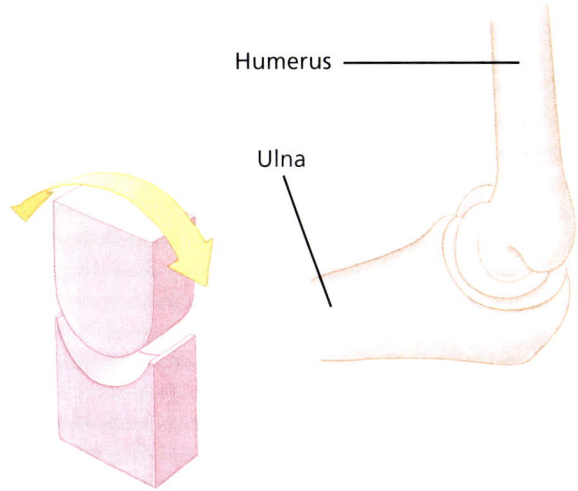

Hinge joint: found at the elbow and knee. The range of movement is limited to one plane, such as a door hinge

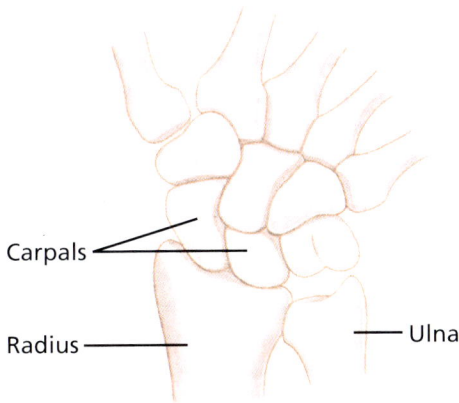

Carpals

Radius

Ulna

Vertebrae

Condyloid joint: found at the wrist and ankle. Movement in two planes, but not such a full range as in the ball and socket joint

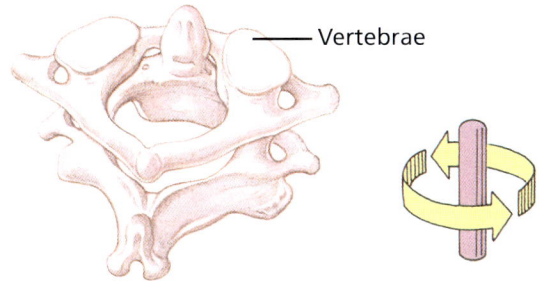

Pivot joint: found in the neck. Part of the bone fits into another ring of bone as intake atlas and axis, allowing rotation of the head

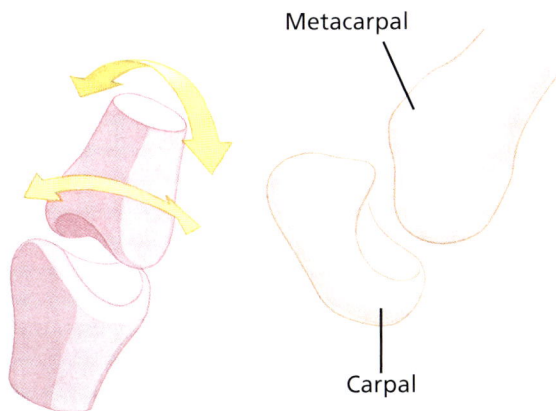

Metacarpal

Carpal

Saddle joint: found at the base of the thumb. This joint allows the thumb to be moved in two directions

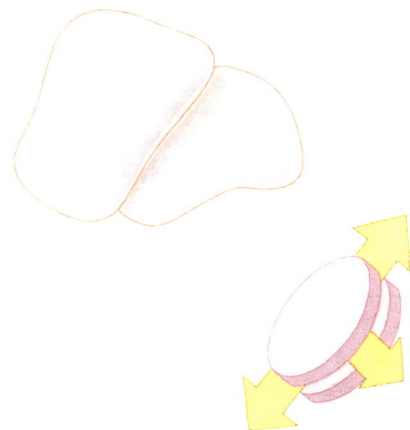

Gliding joint: found in the wrist and vertebral column. Two bones have a small range of movement limited by connecting ligaments

CARTILAGE

Cartilage is found in all joints. There are two main types of cartilage:

- articular or hyaline cartilage – this is found on the ends of long bones in the joints. It is smooth and tough and both protects the bone and reduces friction between the bones. It also produces synovial fluid in the joint
- fibro-cartilage – this is located in the spine between the vertebrae, where it acts as a shock absorber. In the knee joint this cartilage is sometimes known as menisci, acting as a shock absorber between the tibia and the femur.

LIGAMENTS

Ligaments are strong connective tissues which have very little elasticity. Their purpose is to hold bones together at the joints. In more complex joints such as the knee joint there are special arrangements of ligaments which maintain the stability of the joint and allow specific movement.

Types of body movement

Because of the range of movements required in sport, it is useful to be able to describe them technically.

Abduction – the limbs are moved away from the centre line of the body

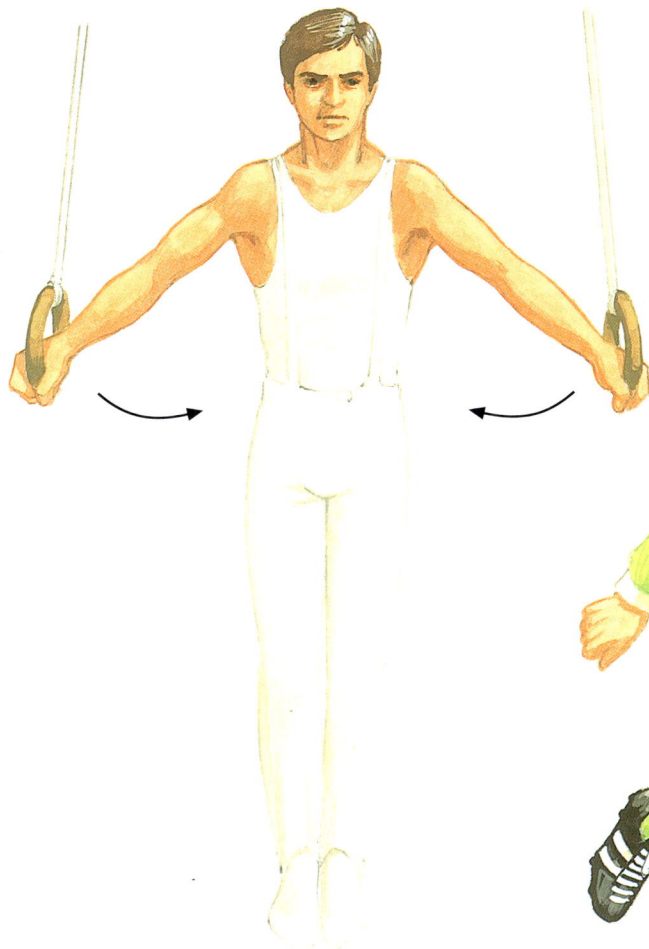

Adduction – the limbs are moved towards the centre line of the body

Flexion – bending at a joint

Extension – straightening arms or legs or the whole body from a flexed position is known as extension. Hyper-extension is when joints are extended excessively in the opposite direction to flexing the joint

Rotation – this occurs with the head, although the whole of the body could be rotated in a somersault

Circumduction – this is the movement of a limb such as arm circling

Questions on the skeletal system

1 Where does blood production take place?
  a in the vertebral column
  b in the marrow of the long bones
  c in the cranium
  d in the carpals.

2 Which of the following joints are hinge joints?
  a elbow
  b shoulder
  c hip
  d neck.

3 Complete the table below:

4 Draw and label four features of a long bone.

5 Name four functions of the skeletal system.

6 Describe how bones grow.

7 Name four types of joints and give one example of each.

8 Name four characteristics of a synovial joint.

9 What holds joints together?

10 Describe flexion and extension of a named joint.

Type of bone	Name of bone	Location	Main purpose
Irregular		Spine	
	Radius	Arm	
Flat			Protection
	Femur		

Exam-style questions

1 There are five regions of the vertebral column. The one nearest the head is the cervical region; name the other four in descending order. (5 marks)

2 a What is meant by a joint? (2 marks)
  b Draw and label four features of a knee joint. (8 marks)

3 Name five types of body movement and give sporting examples of each of these. (15 marks)

4 a State four functions of the skeleton. (4 marks)
  b The vertebrae are irregular bones. Give two other types of bone and an example of each. (4 marks)
  c Give
    i two types of joints. (2 marks)
    ii the location of each of these joints and the type of movement related to a sporting activity. (5 marks)

Quality of written communication (5 marks)

2

Muscular System

Attached to the skeleton are the muscles of the body. Although the skeleton provides the underlying framework, the muscles give the body its unique appearance. The importance of muscles is that they are needed for all body actions, ranging from movement to digestion and breathing.

LEARNING OBJECTIVES

- types of muscle
- muscle contractions
- body movement
- levers

Types of muscle

SMOOTH OR INVOLUNTARY MUSCLE

This type of muscle is found in the bowel, the gut and internal organs. There is no direct control of this muscle as it works automatically. When food is swallowed, it travels through the digestive system by muscular activity which cannot be consciously controlled.

CARDIAC MUSCLE

The heart is a specialised type of muscle which contracts regularly and automatically. Some factors can influence the speed of contractions such as drugs and stress, but the rate cannot be controlled voluntarily. When the body is excited and adrenaline is produced, the heart rate increases.

Deltoid
(raises arm
sideways)

Pectorals
(move arm and
shoulders)

Biceps
(bend/flex arm
at the elbow)

Abdominals
(strengthen abdominal
wall, flex the trunk
to bend forward)

Quadriceps
(straighten/extend leg at
the knee, keep leg
straight)

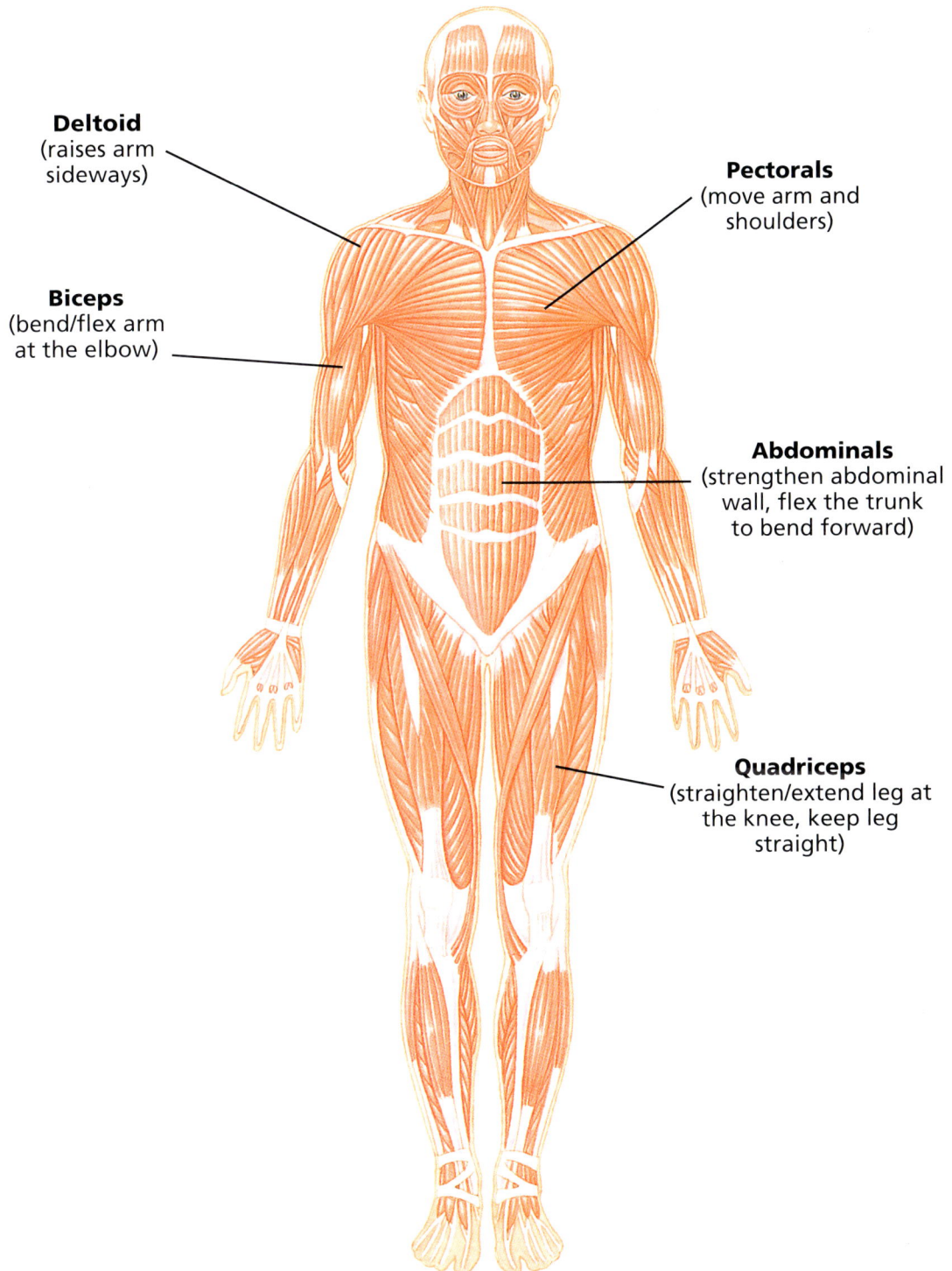

Front view of skeletal muscles

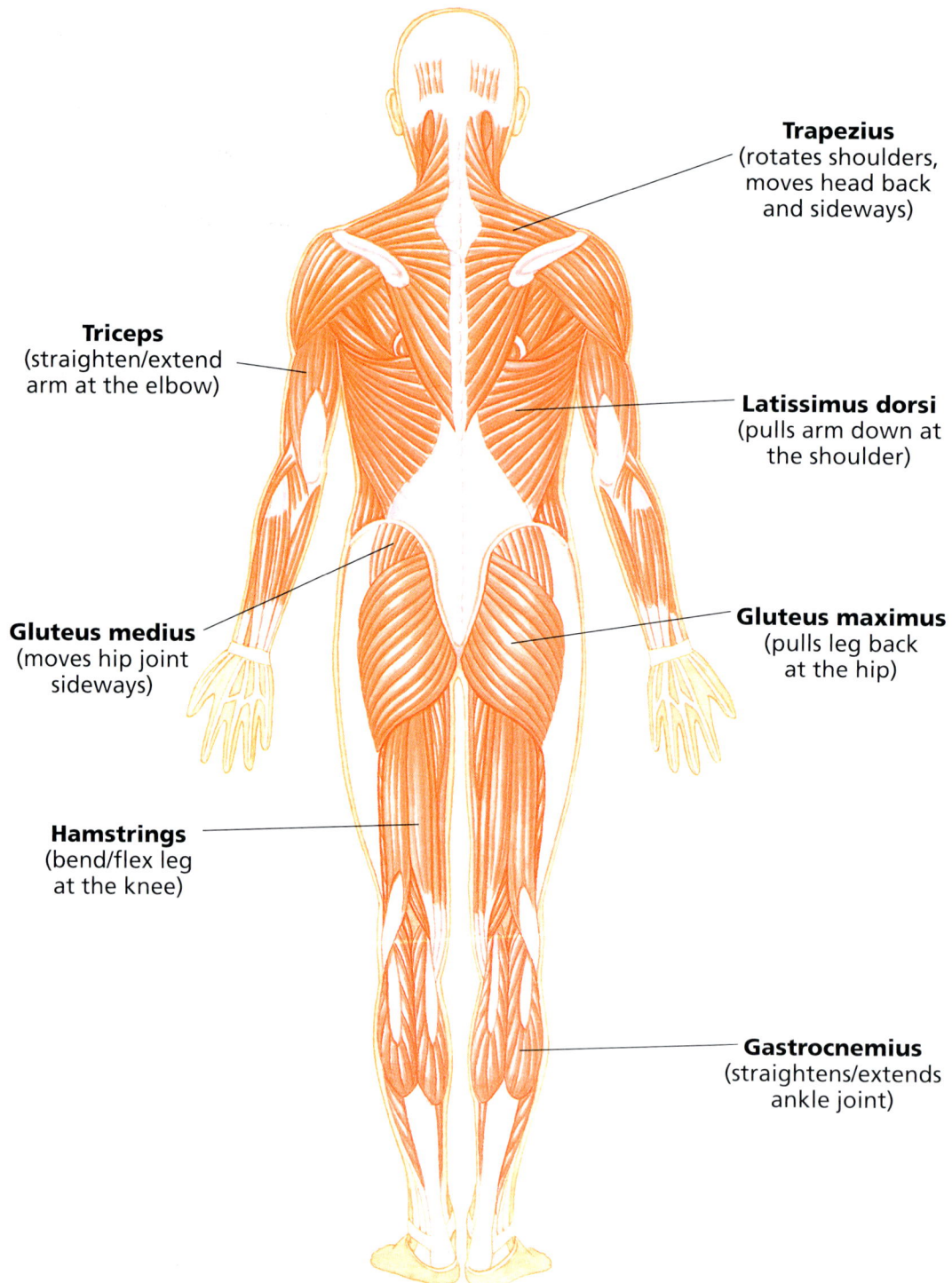

Trapezius
(rotates shoulders,
moves head back
and sideways)

Triceps
(straighten/extend
arm at the elbow)

Latissimus dorsi
(pulls arm down at
the shoulder)

Gluteus medius
(moves hip joint
sideways)

Gluteus maximus
(pulls leg back
at the hip)

Hamstrings
(bend/flex leg
at the knee)

Gastrocnemius
(straightens/extends
ankle joint)

Back view of skeletal muscles

SKELETAL MUSCLE

This is the muscle which can easily be seen as a shape under the skin, and there are 600 examples of it in the human body. This muscle is attached to bones and is called voluntary because it can be controlled. Because of its composition it is sometimes known as **striated** (striped) muscle.

Skeletal muscle is composed of thousands of long, narrow muscle **fibres** or cells which are able to **contract** (shorten in length). When muscle fibres contract, they cause the whole of the muscle to contract. The muscle fibres are enclosed inside a strong connective tissue called the **epimysium**.

Each muscle fibre is made up of large numbers of very small thread-like structures called **myofibrils**. Each myofibril consists of rows of microscopic protein molecules, **actin** and **myosin**, which are interleaved. These molecules are linked by thread-like nerves to the central nervous system. At the **motor end plate**, the nerves which activate the muscle fibres are to be found.

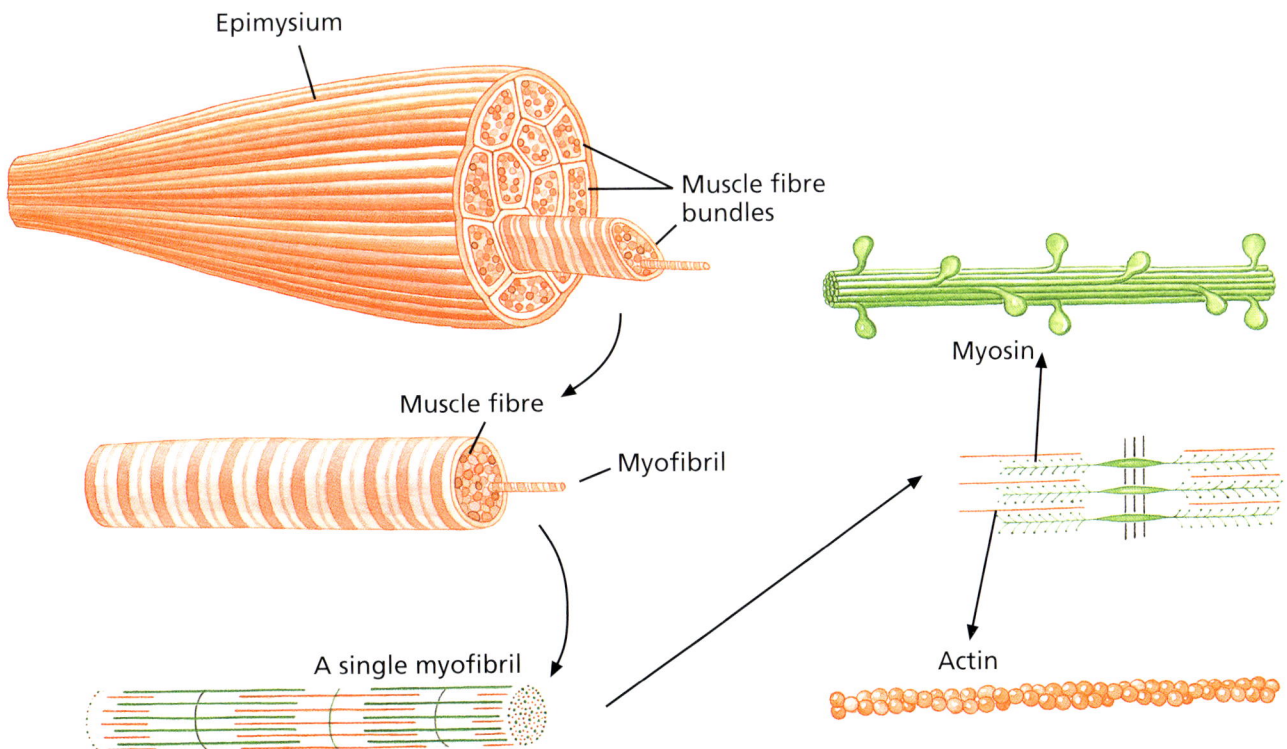

Epimysium

Muscle fibre bundles

Muscle fibre

Myofibril

Myosin

Actin

A single myofibril

How skeletal muscle is constructed

Muscle contractions

The heavier the weight to be lifted, the more force is required; therefore, *more* muscle fibres contract when lifting a heavy weight. However, a light weight requires *less* fibres to contract. When muscle fibres contract, they obey the **all or none** principle. This means that a muscle fibre contracts fully or not at all; it cannot partially contract.

MUSCLE FIBRE TYPE

There are two types of muscle fibre: **slow** and **fast twitch**. Each type is suited to certain sporting activities.

Slow twitch

These contract slowly with little force, but they do not tire easily. Therefore, activities which require endurance such as

- jogging
- long-distance running
- swimming

rely on slow twitch fibres. These are called **aerobic** activities.

Fast twitch

These contract quickly to produce fast and powerful actions for sporting activities. Because of the energy they produce, these fibres tire quickly. Therefore, **anaerobic** activities such as

- sprinting
- throwing

are best carried out by fast-twitch fibres.

Slow and fast-twitch fibres are used during a triathlon competition

With a partner, identify two sports where fast-twitch fibre is important, and two sports where slow-twitch fibre is important.

All muscles have a mixture of both types of fibre. In many sporting events we often need to use both types at different times during the event: a marathon race might depend on *slow*-twitch fibres for most of the time, but a sprint at the finish will require *fast*-twitch fibres to be brought into use.

Fast- and slow-twitch fibres are distributed fairly equally in the body, although there are some variations. It appears that we are unable to alter the ratio of fast- to slow-twitch fibres we are born with, but training for specific sports can develop either type, enabling them to contract more often or more powerfully.

MUSCLE TONE

The fibres in muscles are never completely relaxed. There is always some tension in the muscle, which maintains the shape even though there is no movement. The *partial* contraction of muscles is called **muscle tone**. Muscle contraction without movement is needed for the human body to stay erect, for the head to be kept up.

Muscle tone is important for good posture of the body, which places the minimum amount of stress on the skeletal and muscular system. Posture is important in a number of situations such as

- standing
- sitting
- walking or running
- lifting and carrying.

Muscle tone!

Standing

Soldiers on guard duty have to stand very straight and upright. They need to have good posture when standing for long periods of time, in order to avoid excessive muscular contraction and to maintain a stable upright position.

Sitting

When sitting at a desk or computer, it is important to sit correctly. Leaning over the keyboard with an arched back or lounging in chairs will not help good posture.

Walking and running

When moving, dynamic posture is an important factor to prevent undue stress on muscles and joints. An upright position with head held looking forward is usually best, although there are many varieties of running styles.

Lifting and carrying

It is important when lifting a heavy object to take its weight on your legs, and to keep the spine as straight as possible. Putting pressure

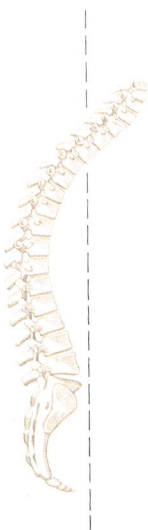

Kyphosis – extreme curvature of the spine when standing

on the spine when it is in a curved position can result in damage to the discs between the vertebrae (see page 8).

Heavy objects should be carried as close to the body as possible. The best way is directly above the spine, as the weight is above the centre of gravity.

Try lifting a light box the correct way. Your partner should check that you are doing it correctly.

Correct/incorrect lifting methods

Body movement

Antagonistic muscle action – muscles can only contract, so to produce a range of movements at the joints, there are usually two or more muscles working opposite each other. This is known as antagonistic muscle action. A good example of this is the upper arm where the biceps and triceps are located at either side of the humerus:

- as the biceps contract, the radius moves up towards the muscle
- at the same time, the triceps must relax to allow this movement to take place.

In this action the biceps is the prime mover, or **agonist**, while the triceps is the **antagonist**. The muscle actions are reversed when doing a backward pull over with a weights bar. In this action the triceps is the agonist and the biceps the antagonist.

Synergists – often certain parts of the body need to be kept still to allow other movements to take place. Synergists are muscles which work to maintain body position. When doing a biceps curl with a weights bar, the back and shoulders are kept fixed by this type of muscle action.

Tendons – muscles are attached to bones by tendons. These are strong flexible cords which have to transmit considerable amounts of energy from the muscle to a bone to create movement. The largest and strongest tendon in the body is the Achilles tendon which attaches the gastrocnemius to the heel bone.

Origin – the point of origin of a muscle is where the tendon joins a bone which is stable and does not move.

Insertion – the point of insertion of a muscle is where the tendon joins a bone which the muscle can move.

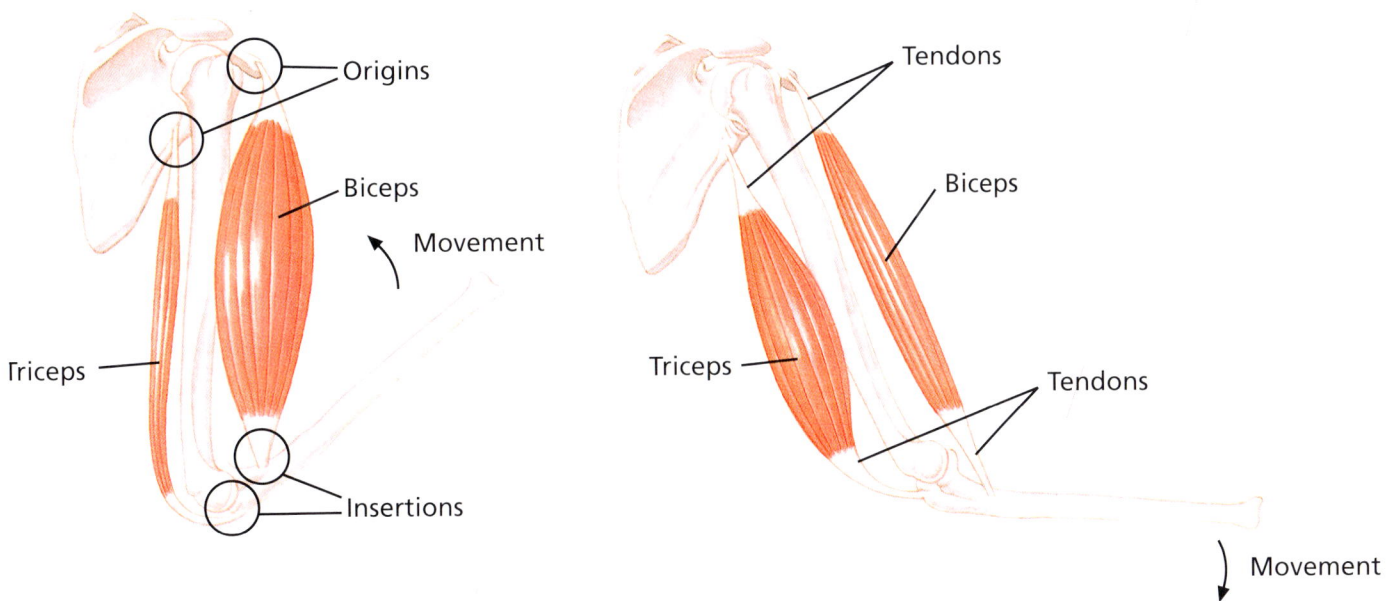

Origins

Biceps

Movement

Triceps

Insertions

Tendons

Biceps

Triceps

Tendons

Movement

Shoulder/elbow joint in two positions showing both bicep and tricep as prime movers

Working with a partner, watch each other doing press ups. Draw the body position when arms are straight and then bent. Identify the prime movers and synergists.

Press ups

MUSCLE CONTRACTION FOR MOVEMENT

There are three types of muscle contraction

- isometric
- isokinetic
- isotonic.

Isometric

In isometric contraction, the muscle remains the same length throughout. Often certain parts of the body need to be kept still while other parts are working. In curling a weights bar, the biceps are the prime movers, but the body must be kept still. The back and shoulder muscles are under isometric contraction stabilising the body. These muscles are working as **synergists**, enabling other muscles to work effectively.

Muscle length is unchanged

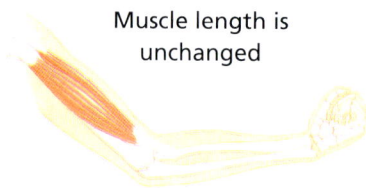

Isometric contraction

Isokinetic

Isokinetic contraction occurs when the speed of movement stays the same throughout the movement. In swimming front crawl, the arms are moving at a relatively constant speed, although the forces applied by the arms alter during the stroke.

Isotonic

Isotonic contraction can be divided into two types

1. **Concentric:** the muscle shortens as it contracts, as the biceps does in a curl movement with a bar.
2. **Eccentric:** the muscle lengthens but is still under tension, such as lowering a bar in the curl.

Pretend you are lifting a heavy weight with one hand. With the other hand check on the tension of both your biceps and triceps. Are they both under tension?

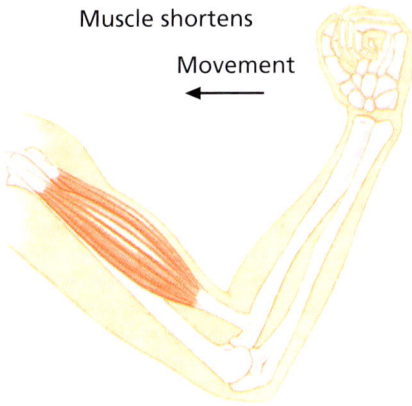

Muscle shortens

Movement

Concentric contraction

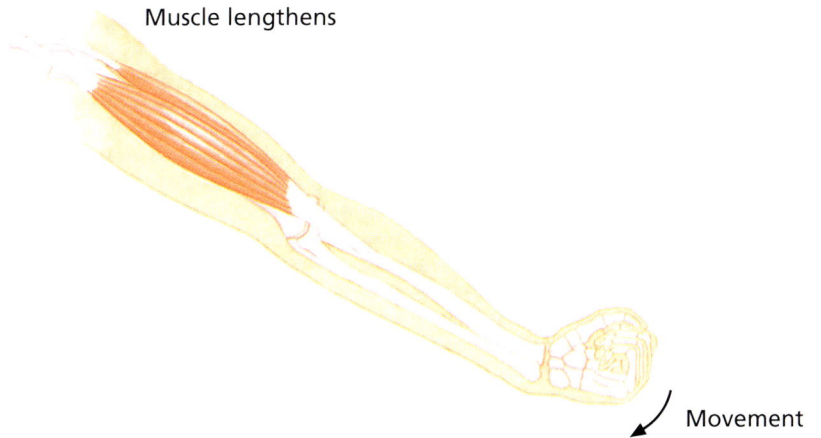

Muscle lengthens

Movement

Eccentric contraction

Levers

The purpose of muscle contraction is to cause movement in some part of the body. This is done by a system of levers. There are three classifications of levers, but each lever has

① a **fulcrum** – the point of movement or pivot, usually the centre of a joint in the body

② a **load** – the body weight or some external object

③ an **effort** – a muscular force to move the load.

FIRST-ORDER LEVERS

The fulcrum is between the effort and the load.

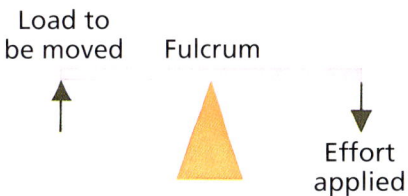

Load to be moved   Fulcrum   Effort applied

Lever

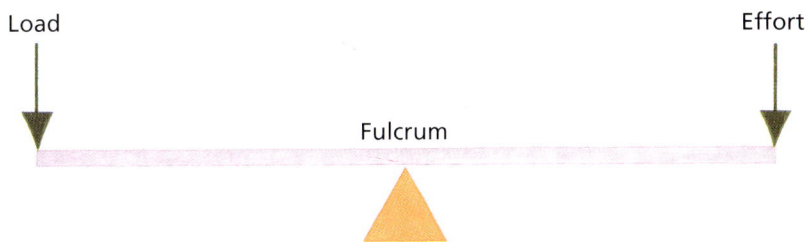

Load   Fulcrum   Effort

First-order levers

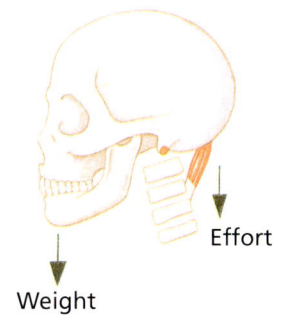

Effort

Weight

SECOND-ORDER LEVERS

The load is between the fulcrum and the effort. This is the most effective lever as a relatively small force can move a larger weight. This is transmitted through the very strong **Achilles** tendon.

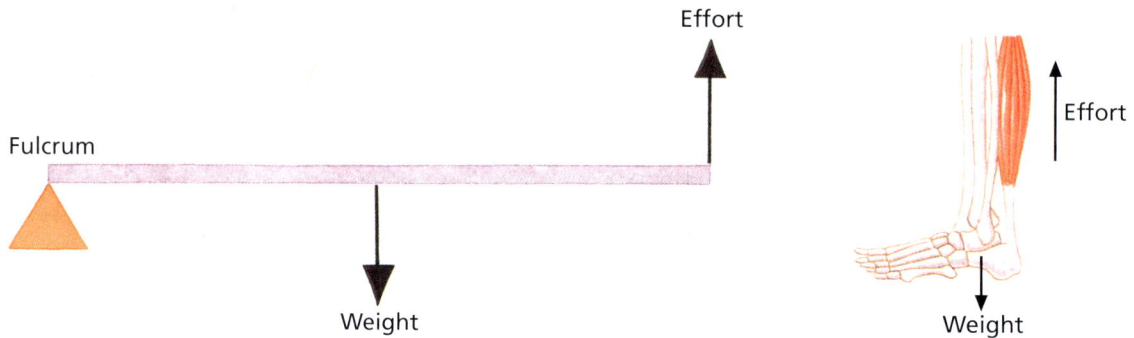

Second-order levers

THIRD-ORDER LEVERS

The effort is between the load and the fulcrum. This is not as efficient as a second-order lever, but a small muscle movement creates a long lever movement.

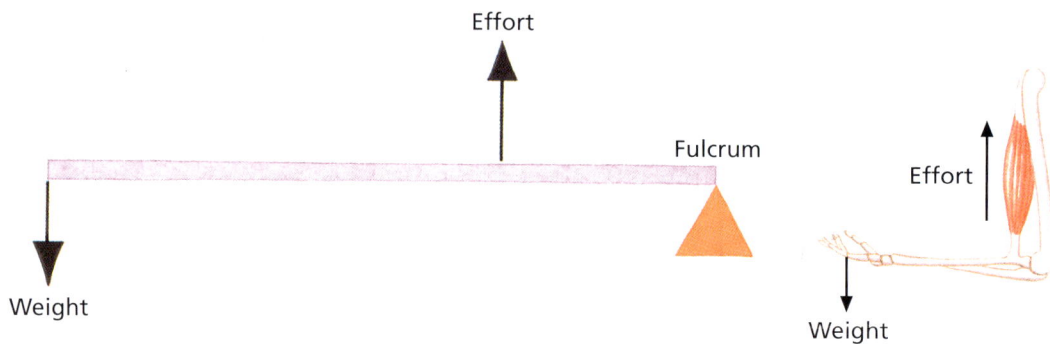

Third-order levers

Write down three examples from sporting activities where the three lever systems are used. Select one of these examples, and draw a labelled diagram showing the bones and muscles in the lever system.

Questions on the muscular system

1 When contracting, the biceps muscle
   a straightens the leg at the knee
   b flexes the abdomen
   c raises the arm at the shoulder
   d flexes the arm at the elbow.

2 Isometric muscle action is where
   a the muscle remains the same length throughout
   b the muscle shortens
   c the muscle stretches
   d the muscle works at the same speed throughout the movement.

3 Name three types of muscle.

4 Why is skeletal muscle sometimes called voluntary muscle?

5 Name three muscles in the leg.

6 What is meant by a synergist in muscle action? Give an example from an activity.

7 Name two muscles which work as agonists and antagonists and describe the action in detail.

8 Give an example from sport where slow- and fast-twitch muscle action is important.

9 What are the origin and insertion of muscles?

10 The Achilles tendon is extremely strong. With a diagram show the lever system at the ankle joint and the placement of this tendon.

Exam-style questions

1 a Why is skeletal muscle known as voluntary muscle?   (2 marks)
    b What is meant by muscle tone and why is it important?   (3 marks)

2 a Name the muscles labelled in the body.   (6 marks)

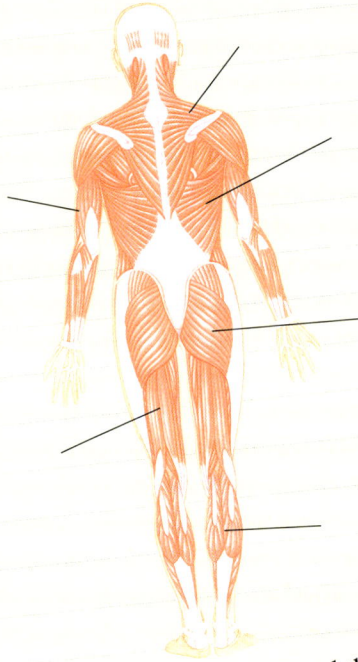

    b Which muscles flex and extend the knee joint and how is this applied to sporting activities?   (4 marks)

3 a On the diagram, indicate the names of the muscles and mark their origin and insertion.   (6 marks)

    b Explain how both of these muscles can be prime movers during different actions.   (4 marks)

    c What is a synergist and why is it important in this activity?   (5 marks)

4 a Give a brief description of isometric, isotonic and isokinetic muscle action.   (6 marks)

    b Describe the difference between fast- and slow-twitch muscle action, giving examples from sport.   (9 marks)

Quality of written communication.   (5 marks)

3

Cardiovascular System

The cardiovascular system consists of the heart and blood vessels. Blood which contains essential nutrients and oxygen is carried around the system to where it is required to release energy in the muscles. Blood then transports waste products from muscles and other locations in the body. The cardiovascular system ensures a constant supply of blood where needed throughout the body.

LEARNING OBJECTIVES

- functions of the circulatory system
- blood vessels
- heart
- blood
- effects of exercise

Functions of the circulatory system

- Transport – blood carries nutrients, oxygen and waste products around the body.
- Temperature control – blood absorbs and transfers heat from warmer to cooler parts of the body.
- Protection – blood carries antibodies, mainly in white blood cells to fight infection and platelets which help the blood to clot at wounds and cuts.

There is a double circulatory system.

SYSTEMIC CIRCUIT

This is the main circuit and responsible for taking oxygenated blood from the heart around the body through the arteries. Deoxygenated blood is returned through veins to the heart.

PULMONARY CIRCUIT

This circuit includes the heart and the lungs. Deoxygenated blood is pumped from the heart to the lungs where it is oxygenated. From there it is returned to the heart, to be pumped around the body in the systemic circuit.

Blood vessels

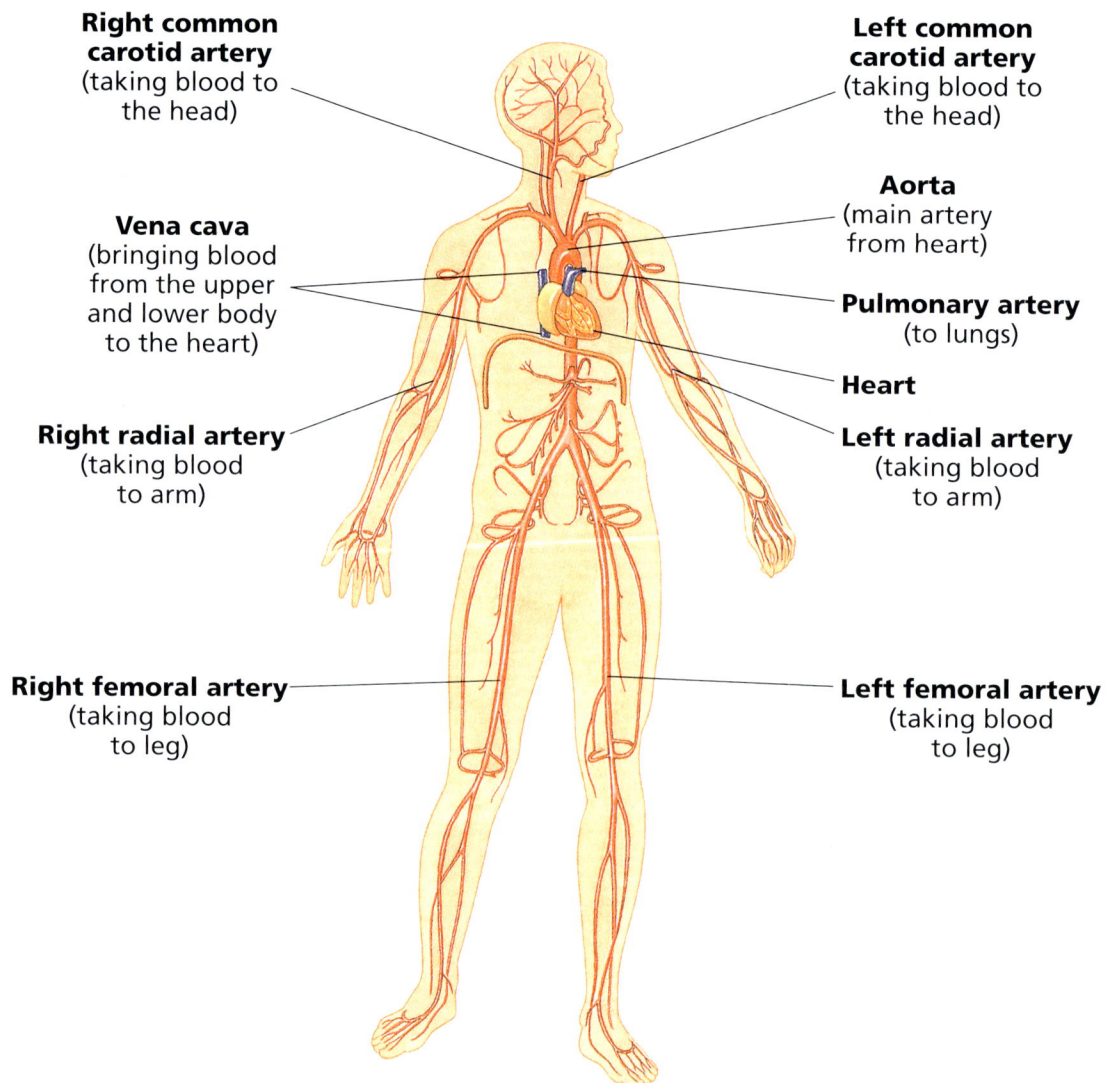

Right common carotid artery
(taking blood to the head)

Left common carotid artery
(taking blood to the head)

Vena cava
(bringing blood from the upper and lower body to the heart)

Aorta
(main artery from heart)

Pulmonary artery
(to lungs)

Heart

Right radial artery
(taking blood to arm)

Left radial artery
(taking blood to arm)

Right femoral artery
(taking blood to leg)

Left femoral artery
(taking blood to leg)

Major arteries of the circulatory system

These are tubes through which blood flows around the body. They differ in size and function and are divided into

- arteries
- capillaries
- veins.

ARTERIES

These carry **oxygenated** blood away from the heart under high pressure. There is one exception to this: the **pulmonary** artery which carries **deoxygenated** blood between the heart and lungs (see Chapter 4).

Arteries not only carry blood but they also assist with its movement. The inner wall of arteries is involuntary muscle, which controls the diameter of the tube as it expands or contracts to control the flow of blood. Arteries branch into smaller tubes called **arterioles** which further subdivide into **capillaries**.

CAPILLARIES

These are tiny tubes, only one cell thick. The walls are extremely thin, allowing food and oxygen to pass **out** to body cells, and carbon dioxide and waste products to pass **into** the bloodstream through the capillary walls.

VEINS

As carbon dioxide and waste products pass into the bloodstream through the capillary walls, they enlarge into **venules**. These flow into veins which carry blood back to the heart. There is a reduction in blood pressure as the blood passes out of the venules into the veins; the veins have valves which prevent the blood from flowing backwards. Veins have a similar construction to arteries but are thinner. Muscles in the body contain veins, and muscular contractions help to force deoxygenated blood through the veins and back to the heart.

Check the valves in your veins. Have a partner put a finger on a vein in your arm. Run your finger down the vein towards your hand, then run your finger along the same vein towards your body. Describe what has happened and give an explanation.

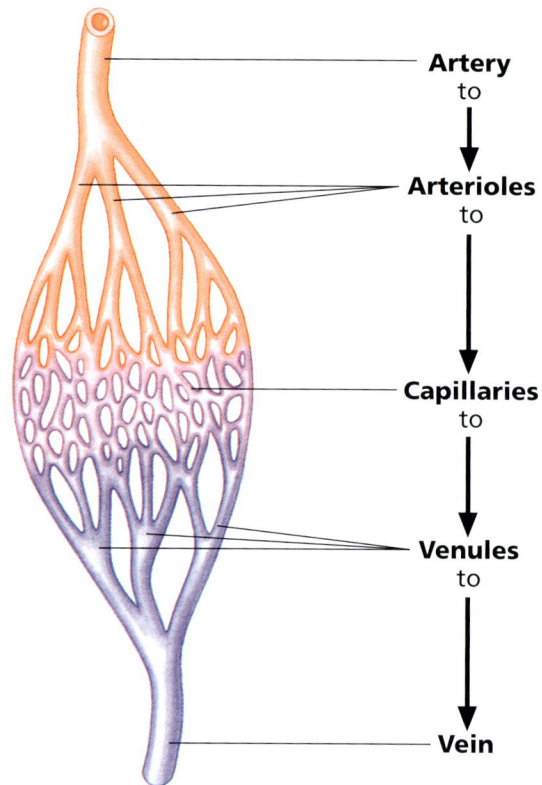

Artery
to

Arterioles
to

Capillaries
to

Venules
to

Vein

From artery to vein

Heart

The function of the heart is to pump blood around the body. It is internally divided into four sections:

- the two upper chambers, the **atria**
- the two lower chambers, the **ventricles.**

Oxygenated blood is passed through the left atrium and left ventricle and on to the systemic circuit, whilst deoxygenated blood passes through the right atrium and right ventricle to the lungs. Inside there are valves which control the direction of blood flow.

The heart is a muscle and each section performs a series of powerful contractions in sequence, which pumps blood around the body. Each cycle of contractions is known as a **heartbeat**. The human body contains between 4/5 litres of blood, which is pumped around the system every minute.

BLOOD FLOW

① Oxygenated blood leaves the heart after being pumped out of the left ventricle, through the **semilunar** valve into the **aorta**.

② Blood then flows around the body through **arteries** then **arterioles** and then **capillaries** where it is deoxygenated. The blood then flows back to the heart through the **veins**.

③ Deoxygenated blood enters the right atrium of the heart from the **superior** and **inferior vena cava**.

④ Blood is then pumped into the right ventricle through the **tricuspid** valve.

⑤ From the right ventricle blood is pumped through a **semilunar** valve into the **pulmonary artery** and into the lungs to be reoxygenated.

⑥ Oxygenated blood is passed through the **pulmonary vein** into the left atrium.

⑦ From the left atrium blood passes through the **mitral** valve into the left ventricle where it begins its circuit again.

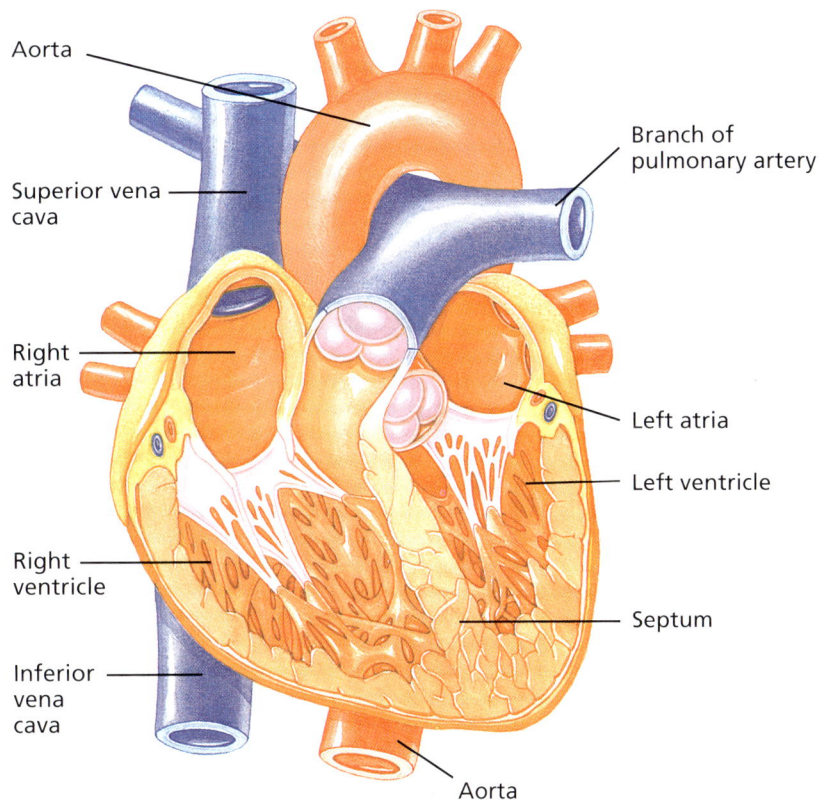

Aorta

Branch of pulmonary artery

Superior vena cava

Right atria

Left atria

Left ventricle

Right ventricle

Septum

Inferior vena cava

Aorta

Heart

HEART RATE

The **rate** of the heart is determined by a number of factors, but at rest it beats between 50 and 80 times per minute. When more blood is required at the muscles during exercise, the heart rate can increase to over 200 beats per minute, pumping 45 litres around the body in a minute.

Blood

COMPOSITION OF BLOOD

The composition of blood is complex. It consists of

- red cells
- white cells
- platelets
- plasma.

The cells and platelets form the *body* of the blood; the plasma forms the liquid part.

Red cells

The most important function of the red cells is their ability to *carry oxygen*. **Haemoglobin**, a chemical compound of iron and protein, combines with oxygen in the lungs to form **oxyhaemoglobin**. Millions of these blood cells are made in the marrow of bones such as the vertebrae, the ribs and the femur. About 200,000 cells are replaced each day. The cells pick up oxygen where there is plenty (eg in the lungs), and give up this oxygen where there is little or where it is required (eg in working muscles).

White cells

These are larger than red cells, and their chief function is to defend the body against disease. Certain white cells called **phagocytes** pass through the capillary walls and surround germs. They then produce enzymes which destroy the germs. Other white cells form **antibodies** which fight against germs and infections. White cells are produced in the bone marrow and in lymph glands.

Platelets

These fragments or particles help to clot the blood. They stick together in clumps where the skin may be broken, or on small damaged blood vessels. Platelets are produced in the bone marrow.

Plasma

Ninety-two per cent of plasma is water; the remainder consists of fibrinogen, protein, glucose, amino acids and waste products such as carbon dioxide and urea. Protein and amino acids are transported to cells in the body, and are used for growth and repair. Glucose is used to supply energy.

BLOOD FUNCTIONS

Blood has the capacity to carry essential items around the body. These are

- oxygen from lungs to body cells
- carbon dioxide from body cells to lungs
- waste products and water from cells to kidneys
- glucose and nutrients from digestive system to cells
- hormones from glands to where they are needed
- white blood cells to sites of infection
- platelets to damaged capillary areas
- heat from warmer to cooler parts of the body.

BLOOD PRESSURE

Blood is under pressure in the circulatory system. The pumping action of the heart creates this pressure, which varies in different parts of the body. The highest pressure is in the **arteries**, and the pressure reduces by the time it reaches the veins (the widest blood vessels).

Blood pressure is easily measured, by taking the pressure at an artery in the arm. A cuff is put around the arm, and this is pressurised enough to stop the blood flowing. As the pressure reduces, the blood starts to flow again. A doctor listens to this through a stethoscope, and reads the pressure from the gauge. Modern equipment gives a digital display and print-out of blood pressures.

There are two pressures to correspond with the contraction and relaxation of the heart. These are known as systolic (contraction) and diastolic (relaxation) pressure. This is why the pressure is given as two numbers such as $\frac{120}{80}$, the average for a young adult.

If your school or college has a blood pressure tester, ask if you can be tested. Some sports centres and chemists have blood pressure testers; see if you can be tested there.

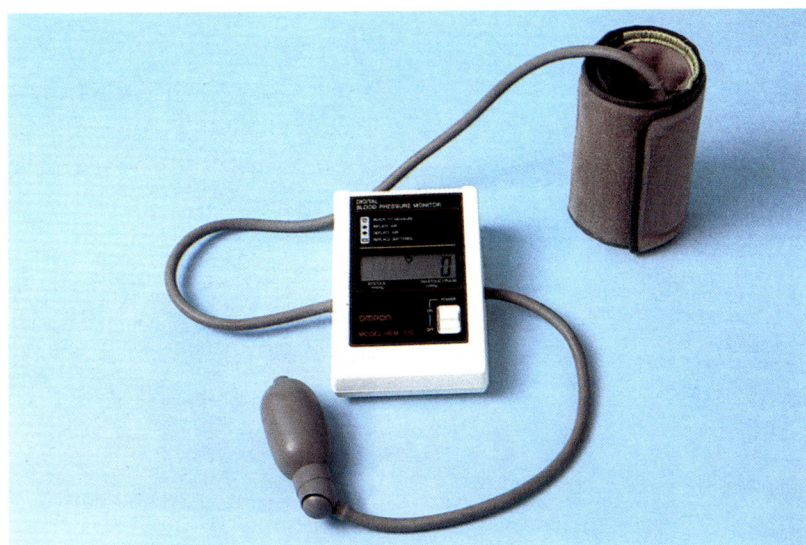

Modern blood pressure tester

Blood pressure is often taken to give an indication of general health. There are other factors which affect blood pressure

- exercise – increases the blood pressure
- age – young people have a lower blood pressure than adults
- sex – there are variations between the blood pressure of men and women
- stress – a person under stress or emotional tension might have increased blood pressure
- poor condition of the circulatory system can increase blood pressure.

Heart disease

In the western world, heart disease is one the biggest causes of death. Fat is deposited on the artery walls from a young age. Depending on diet, this fat build-up can continue to a point where the arteries become very restricted. This means that the heart has to work harder to pump blood through much narrower tubes, thus causing a high increase in blood pressure. The heart itself may not get sufficient oxygen to work properly, and a sharp pain, **angina**, is a warning signal. In more serious cases, a **heart attack** occurs, where the heart stops completely. It can sometimes be started again by physical massage, drugs or a powerful electric shock.

Although diet and non-smoking are very significant factors in preventing heart disease, other methods can be used such as regular exercise and avoiding unnecessary stress.

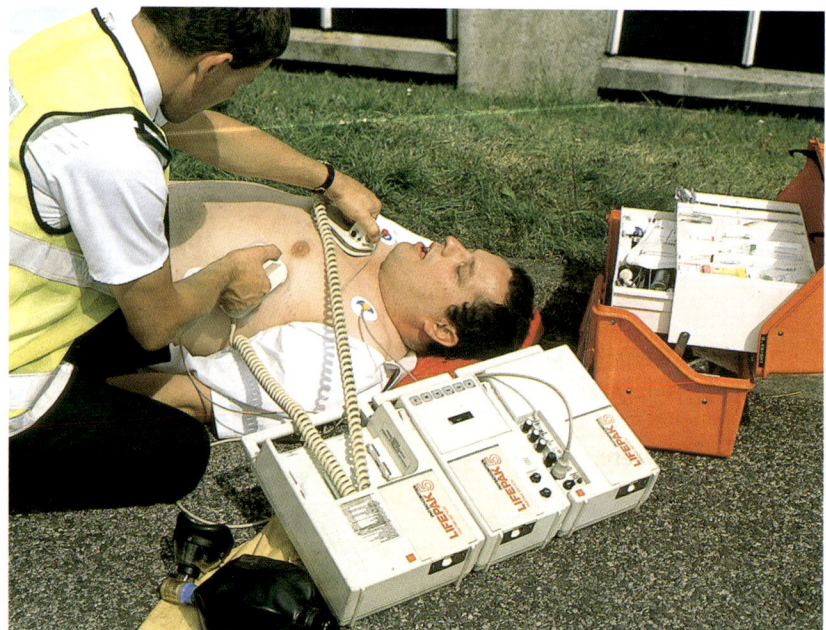

Electric shock to restart the heart

Effects of exercise

HEART

Like any muscle, the heart can grow in strength when exercised. Also endurance training can increase the size of the heart. Two factors affect the heart's efficiency:

- heart rate
- stroke volume.

Measuring the heart rate

The faster the heart pumps, the more blood can be circulated in a given time. During exercise the heart rate increases rapidly to provide the muscles with oxygen and other nutrients. The heart rate is easily measured, as there is a pulse each time it beats. There are a number of sites in the body where the pulse can be felt:

- radial pulse – below the thumb in the wrist
- carotid pulse – in the groove on either side of the windpipe in the neck
- temporal pulse – on the temple at the side of the head
- femoral pulse – in the groin.

During or after exercise, the heartbeat can also be felt on the chest.

Take your partner's pulse rate at wrist and carotid artery, using two index fingers.

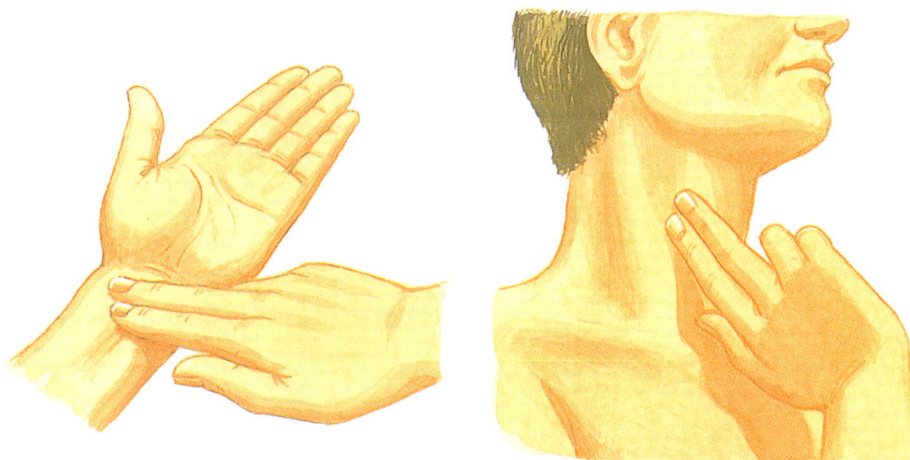

Taking different types of pulse – radial, carotid

Stroke volume

This is the amount of blood leaving the ventricle on each beat. During exercise, the stroke volume increases because

- more blood is sent back to the heart, due to the muscles squeezing blood in the veins
- as the heart fills up, it stretches
- as the muscle fibres stretch, they contract more strongly, pumping out more blood.

Endurance Training can increase the Stroke volume.

Cardiac output

Under exercise conditions, cardiac output is increased considerably. The rate of heartbeat and the stroke volume determine the **cardiac output**:

Intense activity requires considerable amounts of blood to the muscles

Cardiac output = stroke volume $\times$ heart rate

An example of this is a person at rest with a stroke volume of 75 ml per beat and a heart rate of 70 beats per minute:

Cardiac output = 75 ml $\times$ 70 bpm
    = 5.250 litres per minute

When exercising, the same person could have a heart rate of 150 bpm and a stroke volume of 150 ml per beat.

Cardiac output = 150 bpm $\times$ 150 ml per beat
    = 22.500 litres per minute

After someone has exercised hard and looks hot, put your hand close to their face, but do not touch the skin. Can you feel the radiated heat?

Many inexperienced long-distance runners take off their shirts when running in hot weather. Discuss with a partner whether this is a good thing or bad, and how it might or might not help keep the body cool.

BODY

As seen above, considerably more blood is pumped during exercise than at rest. Where does this extra blood come from? The amount of blood in the body is a fixed volume, therefore extra blood needs to be taken from other organs of the body. During intensive exercise, blood is taken from the **gut** to the **muscles**.

Homeostasis is the way the body temperature is regulated despite changes in the external environment. As the intensity and duration of exercise increases, so does the heat produced by the body. The hypothalamus is sensitive to blood temperature and relays messages to the skin, where sweating takes place. Blood is diverted to the capillaries just below the skin. This causes the skin to redden, a common sight when someone is exercising. Heat from the blood is then radiated from the skin. Losing heat through sweating (which is formed in sweat glands under the skin) is caused by the evaporation of sweat from the skin's surface.

In hot dry conditions **sweating** is an effective way of losing heat. When the air is humid (moist) then sweating is not as effective as the sweat does not evaporate as readily. In cold climatic conditions there is little sweating and less blood in the capillaries near the skin.

Shivering is involuntary muscle action and is the body's attempt to create heat in the muscles and surrounding tissues.

Questions on the cardiovascular system

1 The cardiovascular system consists of
   a   the heart and lungs
   b   the heart, blood vessels and lungs
   c   the heart , blood and lungs
   d   the heart, blood and blood vessels.

2 The pulmonary vein carries
   a   oxygenated blood to the heart
   b   deoxygenated blood to the lungs
   c   oxygenated blood from the heart
   d   deoxygenated blood from the lungs.

3 Name the three components of the cardiovascular system.

4 Name two types of valves in the heart.

5 What is meant by stroke volume?

6 What difference is there between blood pressure in the arteries and in the veins?

7 What is the name of the main artery from the heart to the rest of the body?

8 Name the four constituents of blood.

9 What in blood combines with oxygen and carbon dioxide?

10 Give five functions of blood.

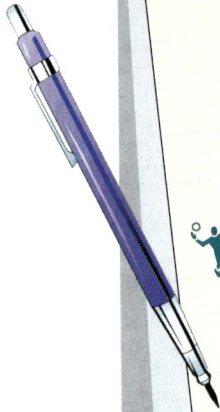

Exam-style questions

1 Give five functions of blood. (5 marks)

2 What is (2 marks)
   a Stroke volume? (2 marks)
   b Cardiac output? (2 marks)
   c What effect does exercise have on the heart? (6 marks)

3 Using the diagram of blood circulation below

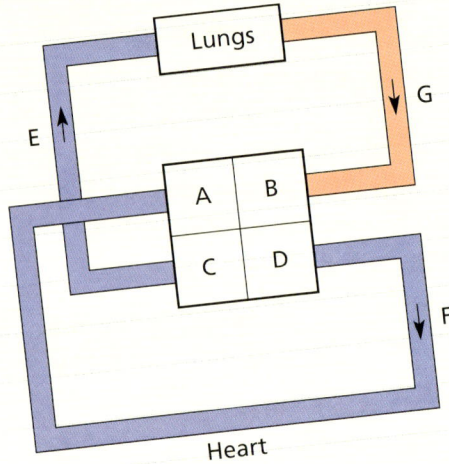

   a i what letter represents the left ventricle? (2 marks)
      ii what letter represents the left atrium? (2 marks)
   b Name the blood vessels E , F and G. (3 marks)
   c Name two valves in the heart. (2 marks)
   d What two things happen in the capillaries? (2 marks)
   e Why are the walls of arteries fairly thick? (2 marks)
   f Why are their valves inside veins? (2 marks)

4 Discuss what is meant by having a healthy heart, and give possible causes of heart disease. (15 marks)

Quality of written communication. (5 marks)

4

Respiratory System

The human body needs a constant supply of oxygen to enable energy to be released and also a means of removing waste product of carbon dioxide which is produced by this process. The respiratory system can be considered in two parts. The first is the mechanical process, whereby oxygen from the air is transported to the muscles, and carbon dioxide is removed from the body. The second part is a biochemical one; how muscles contract as a result of chemical action and the importance of oxygen and other chemicals in the body.

> **LEARNING OBJECTIVES**
>
> - components of the respiratory system
> - breathing action
> - breathing and exercise
> - gaseous exchange
> - muscle contraction and energy

Components of the respiratory system

The respiratory system is made up of the

- air passages
- lungs
- diaphragm.

AIR PASSAGES

A series of air passages allow air and the oxygen it contains to be transferred to the bloodstream, and also remove waste products such as carbon dioxide from the body.

Tense the muscles in your
stomach. Keep them tense,
then try to take a deep
breath. Why do you think
this is difficult?

LUNGS

The two lungs are found in the thorax. They are sac-like with thin
walls, and are very flexible. The right lung is slightly larger with three
sections, compared to the left lung which has two sections. To keep
the lungs moist and to lubricate them on their outside surfaces, the
thoracic cavity is lined with the **pleural membrane**.

Air is taken into the body
through the **mouth** and
nasal cavity. In the nostrils,
the air is filtered by tiny
hair (**cilia**), warmed, and
moistened by **mucus**.

Air passes through the **larynx**,
which is sometimes known as
the voice box. Sound is produced
by passing air over the vocal
chords in the larynx.

At the top of the throat is a
flap of skin, the **epiglottis**,
which prevents food or other
particles entering the lungs.

The **trachea** is a large,
flexible but strong tube,
also known as the windpipe.
Rings of cartilage maintain
its shape.

The trachea branches
into two to enter the
lungs as **bronchi**.

Lung

The bronchus in each
lung divides into
bronchioles.

Bronchioles sub-divide into small
air sacs, **alveoli**. Most of the lung
tissue is made up of millions of
alveoli, which is where the exchange
of oxygen *into* the blood and carbon
dioxide *out* of the blood occurs.

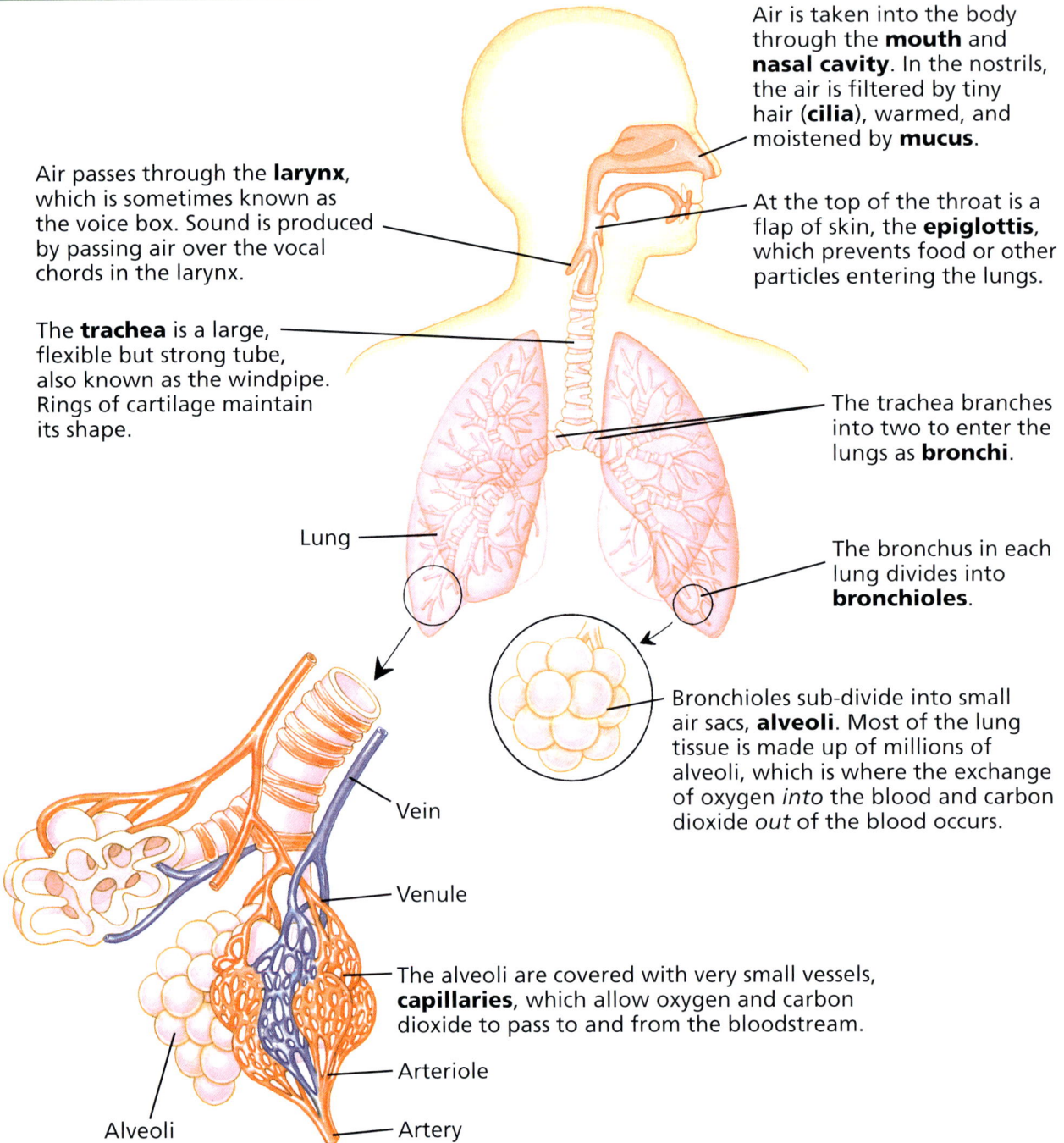

Vein

Venule

The alveoli are covered with very small vessels,
capillaries, which allow oxygen and carbon
dioxide to pass to and from the bloodstream.

Arteriole

Alveoli

Artery

Respiratory system

DIAPHRAGM

This is a sheet of muscle which encloses the bottom of the thorax. Contraction and relaxation of the diaphragm, combined with the intercostal muscles, enables breathing.

Breathing action

There are two phases in breathing: **inspiration** (breathing in) and **expiration** (breathing out). As shown on page 42, the lungs are enclosed in the sealed but flexible cavity of the thorax. When the diaphragm contracts, a vacuum is created inside the thorax. The lungs expand to fill the space created, as air pressure allows air to expand the lungs. At the same time, the intercostal muscles contract in the chest and lift the rib cage, further increasing the thoracic space.

During expiration, the diaphragm and intercostal muscles relax. As the lungs are elastic, they contract to their original size, thus forcing air out of the lungs. Although there is no need to think about breathing (it is involuntarily controlled), breathing can also be consciously controlled:

- larger breaths can be taken
- the speed of breathing can be increased
- the action can be stopped altogether by holding the breath.

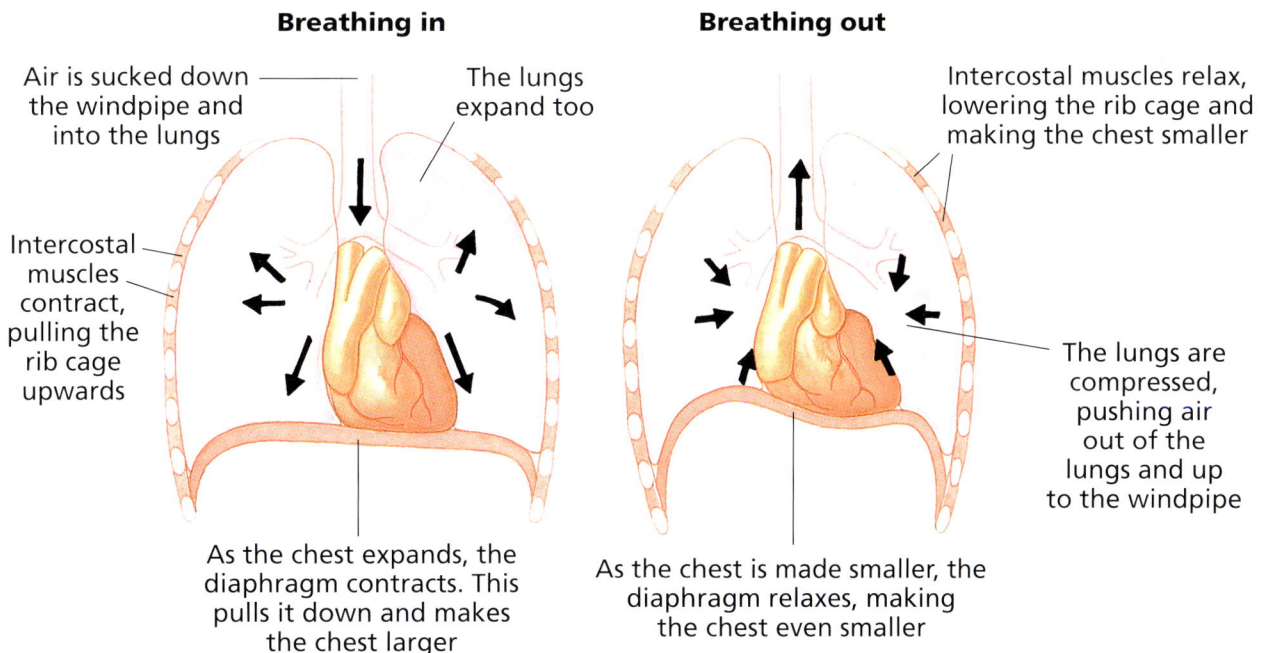

Breathing in

Air is sucked down the windpipe and into the lungs

The lungs expand too

Intercostal muscles contract, pulling the rib cage upwards

As the chest expands, the diaphragm contracts. This pulls it down and makes the chest larger

Breathing out

Intercostal muscles relax, lowering the rib cage and making the chest smaller

The lungs are compressed, pushing air out of the lungs and up to the windpipe

As the chest is made smaller, the diaphragm relaxes, making the chest even smaller

Lungs expanded and normal

Breathing and exercise

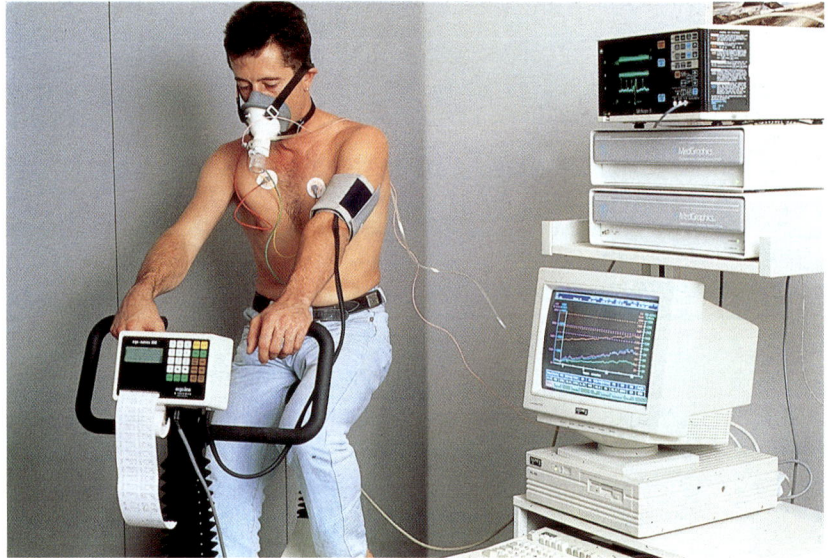

Measuring lung efficiency

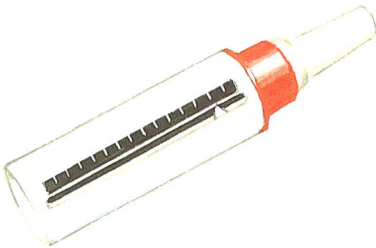

A peak-flow meter tests the vital capacity of the lungs

Sit down and have a partner take your breathing rate. Exercise gently on the spot for two minutes, and have the rate taken again. Increase your work rate and have the breathing rate taken every two minutes on four further occasions. Warm down for two minutes and again check breathing rate. Graph your results and examine the slopes of the graph. What conclusions can you make?

A number of factors determine how much air is breathed in a given time:

- **vital capacity** is the maximum amount of air that can be breathed out in one breath, usually about 4.5 litres in adults
- the **residual volume** is the amount of air left in the lungs, as they cannot be completely emptied. There is usually about 1.5 litres of air remaining in the lungs
- **respiratory rate** is how many breaths are taken per minute
- the **tidal volume** is the amount of air taken in or out with each breath, and is dependent on the vital capacity. The larger the person, the larger the lungs, the greater vital capacity and therefore the greater tidal volume
- the **minute volume** is the amount of air breathed in a minute:

$$\text{Minute volume} = \text{tidal volume} \times \text{respiratory rate}$$

During exercise, the body needs a supply of oxygen to release energy in the muscles. Respiration must be increased to provide that oxygen and remove carbon dioxide from the muscles. This is done by

- increasing breathing rate considerably, about three times the normal rate
- increasing tidal volume by five times the normal rate
- increasing blood supply to and through the lungs
- increasing oxygen take-up.

A slow steady supply of energy is needed throughout the race

Learn the three energy systems and explain to a partner in detail one of these systems.

Use the results of the last task from others in your class. Compare all the results and relate these to gender, body size and type of exercise chosen for the experiment.

The amount of oxygen used during exercise increases rapidly as the level of exercise increases. As athletes get fitter, their bodies become more efficient at using oxygen. This is known as a $\dot{V}O_2$ **max** and can be accurately tested.

$\dot{V}O_2$ max is the maximum amount of oxygen that can be used during exercise. It is a test of aerobic capacity. Top athletes can work at about 85 per cent of their maximum, whereas non-athletes might only work at 65 per cent.

Gaseous exchange

Small air sacs called alveoli are in the bronchioles. The walls of the alveoli are thin and well supplied with red blood cells as each alveoli is connected to its own capillary. This allows the haemoglobin in the red blood cells to absorb oxygen, to form oxyhaemoglobin, as well as carbon dioxide being released by the blood, into the alveoli, through the bronchioles and out of the body through the lungs and mouth.

Muscle contraction and energy

Muscles need energy to work, and this is provided by a substance called adenosine triphosphate – ATP – which is in the muscle fibre. Muscle action quickly uses up the store of ATP which is converted into adenosine diphosphate – ADP – and some energy is released:

ATP = ADP + energy

However, there is only a small store of ATP and therefore when it is used up it needs to be replaced, by converting the ADP back into ATP. The body has three systems for doing this.

ANAEROBIC – CREATINE PHOSPHATE SYSTEM

Anaerobic means without oxygen. Creatine phosphate (cp) occurs in the muscles and combined with ADP creates ATP. The equation below shows that no oxygen is required to produce this energy:

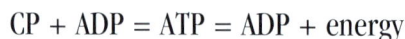

CP + ADP = ATP = ADP + energy

This system only produces short bursts of energy lasting between eight and ten seconds. Short sprints in games, vaulting in gymnastics, throwing and jumping events in athletics are short but intensive activities using this anaerobic system.

ANAEROBIC – LACTIC ACID SYSTEM

When stores of creatine phosphate have been used up the lactic acid system is brought into use. ADP is combined with **glycogen** (GL) which the body creates from carbohydrates in the digestive system which produces more ATP and a by-product called **pyruvic acid**. Without oxygen, pyruvic acid becomes **lactic acid**:

GL + ADP = ATP + pyruvic acid
Pyruvic acid = lactic acid

As lactic acid builds up in the muscles it becomes more difficult for them to contract and pain is felt. To overcome this, lactic acid has to be converted back to pyruvic acid. However, this needs a supply of oxygen, and if this is not available then **oxygen debt** occurs. This system can produce energy for up to two minutes in athletics events of between 400 and 800 metres depending on the athlete.

AEROBIC SYSTEM

In most of the everyday activities such as walking, gardening or similar, sufficient energy is available to keep up the activity for some time. These activities are often slow and require a steady supply of energy. There is sufficient oxygen available through breathing, and this is carried to muscles by the blood. The muscles have sufficient oxygen and can break down carbohydrate and fat and supply the energy needs as required. Pyruvic acid is created but is broken down by oxygen to form water and carbon dioxide:

GL + ADP = ATP + pyruvic acid
Pyruvic acid + oxygen = water + carbon dioxide + heat

When oxygen is available then continued muscular action such as jogging, long-distance running or swimming can take place.

Although there are three systems, energy ultimately comes from the food we eat. Carbohydrate is broken down and stored in the body as glycogen. The following equations summarise aerobic and anaerobic energy production:

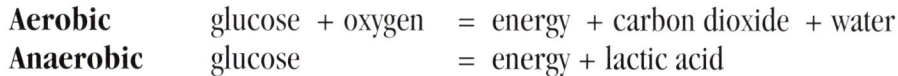

Aerobic   glucose + oxygen = energy + carbon dioxide + water
Anaerobic   glucose = energy + lactic acid

AEROBIC AND ANAEROBIC ACTIVITIES

Some activities use either one or sometimes both of these energy systems in different phases of an activity. In team games such as hockey and soccer, players are moving for much of the game at constant speeds, and are using the aerobic energy system. A sprint up the wing or to get back to help the defence will require a short burst of high intense energy, so using the anaerobic system. Longer endurance events, distance walking and swimming are aerobic for most of the time, although competitors may use an anaerobic burst at the end of a race. Explosive events such as throwing or jumping, or short sprints are anaerobic.

Questions on the respiratory system

1 Gaseous exchange in the lungs takes place in the
   a bronchioles
   b trachea
   c alveoli
   d bronchi.

2 The maximum amount of air that can be breathed out in one breath is the
   a tidal volume
   b vital capacity
   c minute volume
   d residual volume.

3 Name three components of the respiratory system.

4 What prevents food and debris from entering the lungs?

5 What is the diaphragm?

6 What is $\dot{V}O_2$ max?

7 Where are the intercostal muscles?

8 What is lactic acid and what effect does it have on performance in sport?

9 Complete glucose + ... = ... + carbon dioxide + water

10 Give examples from **one** sporting activity where both aerobic and anaerobic systems are used.

Exam-style questions

1 Describe each of the following
  a diaphragm
  b alveoli
  c trachea   (5 marks)
  d tidal volume   (4 marks)
  e vital capacity.

2 a Explain
   i how air is inspired using muscular contraction.   (2 marks)
   ii how air is expired from the lungs.
   iii where oxygen and carbon dioxide are exchanged in   (2 marks)
     the lungs.   (2 marks)
  b How does this occur?

3 a Label the diagram of the respiratory system.

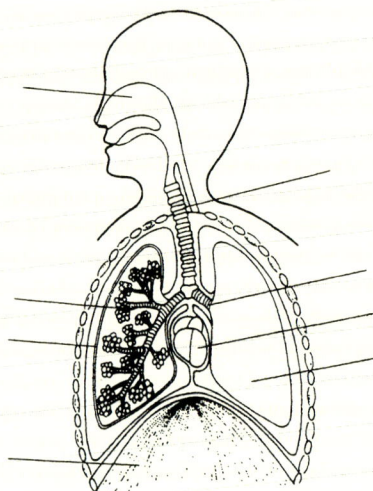

                                        (6 marks)
                                        (2 marks)
                                        (7 marks)

  b State two functions of the respiratory system.
  c What is $\dot{V}O_2$ max and describe how it can be tested?

4 a To produce energy the body uses glycogen which it creates from
    glucose. Complete the equation below: (2 marks)
    Glucose + oxygen = energy + ……….. +……………
  b What is formed from pyruvic acid during anaerobic
    respiration and what is its effect on muscular contraction?   (2 marks)
  c Write an equation showing the relationship between   (3 marks)
    ADP, ATP and energy.
  d Briefly describe the differences between aerobic and
    anaerobic energy systems. Give examples and reasons for
    three sporting activities, one of which uses the aerobic system,
    one which uses the anaerobic system and one which   (8 marks)
    uses both systems.   (5 marks)

Quality of written communication.

B

5

Acquisition of Skill

All of us have different skills. In sports special skills are required to perform well and effectively. The words 'skill' and 'technique' can be confused. Technique is a particular way of performing a physical activity. Skill is the ability to know when and how to perform an activity with the correct technique. Learning skills requires both mental and physical processes.

LEARNING OBJECTIVES

- types of skill
- learning skills
- practice and learning
- information processing systems
- performance of skills
- motivation
- arousal
- goal setting
- aggression
- personality

Types of skill

Most sports require physical performance and mental activity. Repeating a swimming stroke requires little mental planning *after* the stroke has been learned. In orienteering, running over rough ground, reading a map correctly and planning where to run are all skilful activities necessary for this sport.

Physical and mental skills are required for this sport

Select a team game and give an example of a basic skill and a complex skill in the game.

PHYSICAL SKILLS

These are often known as **motor** skills and they form the basis of all sports. Some of these skills are simple: they do not require intricate body movements, and are similar in many sports. Running is a *basic* skill in many sports; hitting, throwing and catching are basic skills in ball games. Although most sportspeople can perform these basic skills easily, they are still learned and require considerable coordination of muscles.

Some skills involve more movements and finer control of many parts of the body. These are known as **complex** skills. For example, high jumping using the Fosbury technique requires the athlete to know and practise

- the exact length and direction of the run-up
- the precise distance of the take-off foot from the bar
- the angle of the leg
- the movement of the arms
- the arching of the back during flight
- the change of body shape over the bar
- a safe landing.

MENTAL ACTIVITY

Very few sports and activities are performed without some mental activity. Activities such as running and jumping need little mental input, whereas activities such as trampolining or gymnastics, where a series of complex movements are put together, need considerable mental activity. Top performers in sports and games practise movements over and over again, until they can perform accurately with very few errors.

When to perform certain skills in a competitive situation requires mental input. No matter how good a tennis player's groundshots might be, the important thing is to play them at the right time during the game, depending on where the opponent is standing.

The ability to 'read the game' is an important part of playing sport at all levels. Knowing when to lob the ball in tennis or to join the line from the fullback position in rugby, is as much a mental activity as a physical skill.

Working out why errors might be occurring, eg in high-jump technique, and correcting them before the next jump, are mental processes necessary to improve performances.

The top performers in sports and games not only have the ability to perform skills at the highest level; they also have the ability to select the right skill at the right time.

CLASSIFYING SKILLS

Some sports require very similar skills, eg tennis, badminton, squash, while quite different skills are needed for others, eg diving and playing rugby. If skills can be put into similar groups then it might be easier to understand how learning one might help in the learning of another.

Transfer of skills

If a learned skill *enhances* the way another skill is performed, it is known as **positive transfer**:

- learning to kick in soccer might be useful in tackling a rugby ball
- passing the ball in netball could help in a game of basketball.

On the other hand, if a previously learned skill *spoils* the way another skill is performed, this is known as **negative transfer**:

- a loose wrist in a badminton service will not help in a tennis service.

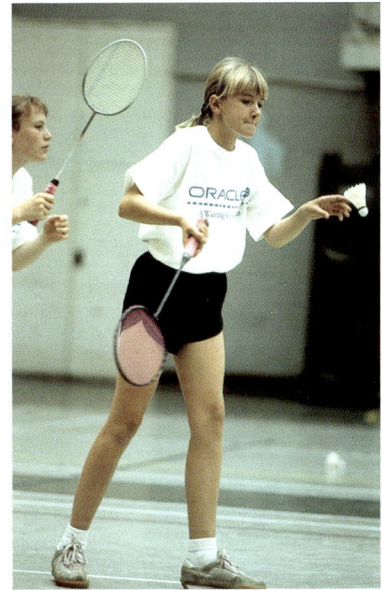

Rackets are needed to play these games, but not all the skills are the same

Open and closed skills

Skills which are affected by the environment or by others taking part at the same time are known as **open skills**. They are found in most sports where there is an opposing player or team. In games such as hockey and rugby there is always some element of unpredictability – what a defending team does, affects how the attacking team play; how an individual dribbles a ball, determines how a defender makes a tackle.

In some sports, an opponent's actions do *not* always determine the actions of others. Skills where the performer has nearly complete control of their performance are known as **closed skills**. In a high-board diving competition, each competitor performs their own dive,

Using one game only, describe three skills which are open, closed and in between.

in the same circumstances as each other, and in conditions very similar or identical to their practice situations. The performance of one diver usually has little effect on another. But if a diver has a lower score than his/her rival, s/he may well try a harder dive to improve their marks.

All skills lie somewhere between these two extremes, and in some sports there are both open and closed skills. A tennis player is in a closed skill situation when serving, but once the ball is in play the skill becomes open, as their opponent returns the serve. It is useful to use a **continuum** to classify each sport.

Open ◄──────────────────────────────────────► Closed

A continuum of sports showing open and closed skills

Pacing continuum

The pacing continuum is based on the degree of control that the performer has over the skill being carried out. It is similar to the open and closed continuum:

- **external pacing** takes place when an external source determines performance; eg a starting pistol in athletics, the reaction of a goalkeeper to a shot in hockey, or the strength of the wind in sailing
- in a **self-paced** situation the performer decides when they are going to perform their skill; eg when to hit the ball in golf, or throwing a javelin.

Serial continuum

The serial continuum is used to describe skills which range from **continuous**, such as swimming or running, to **discrete** skills which have a clear start and finish, such as a somersault in gymnastics.

Learning skills

Learning new skills is a complex process. People are not born with specific skills and abilities, although everyone inherits physical characteristics of size and shape. There are three recognised phases in skill learning:

- cognitive
- associative
- autonomous.

COGNITIVE PHASE

The first stage in learning a skill is to understand what has to be done. Beginners need to be told or shown what actions they have to perform and what results from these actions. At this stage many mistakes are made and help is often needed. Simple things such as holding a racket in the correct way may improve performance considerably:

- example – to perform a badminton serve, the shuttle needs to be hit over the net to start the game.

ASSOCIATIVE PHASE

Performance of the skill improves considerably. There are fewer mistakes, and there is some ability to understand and correct these mistakes. More use is made of the information received from the senses:

- example – to perform a badminton serve well, the shuttle should be hit low over the net and into the opposite service box.

AUTONOMOUS PHASE

The skills are performed almost automatically without much thought or attention. This means that more mental decisions can be made about strategies and tactics in the game. Very few errors occur, and coaching is only needed for fine adjustment to performances:

- example – during a badminton serve, the service is hit either low or high depending on where the opponent is standing. If low, it must be travelling downwards as soon as it has crossed the net; if high, it must have sufficient length to send the opponent to the back of the court.

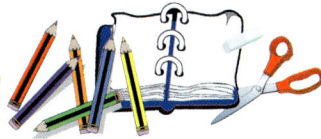

Look at the example of the three phases of learning in badminton. Select any other game (except tennis) and give a detailed description of how these phases apply to learning a skill or technique.

Practice and learning

When learning a new skill or improving a previously learned skill, you need to repeat it over and over again so that it becomes automatic. Because many sports skills are complex, sometimes the skills have to be broken down into smaller units during learning and practice. Triple jump in athletics is a good example where the whole event can easily be broken into different phases to be learnt and practised. This is known as the **part** method of learning.

A front somersault in gymnastics would be *more* difficult to break into parts, and therefore it is best learned and practised as a **whole** event (**whole learning**).

> **Can you think of two sports where part learning would be a good method to use?**

Extreme physical effort cannot be repeated again and again

Some activities can be practised for a long time, while others can only be practised for a short time because of physical demands.

- a basketball player may practise shooting over a fairly long period of time. This is known as **massed practice**
- an athlete practising shot put may not be able to repeat the action frequently as their muscles will tire. Therefore they will have a short practice session, a rest and then repeat the activity again. This is known as **spaced practice**. In very strenuous events such as long-distance running, the practice session may be even less frequent, once a day or even at longer intervals.

GUIDANCE

When learning or practising a skill, some help is needed to ensure that the skill is being done correctly and that improvements are being made. Guidance is often given by a teacher or a coach. There are different types of guidance:

1. visual
2. verbal
3. manual.

In a routine each move needs to be learned separately and then joined together

Visual guidance

When learning sports skills, a demonstration is often given by a teacher or coach. The learner sees what needs to be done and copies the action. Wall charts and diagrams have limited use because they do not show movement, but videos are popular and effective.

Verbal guidance

When learning a new skill, the teacher or coach will talk about it both before and during a demonstration. S/he can explain the finer details of the skill, emphasising important points. Verbal explanations should be short with young learners.

Manual guidance

Often a teacher or coach helps someone to do a movement by holding them. In very dangerous or difficult skills, such as a double back somersault on the trampoline, the learner may be in a belt or rig to give support and safety.

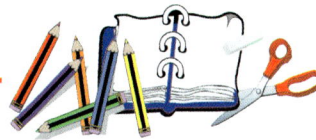

Describe how visual, verbal and manual guidance can be used in three different sports.

Strength

Middle stomach muscles
Move up and down in control, lifting head and shoulders off floor then returning to start positions with shoulders and head flat on floor

Arm and chest muscles
Lower and raise body with control bending and straightening arms.

Upper leg muscles Bend and straighten legs in controlled manner, keeping heels on the floor. With lunges (middle diagram) alternate legs

Lower back muscles
Gently raise and lower head and shoulders. Keep legs in contact with the floor

Many charts show skills but there is no movement

Information processing systems

Information is constantly being received by the brain from our senses – mainly through the eyes, but also through hearing, smell, touch and muscular activity. This system can be represented by the diagram below, which is known as a **model**. It represents what is happening during the learning and performance of a skill.

INPUT

This is the information coming through the senses to the brain. In most games it is important to see the ball and the players of both teams. Sometimes sound is important – a runner may hear someone close behind them. Often in sport, information coming from the skin, joints, tendons and muscles is equally important. A gymnast is unable to see themselves vaulting, but they have sufficient information from the receptors in their muscles and joints to tell the brain the position and shape of the body.

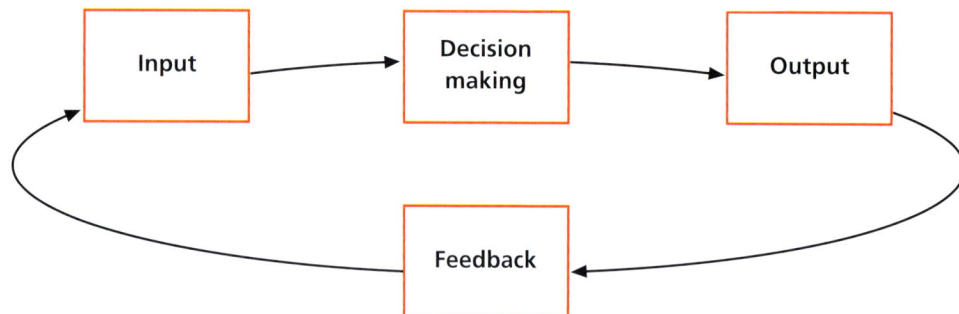

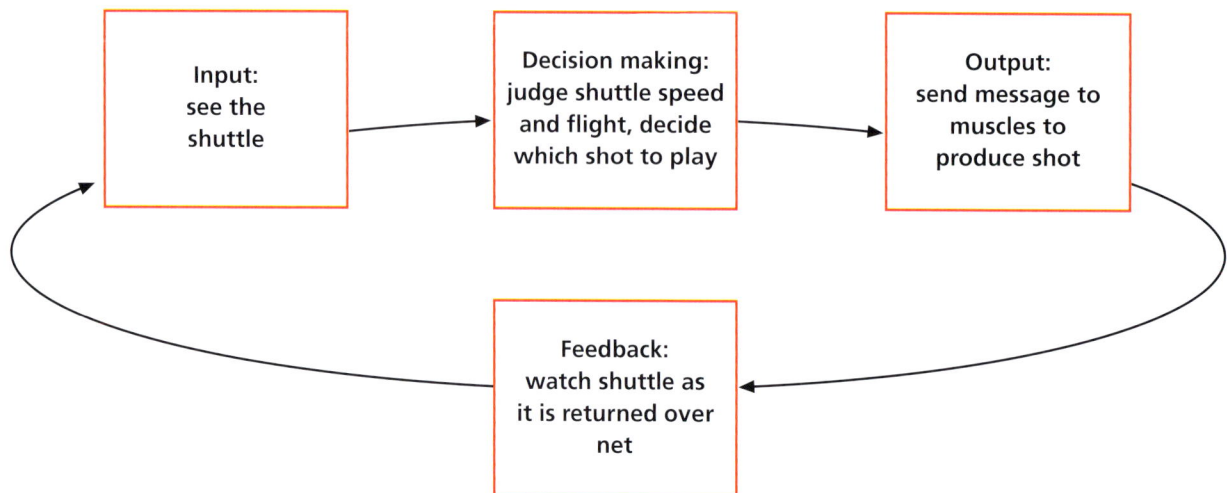

Study the diagram below. Work out the information processing that occurs in another game.

Input → Decision making → Output → Feedback → (back to Input)

Input: see the shuttle → Decision making: judge shuttle speed and flight, decide which shot to play → Output: send message to muscles to produce shot → Feedback: watch shuttle as it is returned over net → (back to Input)

Basic and applied (for badminton) model of information processing systems

When performing a dive, you cannot see your body shape but you know how it looks

Test your short-term memory with a partner. Write down ten nonsense words of three letters each. Show them to your partner for ten seconds, cover them up and ask your partner to write them down. Change over, and this time ask your partner to wait for three minutes before writing down the words.

DECISION MAKING

Often too much information comes through the senses, creating **information overload**. Some of this information may be important (the speed and direction of a ball in tennis), while some of it may be of little use (the colour of the opponent's shirt). The brain has to decide what is and what is not important, and in most sports this has to be done very quickly. Facing a tennis serve of a top player at over 100 mph means that there is little time to take in the information about the direction in which the ball is travelling, letalone decide which shot to play. Two processes occur to reduce the amount of information.

Limited channel capacity

Although the senses are bombarded with information which is then sent to the brain, this information reaches a bottleneck, allowing only part of it to go further for processing. While one piece of information is being processed, other information cannot be acted on. In returning a shot in tennis, a stroke will have been worked out as the ball leaves the opponent's racket, and the flight path has been determined. If the ball hits the top of the net which alters its flight, the brain may not be able to work out the new flight until the system is clear of the first process. There may not be enough time for the player to react to the new information.

Selective attention

This enables sense to be made of all the information available, so that only useful information is acted on. Making sense of the information is done by **perception** and **memory**. For skilled performers, perception allows some anticipation. How else could a tennis ball be returned after a 100 mph serve?

Memory is equally important, but there are two types of memory to be considered:

- **short-term memory** allows information to be stored for a short time. If it is not used, then within about two minutes it will have gone. Important information coming into the short-term memory will be transferred to the long-term memory
- **long-term memory** has a huge capacity to store all kinds of information. In sport, long-term memory will not only hold the rules of the games, but how to play them, what shots to use and how the player performed against an opponent in previous competitions.

OUTPUT

Decisions about the desired output are based on the information received. At this point, the brain sends messages to the muscles to contract in coordinated ways. It may be a lob in tennis, an off drive in cricket or even just standing still and letting a ball roll out of play.

FEEDBACK

As a result of action taken during the output phase, the brain receives further information. This is known as a **feedback loop**, and enables further decisions to be made. There are two main sources of feedback:

1. internal
2. external.

Internal

Internal feedback is gained mainly from the proprioceptors in the muscles which convey information to the brain about muscle tension and joint flexion. There is a feel to a movement, particularly valuable in gymnastics and trampolining, both during and after the event. The receptors also can send messages to the brain about incorrect movements, perhaps in shot putting where the wrong grip and action can cause pain.

External

Feedback comes from outside the body through sound and vision. It could be a video of a performance (a top athlete may receive the information as his/her performance is shown on a large screen in a stadium). Verbal feedback may be given by a teacher or coach, both during and after the performance. Knowing both performance and results provides a sportsman or woman with valuable information during, after and for the next time the event will be performed:

- **knowledge of performance** (KP) generally comes internally through feel and body awareness. But a teacher or coach can talk about performance as well as show it on video. In sports which have an **aesthetic** element such as gymnastics, dance or trampolining, performers are often aware of how well they have performed without their coach or teacher telling them
- **knowledge of results** (KR) gives the final outcome of a performance. A rugby player might be well aware of a number of sidesteps which have taken him/her to the try line, but the result of grounding the ball is the outcome of previous actions. Results are usually obvious, such as a goal, a winning shot in tennis or a hit for six in cricket. Sometimes the results are not always as immediate. After finishing the final race in a decathlon, times have to be converted to points and added to the previous nine events to work out the winner.

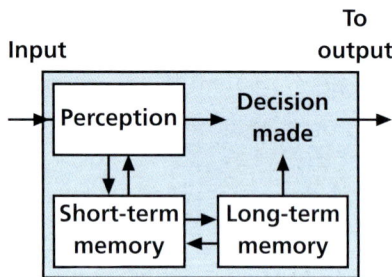

Input — To output

Perception → Decision made

Short-term memory ↔ Long-term memory

Advanced model of information processing

Not only spectators benefit from a screen like this

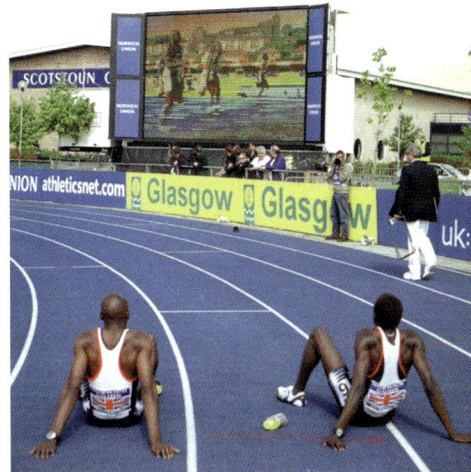

Positive and negative feedback

Having a good performance in a gymnastic routine, or a personal best in long jump, has a positive effect on the next time. Even a good word from a coach can have a very positive effect. Failure to hit services into court in tennis or losing to a weak opponent, might give negative feedback which may have an effect on future performances.

Performance of skills

All sports and activities involve some physical performances of specific skills. This is the final outcome of the information processing system. As a result of practising skills and techniques, sportspeople are able to perform these skills.

Every sport and activity has its own special skills; think of the variety of strokes in just two sports such as badminton and cricket. As a result of practice, special skills and skilled movements are learned, to be reproduced at the correct time during the game. These are sets of movements stored in the brain. A service in badminton requires a series of coordinated movements:

- positioning on the correct place on the court
- holding the racket in one hand and the shuttle in the other
- releasing the shuttle as the racket is swung through with the correct amount of force
- contacting racket and shuttle to send the shuttle in the desired direction with the correct trajectory for the type of service.

Select a skill or technique from a sport and work out the different movements or sub-routines needed to perform that action. Copy the diagram on page 62. (You may need more boxes if the action is complex.)

```
                    Volleyball
                      game
                        ▲
                        │
                  Volleyball serve
                ▲    ▲    ▲    ▲
              ╱     │    │     ╲
```

| Stand behind line | Throw ball in air | Take arm back and then forward | Strike ball with hand |

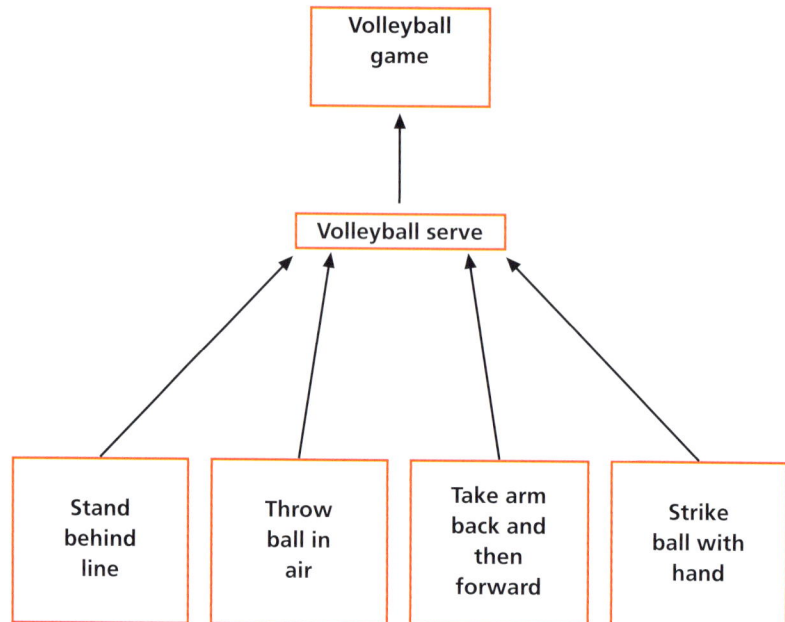

One of the sub-routines that contribute to a volleyball game

These learned series of movements are known as **motor programmes** or **action plans**. They may consist of just a few simple movements, or a series of complex ones. Look at the diagram above of a volleyball serve: it is divided into a series of separate movements or sub-routines, which make up the whole service.

Motivation

No matter how good the coach, the equipment or the facility, learning will not take place if a person lacks the motivation to take part in the activity. Motivation is the driving force that compels people to do something, such as climb a mountain or go to a fitness class. People are motivated by different things: for some it is money, for others the satisfaction of finishing the event (eg many London Marathon runners). Motivation can be

- intrinsic
- extrinsic.

INTRINSIC MOTIVATION

For many people taking part in a sport or some activity is sufficient motivation for them to participate many times. They value the activity and enjoy being with friends and playing the game.

Can you find out the names of other award schemes, and which sports they are used in?

EXTRINSIC MOTIVATION

For professional sportspeople, the main external source of motivation is financial reward. Trophies, medals and the possibility of playing for your country are also powerful motivators. In schools, award schemes and badges exist to encourage and motivate pupils to take part in activities. See the below for an award certificate.

Taking part in a sport or activity for rewards may increase motivation at the early stage of a professional career, but it is harder to maintain this when sport becomes work. However, many highly paid sports professionals could retire early, but choose to continue to play. Professional basketball players, some of the highest-paid sportspeople in the world, have played in the Olympic Games motivated only by an Olympic medal (there are no money prizes at the Olympics – see Chapter 16).

Select a sport and describe in detail how you would use extrinsic motivation with a beginner in that sport. Be specific about the age of the beginner, and the exact type of external motivation you would use.

RAINBOW
SWIMMING AWARD SCHEME

This is to certify that

has achieved the **5m** distance of the Kellogg's ASA/ESSA Rainbow Swimming Award Scheme

Examiner   Date

Chief Executive

Kellogg's
ASA AWARD SCHEME

5m

Extrinsic motivation for very young performers

Arousal

During a long game of football, players' levels of commitment to the game seem to fluctuate. At times they seem to be involved in every move, at other times they seem to lack interest and rarely touch the ball – they are lacking **arousal**. For many people, their arousal levels are high at the very start of a game or sport. In club changing rooms, the pre-match talk given by the coach or captain is usually aimed at raising arousal levels. Body changes when arousal levels are raised include

- increased heart rate and breathing rate
- mouth becomes dry and the pitch of the voice is raised
- palms of the hands become sweaty
- person becomes nervous and edgy.

AROUSAL LEVELS IN SPORT

Arousal levels in sport are important. Too little arousal causes the level of involvement to be low; too much arousal could cause control of behaviour to be lost. Research has shown that there is an optimum arousal level which produces the best performance. The link between arousal and performance is explained using the inverted U theory.

Different sportspeople have different arousal levels. In a hockey game, players' arousal will peak at different times. This could have a positive effect on a team, in that a number of players will always be at an optimum arousal level.

Arousal and specific sports

In some sports, an optimum arousal level is important at the very start, and some sports need higher arousal levels than others:

- a long-jumper has to raise his/her arousal level before the run-up. Often s/he will seek the help of the crowd by encouraging them to clap
- a golfer taking a putt will benefit from a lower arousal level than a weightlifter, who would benefit from a high arousal level just before a lift; in performing a fine controlled movement, a golfer needs to avoid loss of control caused by sudden muscle jerk, which can be a product of high arousal levels, whereas a sudden increase of muscle movement is needed for weightlifting
- skilled coaches of individuals and teams may raise and lower arousal levels depending on the circumstances of games. A basketball team winning by a one-point margin with under a minute to go need to be calmed down so as not to commit fouls. The reverse would be true of the losing team.

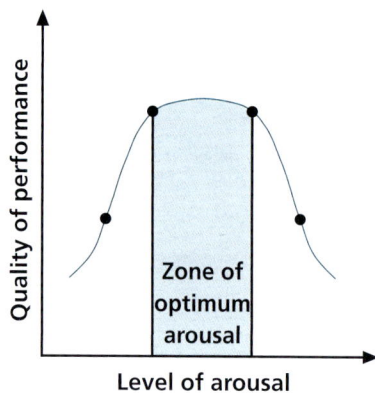

Graph with axes "Quality of performance" (vertical) and "Level of arousal" (horizontal), showing an inverted U curve with a shaded "Zone of optimum arousal".

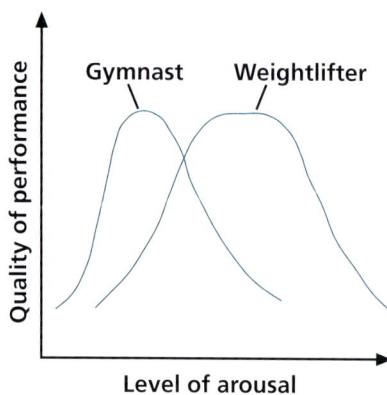

Inverted U graph — showing two overlapping inverted U curves labelled "Gymnast" and "Weightlifter", with axes "Quality of performance" and "Level of arousal".

Too high a level of arousal might spoil the shot

ANXIETY

At the start of an event, arousal levels increase, as does the athlete's anxiety. Anxiety is usually associated with feelings of nervousness, worry and apprehension. Some anxiety may be necessary in order to produce adrenaline and so perform at the highest level but if anxiety is above the optimum level, an athlete may not produce their best performance. Anxiety can be affected by factors such as the level of the match being played, and the reaction of the spectators (particularly the reception of away players by home team supporters).

Goal setting

Setting goals is important for development. You might aim to achieve an academic qualification or a job, to learn a new sport or to improve in an existing sport. The target for a sportsperson might be to win a particular trophy or gain a ranking in the top ten in their sport. For other sportspeople, performance goals may be more important – to improve the time on a previous run, to throw a better distance.

This is not specific to top performers. A beginner in a marathon might set modest targets to improve in his/her first events. The National Coaching Foundation believe that setting goals in sport is important, and use the **SMARTER** system. An example is given in brackets which refers to a tennis serve:

- **S**pecific – goals should be focused and specific (to improve serve)
- **M**easurable – there must be some assessment so that progress can be judged (to reduce double faults in matches to three per set)
- **A**ccepted – the goals must be jointly set between performer and coach (agreed and accepted as necessary)
- **R**ealistic – the performer must be able to achieve the goals (on average, yes)
- **T**ime phased – target dates should be set for goals to be achieved (over the next ten matches)
- **E**xciting – the performer should see the goals as challenging and rewarding (yes)
- **R**ecorded – goals should be written so that coach and performer can judge progress (details of performance at each match recorded).

Aggression

Controlled aggression is necessary in most sports. There is a need to be forceful and assert authority in a team game such as rugby, or in batting and bowling in cricket. In contact sports, aggression is directed against the opposition. Hard contact is made in punching and tackling, yet there must be control to stay within the laws of the game.

A bowler can display aggression in cricket, not by physical contact, but in the way he/she bowls. A bouncer is usually a mark of aggression against a batsman or woman. Equally a batsman or woman may attack a bowler with forceful shots. In athletics, a long jumper is often told to 'attack the board'. There is aggression in the run-up and at the point of take-off.

Can you think of two other sports where there is aggression directed at a player and at an object?

The New Zealand rugby team perform the Haka

A display of aggression before the game

Personality

Studying sports personalities raises many questions: do some people take up sport because of their personality? Does the sport change their personality? Do certain sports attract people with a particular personality?

INTROVERT AND EXTROVERT PERSONALITIES

Personality **traits** determine behaviour in normal life and in sporting situations. People who are quiet, shy, calm and retiring, can be described as **introverts**, whereas **extroverts** are the direct opposite, being outgoing, loud, lively and sociable.

Jonathan Edwards

Triple jumping requires intricate skills but also a lot of body movements. It is not always easy to categorise which sports introverts and extroverts prefer

Can you find two sportspeople who fit into these categories, and two who do not?

It is thought that introverts prefer

- individual sports
- sports with intricate skills
- sports with restricted movements
- routine and repetitive sports.

Extroverts may prefer

- team sports
- whole-body activities
- sports with a lot of movement
- sports with high levels of excitement.

Questions on acquisition of skill

1 Which of the following might be considered a closed skill?
   a   a handstand
   b   receiving a pass in soccer
   c   tackling a player in hockey
   d   catching a ball in rounders.

2 Intrinsic motivation is when a sportsperson takes part in a sport for
   a   enjoyment
   b   money
   c   badges
   d   trophies.

3 Draw a continuum line for open and closed skills, and put the following sports on this line – rugby, archery, high jump.

4 What is the difference between basic and complex skills? Give an example of each of these.

5 What happens in the cognitive phase of learning?

6 What is meant by limited channel capacity?

7 Name two types of motivation.

8 Give an example of both positive and negative feedback.

9 What is meant by arousal in sporting activities? Give two examples.

10 Name one sport which introverts might prefer, and one sport which extroverts might prefer.

Exam-style questions

1 a What is meant by an open skill?   (2 marks)
   b In one sporting activity give an example of a closed and an open skill.   (3 marks)

2 a Describe with examples the three phases of learning skills.   (6 marks)
   b Name two types of guidance and give examples where they might be used in skill learning.   (4 marks)

3 a Draw an information processing model to include input, decision making and output and feedback.   (4 marks)
   b Explain internal and external feedback and give examples of each.   (6 marks)
   c How might long-term memory be useful in a tennis match?   (5 marks)

4 a SMARTER is often applied to goal setting; give a brief description of this.   (7 marks)
   b What is meant by controlled aggression? Give an example from a sporting activity where it is important.   (8 marks)

Quality of written communication.   (5 marks)

6

Health and Fitness

Health and fitness are important in everyday living, and being healthy means more than being ill or sick. The World Health Organisation states that health is 'a state of complete physical, mental and social well being... .'

LEARNING OBJECTIVES

🔍 aspects of health
🔍 health-related fitness (HRF)
🔍 skill-related fitness (SRF)
🔍 testing fitness

Aspects of health

PHYSICAL HEALTH

In a state of good physical health, the body can cope with the demands of everyday living: running for a bus, gardening, decorating the house or walking the dog can be done without any excess strain or demands on the body. The body systems function efficiently and there is no illness or injury.

MENTAL HEALTH

Being in good mental health allows you to cope with the emotional pressures of work and family, adapt mentally to the changing environments of work and leisure, and have a positive outlook on life.

Enjoying healthy activity with friends

SOCIAL HEALTH

Being socially healthy should include having friends and help from others, making a contribution to society and being valued by it, and developing good relationships with a wide variety of people from different classes and cultures.

Fitness

Fitness is a measure of the body's ability to complete activities necessary for everyday life effectively and efficiently. Fitness for sport, however, is often more specific and at a higher level. Fitness has two main components, health-related fitness and skill-related fitness.

Health-related fitness

There are five components to health-related fitness:

CARDIOVASCULAR ENDURANCE

Sometimes known as cardiovascular stamina, this depends on the ability of the heart to pump blood and deliver oxygen to where it is needed. This also involves the lungs and respiratory system, and the function of both systems together is called **cardiorespiratory** endurance. This is a person's **aerobic capacity** (the ability to

Good aerobic capacity and muscular endurance are needed for his event

sustain prolonged activities such as running, swimming or rowing). The heart, lungs and blood vessels need to work efficiently to achieve a good aerobic capacity.

MUSCULAR ENDURANCE

This is the ability of the muscles to contract over relatively long periods of time, without tiring. The two types of stamina are interrelated as the muscles need oxygen which is supplied by the cardiovascular system.

This type of fitness is important for ordinary activities such as walking to work, or doing repetitive manual tasks in industry. In some highly active occupations, there is greater reliance placed on this fitness, such as postmen and women, gas meter readers and farmers. In most sports, the ability to keep active throughout is important, whether it be long distance running or boxing.

SPEED

This is the ability to move the body and limbs quickly. For example, the ability to run for help in an emergency, or run for the ball in a game of cricket. This ability is an important part of most sports.

STRENGTH

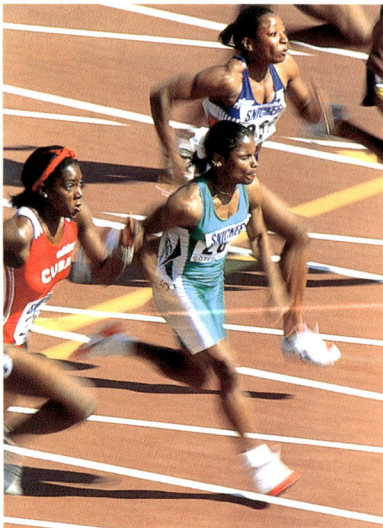

Speed is vital to a sprinter

This is the ability of the muscles to exert force as they contract. Strength is needed in everyday life in many ways. Without good strength, sports such as weightlifting would be impossible. There are different types of strength:

- dynamic
- explosive
- static.

A profession requiring high levels of fitness

Can you think of jobs where different kinds of strengths are needed? Describe these in detail.

Sumo wrestlers need static strength

Dynamic strength

This is required to start and maintain movement of the body. It is related to muscular endurance, but greater effort is required in earlier parts of the activity, eg starting in a cycle or rowing race where considerable effort is required initially, and needs to be maintained until full speed is reached. In rowing, this effort must be continued because the boat will slow down quickly without force being applied.

Explosive strength

This is necessary in many sports. To move the body quickly in gymnastics, or to apply force to an object such as a javelin, requires a special kind of strength. This is sometimes called **power**, and is a combination of **speed** and **muscular strength**. Because of the short time and high muscular activity, fast-twitch fibres and the anaerobic energy system are used.

Static strength

This is the force applied by muscles to a fixed object. Muscle size is important – the larger the size, the more static strength. Activities such as tug of war or pushing in a rugby scrum require high static strength. There is very little movement of the limbs, but considerable internal forces are being exerted against relatively immobile objects.

FLEXIBILITY

The range of movement of limbs at the joints is the **flexibility**, mobility or suppleness of a person. Flexibility is an important part of fitness as it reduces the chances of muscle pulls and allows a full range of movement.

Most sports require a high degree of flexibility. To perform in gymnastics, flexibility at most joints is essential, but there are other sports where flexibility is also very important:

- at the hips in hurdling
- in the shoulder joint in javelin throwing and butterfly swimming.

Javelin throwing is a good example of the importance of flexibility. The bigger the range of movement (the further the arm can be taken back), the longer will be the force applied to the javelin. The more force that can be applied, the further the javelin can be thrown.

Also, in activities such as javelin throwing, the forces exerted on the muscles, tendons and around the joint are considerable. Good flexibility *reduces* the chance of pulled muscles and tendons. In activities which involve short muscle movements, the muscles can become short and susceptible to damage. This is particularly so with soccer players, whose hamstrings shorten as a result of the repetitive kicking actions.

A javelin thrower needs shoulder flexibility

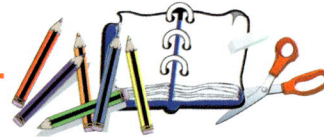

Can you think of sports where there is repetitive and restricted action which might cause flexibility problems?

Skill-related fitness (SRF)

There are five components in skill-related fitness.

AGILITY

Being agile means that a person has the ability to change body direction quickly and accurately. It is dependent on strength, speed and balance. In most sports it is an advantage to be agile; eg to dodge a tackle in rugby, or to change direction quickly to reach a ball in tennis.

Agility is important in volleyball

Balancing on a snow board

BALANCE

A balance can be held (such as a handstand), while cycling or roller blading requires a different kind of balance. A **static** balance is when a position is held without movement; gymnasts need to be good at holding balances using different parts of the body. However, a gymnast has to be balanced when moving on a beam; this is known as a **dynamic** balance. Surfers on water and snow need to have good dynamic balance to maintain control of their boards as environmental conditions rapidly change.

COORDINATION

In many sports, the coordination of limbs and body are important. Moving backwards to play an overhead shot in badminton requires timing and coordination of leg, hand and arm actions, and body movement, in a very short space of time. In pole vaulting, considerable skill is required in coordinating actions after the pole has been planted, until the bar is cleared.

REACTIONS

Being able to react quickly can be a great advantage. For example, a swimmer can gain an advantage over other competitors at the very start of a race, perhaps enough to win the race if the swimmers are equally matched. In these circumstances it is a **simple reaction time**, because the swimmer does not have any choices to make. S/he listens for the 'bleep' and dives as soon as s/he has reacted to it.

In other sports, there may be a number of responses; eg which shot to use when playing a ball in cricket. Because there are different choices, the reaction time becomes the **choice reaction time**. The more choices there are, the longer the choice reaction time will be.

Work out with a partner the maximum number of choices a player may have in a team game.

Quick reactions are needed this close to the net

TIMING

This is the ability to perform a skill at the exact time it is needed. In practice many people can perform skills well, such as heading the ball at the goal. However, the correct *timing* is needed when running from the edge of the box to head in a cross from the corner.

Testing fitness

Most people at some time want to know how fit they are. They might be able to run faster than another person, or do more press ups, but this does not give a measure of fitness; they only appear to be fitter in one aspect than someone else.

Many tests of fitness have been developed scientifically so that the results can be compared between people in different parts of the country and in different countries. It is important that the tests are done exactly as they are described, otherwise the results will not be accurate.

Note: **Some fitness tests are very strenuous, to the point of exhaustion and therefore care should be taken when doing some of these tests. Before taking any fitness test, it is important to work through an appropriate warm-up programme.**

SPEED

The time taken to do a short sprint between 30–50 metres is taken with a stop watch. There needs to be a moving start, otherwise reaction time, explosive strength and sprint start technique become significant factors. Distances longer than 50 metres might involve elements of muscular endurance. The time should be recorded, and when a retest is done, the conditions should be the same.

CARDIOVASCULAR SYSTEM

There are a number of tests for cardiovascular (CV) fitness or aerobic capacity.

Pulse rate

In many of these tests, taking a pulse rate is necessary (see Chapter 3). The pulse rate itself is a guide to basic CV fitness. Resting pulse rates vary, but generally a low pulse rate indicates a better fitness level than a person with a higher pulse rate. Top distance athletes could have a resting pulse rate of 40 bpm. When taking a pulse rate for a minute, miscounts are often made. A 15-second count multiplied by four is a well-tried method.

Extend the time for taking the pulse rate in the Harvard step test for a further two minutes. Make a graph showing your resting pulse rate and recovery rate.

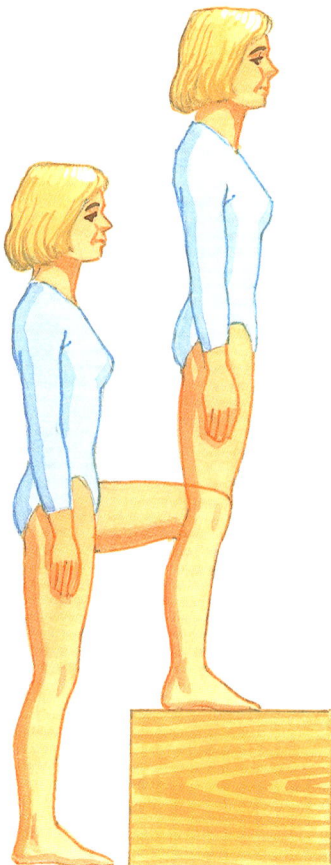

Harvard step test

The Harvard step test

One way of testing CV fitness is to see how quickly a person recovers and gets back to their own normal pulse rate.

Equipment: bench/box 50 cm high, stop watch, metronome or tape with two-second 'bleeps'.

Procedure: take resting pulse rate twice and record the lowest score. The test requires a person to step up and down on the bench/box for five minutes at a rate of 30 steps per minute. After five minutes, the person sits down and the pulse is taken at six, seven and eight minutes. Write down the pulse rate at each interval.

Calculations:

Time of exercise $= 5$ minutes $= 300$ seconds

Total number of pulse counts $= (P1 + P2 + P3) \times 2$

$$\text{Score} = \frac{\text{Time of exercise in seconds} \times 100}{\text{Total pulse counts} \times 2}$$

	High	Above average	Average	Below average	Low
male 15/16 yrs	above 90	90–80	79–65	64–55	below 55
female 15/16 yrs	above 86	86–76	75–61	60–50	below 50

Table 6.1　Ratings for Harvard step test

Cooper 12-minute run

This tests aerobic capacity or $\dot{V}O_2$ max (maximum oxygen consumption).

Equipment: marked track, cones, stop watches.

Procedure: after a warm-up time, run or walk laps of the track for 12 minutes. At the end of 12 minutes, the distance to the nearest 100 metres is recorded.

Score: read directly off the table below.

Age	Sex	Excellent	Good	Fair	Poor
13–14 yrs	male	2,700	2,400	2,200	2,100
	female	2,000	1,900	1,600	1,500
15–16 yrs	male	2,800	2,500	2,300	2,200
	female	2,100	1,900	1,700	1,500
17–18 yrs	male	3,000	2,700	2,500	2,300
	female	2,300	2,100	1,800	1,500

Table 6.2　Ratings for Cooper 12-minute run

Multistage fitness test

This was developed by the National Coaching Foundation (NCF) and is now widely used in schools and colleges. Some national sports teams are tested with this, which measures the $\dot{V}O_2$ max.

Equipment: a firm surface with lines marked 20 metres apart (cones could be used), a tape player with good volume, the NCF tape and tables for scoring.

Procedure: instructions are given at the start of the tape which also identifies the signals for a change of pace. At the start the subject runs slowly from one line to the other. The pace must be judged so the person puts one foot over the line as a beep is sounded. This is repeated a number of times, and then the time between the beeps is shortened requiring a faster pace. There are 25 levels, with the time being reduced each level. When the person can no longer keep up the pace, by arriving at the line after the beep, they drop out. The levels are recorded and fitness is checked against the tables.

Multistage test

STRENGTH

Because there are different aspects of strength, there are a variety of tests. Tests of **dynamic** strength need special machines such as ergonometers, but more simple ways are timed activities such as press ups, pull ups, squat thrusts and dips. Scores for these activities can be compared with others in a group, but it is important that the way tests are done is specified so that everyone does the same action.

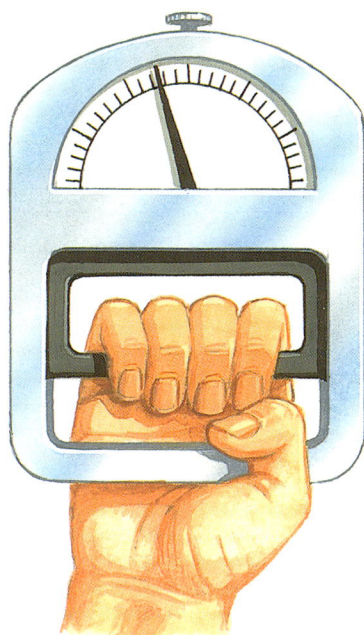
Grip strength dynamometer

Sit-up test

The NCF have developed a sit-up test to measure endurance.

Equipment: mats, tape player, NCF tape and tables.

Procedure: subject lies on a mat with knees at right angles. The ankles are held by a partner. Arms are folded across the chest. When the tape is started the subject does a sit up in time to the bleep from the tape. When the subject can no longer keep in time with the bleep, the level is recorded and the tables used to determine fitness rating.

Grip strength

Equipment: a hand-grip dynamometer.

Procedure: the grip is adjusted to the correct starting point which depends on the subject's hand size. The handle is then squeezed as hard as possible for about two seconds. The best of three scores is taken. A comparison between right- and left-hand strength can be interesting.

Explosive strength can be measured in two easy ways.

Sargant jump

This is a standing vertical jump which tests muscular power.

Equipment: a vertical jump board or chalk, a flat wall, metre rules.

Procedure: the subject stands with both toes against the wall and stretches hands as high as possible while keeping heels firmly on the ground. The height is marked. The fingers of one hand are dipped in chalk, the subject stands with his/her side to the wall. With a slight flex of the legs and swinging of the arms, the subject jumps and touches the wall as high as possible. The distances between the two marks are measured with a metre rule. The best of three jumps is recorded.

Age 15/ 16 yrs	High score	Above average	Average	Below average	Low score
males	above 65 cm	65–56 cm	55–50 cm	49–40 cm	less 40 cm
females	above 60 cm	60–51 cm	50–41 cm	40–35 cm	less 35 cm

Table 6.3 Ratings for Sargant jump test

Standing broad jump

This is very similar to the vertical jump in measuring explosive power, but needs more skill to do correctly.

Equipment: mats, chalk, tape measure.

Procedure: the subject stands behind chalk line, and with flex of knees and swing of arms, jumps two-footed as far along the mat as possible. Mark where the heels land, but if the subject falls back, it is a no jump. Distances recorded, and best score of three is kept.

For **static** strength, machines with captive weight (fixed within a framework) can be used to measure static strength. Loose weight could be used but these require a higher level of skill to be lifted safely. Hand and leg strength can be measured with dynamometers.

Age 15/ 16 yrs	High score	Above average	Average	Below average	Low score
male	2.11–2.01 m	2.00–1.86 m	1.85–1.76 m	1.75–1.65 m	less 1.65 m
female	1.85–1.66 m	1.65–1.56 m	1.55–1.46 m	1.45–1.35 m	less 1.35 m

Table 6.4 Ratings for standing broad jump

FLEXIBILITY

Although the body can be bent and twisted in many ways, measuring flexibility accurately can only be done in a few ways. Hip and shoulder joints are the easiest to measure.

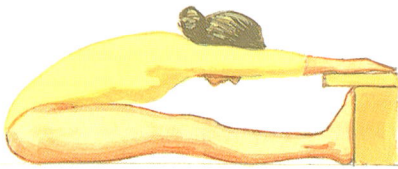

Sit-and-reach test

This measures the flexibility at the hip joint, which is generally restricted in movement by the hamstrings in the back of the leg.

Equipment: a sit and reach box, or bench and metre rule.

Procedure: the subject needs to warm up first with stretching exercises. This will make a difference to the test score in most cases. The bare feet are placed against the edge of the box (or bench), and the back of the legs in contact with the floor. When the subject is ready, s/he reaches slowly along the bench with both hands, fingers outstretched, as far as possible and the distance is recorded. A block of wood can be pushed by the fingers, which makes measuring easier after the event. The best of three scores is taken.

In some cases subjects with very poor hip flexion may have a negative score – they are unable to reach beyond their feet.

Sit and reach

Age 15/ 16 yrs	High score	Above average	Average	Below average	Low score
male	above 28 cm	28–24 cm	23–20 cm	19–17 cm	less 17 cm
female	above 35 cm	35–32 cm	31–30 cm	29–25 cm	less 25 cm

Table 6.5 Ratings for sit-and-reach test

Shoulder hyperextension

This measures the range of movement in the shoulders.

Equipment: metre rules.

Procedure: after a suitable warm up, the subject lies face down, arms outstretched and holding a metre rule shoulder width apart. The chin rests on the floor and the subject lifts the rule against a vertical rule as high as possible. It is important that the wrist remains in a fixed position and is not elevated. The best of three scores is recorded and compared with other group members.

AGILITY

The Illinois Agility Run

This is a well-tried method of testing agility. Its set-up is complicated and exact instructions must be followed.

Equipment: a firm, non-slip surface, six cones.

Procedure: after a suitable warm up, using the course for familiarity, the subject lies face down in the direction of travel. After the starting signal, s/he then runs the exact route as fast as possible. Subjects should have at least two runs, and the best time is recorded.

Age 15/ 16 yrs	High score	Above average	Average	Below average	Low score
male	faster 15.9 secs	15.9–16.7 secs	16.8–18.6 secs	18.7–18.8 secs	slower 18.8 secs
females	faster 17.5 secs	17.5–18.6 secs	18.7–22.4 secs	22.3–23.4 secs	slower 23.4 secs

Table 6.6 Ratings for Illinois agility run

Work with a partner to make up a new agility test, and try it with your friends.

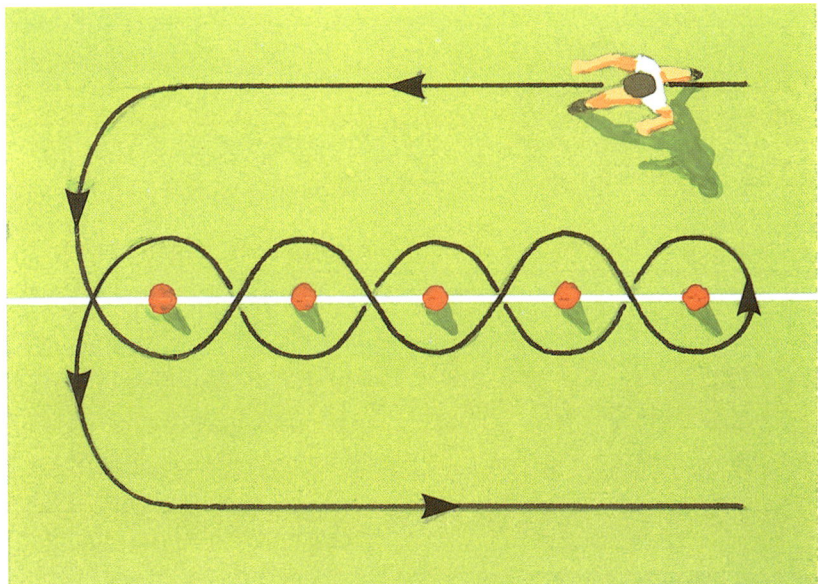

Illinois agility run

BALANCE

Standing on an upturned bench and timing how long this can be held without moving is a simple test of balance.

Stork stand

This is a well-known method of balance testing.

Procedure: stand on both feet, hands on hips. The non-balance leg is lifted so that the toes are placed against the preferred balance leg. The weight is then taken on the ball of the foot and the length of time this is held is taken.

COORDINATION

There are many coordinated movements in the body. Tests of hand–eye coordination can be done by throwing and catching balls.

Alternate hand-wall throw

Equipment: a tennis ball.

Procedure: the subject stands two metres away from a wall. The ball is thrown with one hand and caught with the other. The test lasts 30 seconds and the number of successful catches is recorded.

There are very few tests for coordination. Can you and a partner devise a new test which might be suitable for a racket game?

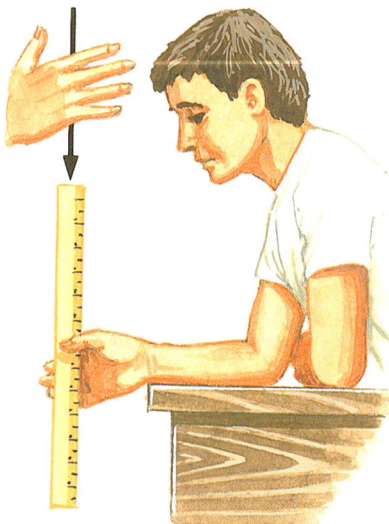

REACTION

Ruler-drop test

Simple reactions can be tested with this.

Equipment: a metre ruler.

Procedure: the subject rests a hand on a table with finger and thumb extended over the edge. A metre ruler is placed between the thumb and forefinger at a marked height. Without warning the partner drops the rule, which must be grasped between the thumb and finger. The height dropped is recorded; the greater the distance, the slower the reaction. This test can be extended to use the other hand, and two rulers can be dropped giving a choice reaction time.

The ruler-drop test

Questions on health and fitness

1 Fitness can be defined as
   a how well a task is performed
   b the ability to meet the demands of the environment
   c the ability to perform a task in a short period of time
   d being healthy.

2 Which of the following is not a component of skill-related fitness?
   a strength
   b agility
   c balance
   d reaction.

3 Name two types of endurance which are important for sportsmen and sportswomen.

4 Give one example of where flexibility in a sport is important.

5 Give an example from one sport where static strength might be important.

6 Name two types of balance.

7 What does the multistage fitness test measure?

8 Name two sports where simple reaction time is important.

9 What is the Harvard step test?

10 How can the pulse rate be a guide to a person's basic fitness level?

Exam-style questions

1 List the five components of health-related fitness. (5 marks)

2 a Give three examples of skill-related fitness taken from sporting activities. (6 marks)
   b Give four examples which might indicate a person's lack of fitness. (4 marks)

3 a Complete the table below:

Sport	Dynamic strength	Explosive strength	Static strength
rugby			
athletics			

   (6 marks)

   b What is meant by flexibility? Describe one test for flexibility. (4 marks)
   c Give an example where improved flexibility can improve performance. (5 marks)

4 a How might improving muscular endurance help with everyday activities?   (5 marks)

b The graph below is taken from the results of a two-people Harvard step test. Describe the differences between A and B.   (10 marks)

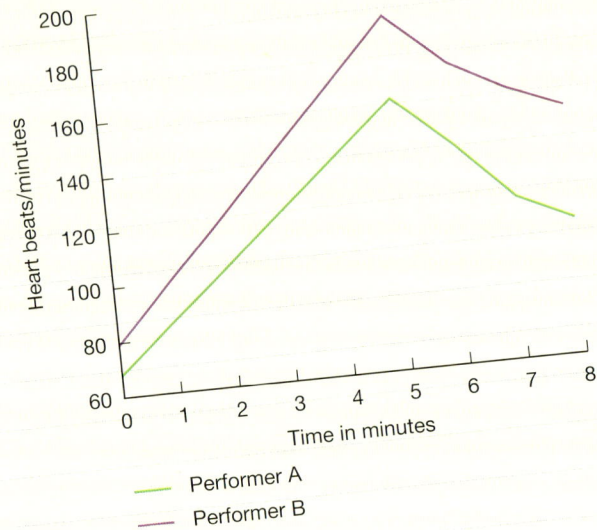

Heart beats/minutes vs Time in minutes

Performer A
Performer B

Quality of written communication.   (5 marks)

7

Training

Training needs to be done to maintain or improve fitness levels and skilled performances. There are general principles for training as well as specific methods.

LEARNING OBJECTIVES

- principles of training
- FITT
- training zone
- planning training
- training methods and effects on the body

Principles of training

There are four basic principles in all training sessions applied to skill and fitness:

- specificity
- overload
- progression
- reversibility.

SPECIFICITY

Training must be specific for a sport or aspect of fitness. Training for tennis may not help improve hockey skills, while improving aerobic capacity will do little to increase flexibility of the joints. This does not mean that training for one sport will have little effect on another. Transfer of training can take place where the sports or parts of a

Think of two sports which could have the same training programmes for one aspect of fitness.

sport have a great deal of similarity (see Chapter 5). Aerobic fitness, muscular endurance and similar elements of fitness are common to many sports. Therefore specific training of fitness elements for one sport may be of considerable benefit in another.

OVERLOAD

Overloading body systems with higher work rates and increased loads, causes the body to respond to these extra demands by improving its performance. There are three ways in which overload can be considered: frequency, intensity and duration.

Frequency

The frequency of training is the number of times training occurs. As levels of performance rise, the frequency of training is often increased. The once-a-week training session and a match on Saturdays is now barely sufficient for many sports. Top performers need to train most days, particularly long-distance runners who need to run considerable distances in training to improve their aerobic capacity. The higher the physical demands in training, the less frequently they occur, so allowing the body to recover.

Intensity

Intensity is increased by raising the workload. This could be the distance run in training, or the number of repetitions. Increasing the weight of an object, such as a shot, is a good form of overload training for the shot putter.

Duration

Duration, or how long training takes place, is determined by the activity and the fitness of the performer. Untrained athletes may only be able to work for a few minutes when they are starting a new event. As athletes improve, they are able to train for longer periods.

Overload is an important principle in weight training

However, the type of event can restrict the duration of training. Excessive physical activity such as weightlifting can only be done for a short period of time. The practising of skills which make little physical demand on the body, such as snooker, can be undertaken for a much longer time.

But duration of training could be determined by the mental pressure as well. In events which are intricate, dangerous and difficult to perform, training time might need to be short.

Training for longer periods of time in a sport can only be achieved by varying the training session, so that fatigue and boredom are eliminated.

PROGRESSION

Progression occurs as the body adapts through overload. Training needs to be progressive. Moving too quickly from basic skills to advanced skills does not enable smooth progression; the body will not be able to adapt to too much overload. Increasing the weight too quickly in weight training does not allow the muscle strength to be built up.

As strength is improved, more weight can be added which then leads to further improvement in strength. In the early stages of fitness and skill training big improvements are seen. As the body adapts, improvements in performance become more gradual. Sometimes a performer seems unable to make progress and stays at the same level for a period of time. This is known as a **plateau**, but performers are often able to improve after some time at this fixed level.

REVERSIBILITY

This is the reverse of progression. Once training and performances are reduced, the body naturally adapts to new circumstances:

- the aerobic capacity can be quickly reduced through lack of exercise
- muscular endurance diminishes when muscles are no longer used over extended periods of time
- skill levels, however, can often remain high, but performances in skills might be reduced because of physical decline.

A javelin thrower might improve his/her technique and performance through training, but after they stop training and practising, the distance they throw is reduced. They will probably have good skills but less muscular power.

Select a sport or activity. Describe examples of training in that sport which, during a training session, can be practised (a) only a few times (b) many times.

Making a comeback after a long lay-off due to injury or for other reasons is often difficult in many sports. Select two sports and suggest why it might be easy to start again in one sport, and more difficult in another.

FITT Principle

Frequency – training sessions should be sufficient to bring about improvements, but there should be enough recovery time, particularly in physical intense activities.

Intensity – training must be set at a sufficient level to bring about change in the body systems.

Time – training time for each session should be judged in accordance with fitness levels. For the same intensity, the time should be gradually increased as cardiorespiratory and muscular endurance increases.

Type – the type of activities included in the training programme must be the same as, or closely associated with, the particular sport or activity.

Training zone

The intensity of training is important; too little, then there is no effective change to the body systems. If the training is too intense then the athlete may not be able to train for the required time, indeed it might be dangerous for the athelete to continue. In most weghts gyms there are charts showing the training zone for appropriate age groups. However, it is possible to work out a safe training zone for an individual. The **threshold**, which is the maximum safe level for an individual, the maximum heart rate, is worked out using the formula:

Maximum heart rate = 220 – age of performer

The older a person is, the lower the maximum heart rate.

The maximum level of heart rate is also dependent on both fitness levels and age. For a 15-year-old it should be just over 120 bpm. This means for a 15-year-old the training zone is between 205 bpm (220–15) and 120 bpm.

The table opposite shows that working between 60–80 per cent, aerobic training takes place; above 80 per cent, the body begins to use the anaerobic system.

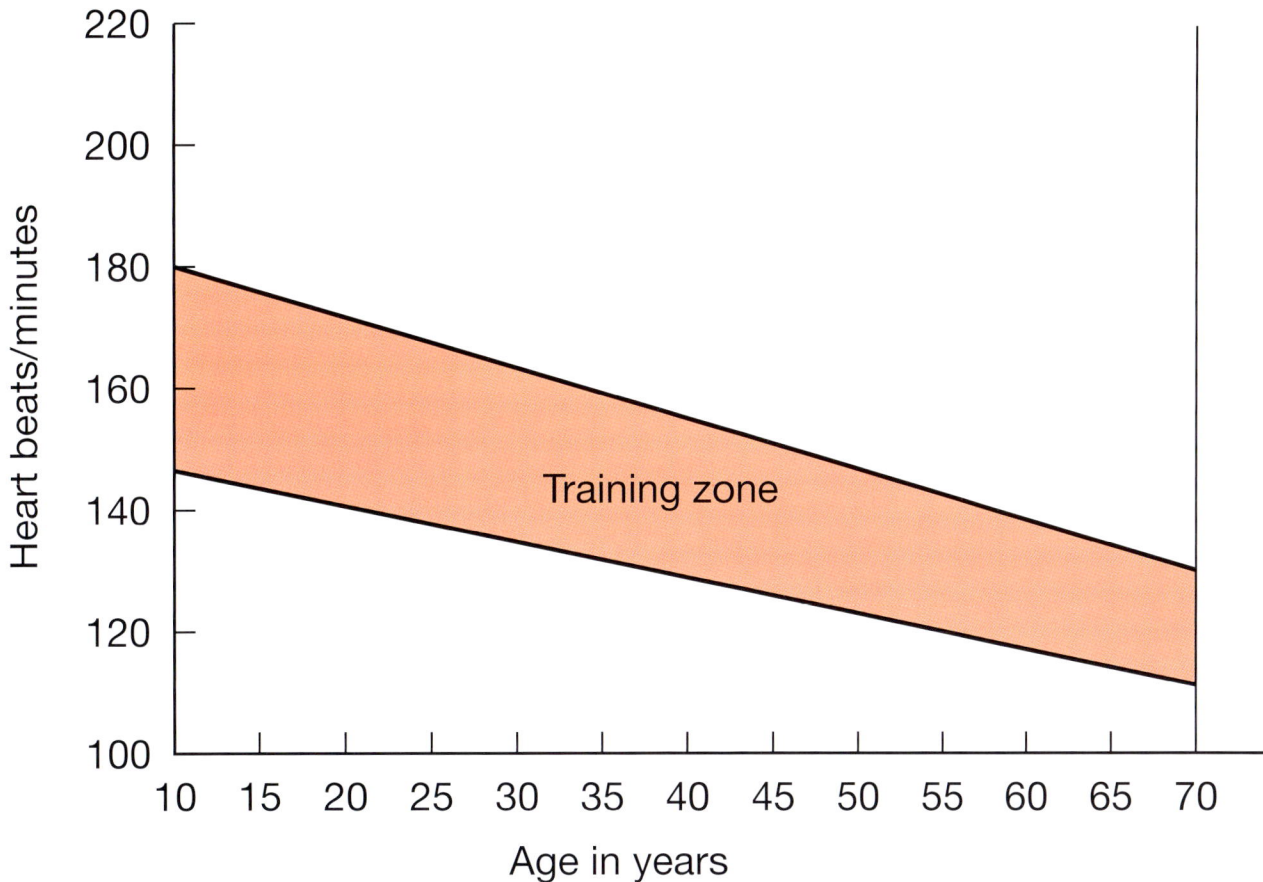

The y-axis is labelled "Heart beats/minutes" with values 100, 120, 140, 160, 180, 200, 220. The x-axis is labelled "Age in years" with values 10, 15, 20, 25, 30, 35, 40, 45, 50, 55, 60, 65, 70. The shaded band is labelled "Training zone".

Planning Training

LONG-TERM PLANNING

When planning a training programme the first consideration is the individual. What are their capabilities? What is the reason for their training? Most sportsmen and women plan their training for a particular purpose; it may be for a season, a series of events, or even just a single event. In many sports there are seasons, although with the growth of indoor and worldwide events sportsmen and women are able to compete throughout the year. Some of our traditional sports have retained their seasons; the soccer season now stretches from August until May, rugby players are now able to play rugby union between September and April, and switch codes to play rugby league in the summer. Athletes are able to compete throughout the year in outdoor and indoor events. However, all sportsmen and women need rest periods and times to prepare more intensely for competitions. They need to structure their training so that they are at their best for a particular competition; it could be the London Marathon, a world championship or the Olympic Games. This is known as **peaking**; they target their training and competition so that they produce their best performances at the right time.

SEASONAL TRAINING PROGRAMME

- out of season – light training, mainly aerobic work and strength training. Participation in another sport helps to prevent mental staleness. Levels of fitness are partially maintained
- pre-season – before the start of competitions. Increase in the intensity of training, particularly muscular endurance and cardiovascular fitness. Improve and refine skills technique. Most sports requiring speed, increase in the amount of anaerobic training
- early season – selected competitions. Continue with aerobic and anaerobic training to maintain levels of fitness. Skills training to refine and improve technique. Mental preparation and physical rest before competitions
- peak season – more regular competitions with appropriate training and rest periods between competitions. Maintain fitness levels. Mental preparation, diet and exercise prior to competitions.

SINGLE SESSION PLANNING

In a single training session the time is often split into a range of different activities:

- warm-up
- fitness
- skills
- cool down.

Warm up

The body needs to be correctly prepared for any activity. The warm-up period serves a number of purposes:

- increases the blood flow to the muscles, increasing the temperature
- stretches muscles and tendons reducing the risk of injury
- increases mental arousal levels.

The warm-up can be considered as a routine in itself. Often it is specific, but a general warm-up could be used:

① flexibility exercises at the start of the session
② pulse-raising exercises such as jogging
③ more specific flexibility exercises, which might be specific to a sport
④ higher levels of exercise using the major muscle groups to maintain and/or raise the heart rate
⑤ skills exercises for the sport, perhaps lay-up routines in basketball or high clears in badminton.

The activity will be the determining factor as to how much time is spent on each activity in the warm-up period. Gymnasts might spend more time on flexibility, whilst runners might work on aerobic warm-up exercises.

Fitness

The amount and importance of fitness depends on the activity. Aerobic fitness is important in most sports, and training sessions will usually include this type of activity. However, some sports demand very high levels of cardiorespiratory fitness, so most of the fitness session will be spent on activities to develop it. Where possible it is important to devise fitness sessions which are based on the game.

Skill phase

This can be individual and team skills. Activities such as athletics (apart from relay), gymnastics and trampolining are **individual** activities. Often groups of athletes will come together for a training session, but will still be working as individuals on their skills. As well as developing individual skills, players in team sports need to be able to work in small groups or units and also in full-team situations. Skill practice should be drawn from game situations: eg passing in pairs, two attackers versus one defender.

Pressure training – combining endurance and skill in a training session has dual benefits. As endurance levels fall, so the level of skill declines. A badminton example: two players are on the same side of the net, playing alternate shots over the net to another player who has to move rapidly right then left, to return shots. This is in effect a short sprint (or shuffle) fitness training, combined with a badminton shot.

Passive and active opposition – when practising very difficult skills or at an early stage, performers have to concentrate fully on the skill itself. A beginner in hockey will find dribbling a ball around cones difficult in the first lesson. As the level of skill improves, the performer may be able to look around. Replacing the cones with pupils is the next step – dribbling around class mates might be more difficult. If they stand still this is known as **passive** opposition. As the skill level continues to improve, the pupils no longer stand still but move, or attempt to tackle the dribbler. Here the opposition has become **active**.

Similarly, whole-team skills can be practised without any opposition. This is known as **unopposed** practice. An example of this is in rugby line-out. The forwards will work together to improve their group skill. Only when they feel they have perfected their line-out technique will they bring in some opposition.

Cool down

This is often the forgotten part of a training session. Many of the exercises used in the warm-up time can be used again. Once an intensive activity is stopped, the body takes some time to respond to this. Remember how long it took for the heart rate to return to normal after the Harvard step test? Also, when the pumping action of muscles contracting stops, lactic acid remains in the muscles longer, causing soreness and pain. This is known as **blood pooling**, commonly occurring in the legs. Gentle exercise is needed to ensure the body returns to its normal state.

Getting it right without the opposition

Training methods and effects on the body

Different sports require different training methods. Even in a single sport such as athletics each event has different training methods; in team games positional play can sometimes determine the most appropriate training.

MENTAL HEALTH AND TRAINING

The mental stress on top-level sportspeople is high. They compete week after week with intensive media coverage, and a string of poor results often brings adverse comments. Top athletes become media stars with all the pressures that this lifestyle brings; personal lives become public property through media coverage.

Some sports governing bodies employ psychologists to work with players. They tend to focus on winning and losing in sport, rather than on personal problems, but often the two are interrelated. Psychologists are able to help players to set goals and to plan for and cope with stressful game situations such as tie-breaks in tennis. They aim to raise players' self-esteem and to help them maintain high levels of motivation during training and in matches.

Imagine you are playing in an important tennis match tomorrow. What mental preparations might you make?

Both batting and fielding require short bursts of effort

ANAEROBIC TRAINING

In many sports short bursts of activity are needed: in netball a fast movement at the centre pass to receive the ball, in athletics the run-up phase in the long jump and in cricket running to field the ball on the boundary. These short bursts of activity rely on the anaerobic system (see Chapter 4). Training is done by repetitions of sprints over short distances of between 10–20 metres, or up to ten seconds sprinting with appropriate rest periods (the work/rest ratio should be around 1:5). The work rate can be increased by sprinting up an incline. If distances are increased then it is important to run at maximum speed.

Effects

- 🏸 the heart walls (particularly the left ventricle) grow stronger and therefore pump blood more effectively
- 🏸 there is a faster dispersal of lactic acid from the muscles, enabling muscle action to continue for a longer time.

Advantages

- 🏸 very specific.

Disadvantages

- 🏸 little variety possible in this type of training.

AEROBIC TRAINING

There are many methods of aerobic training all of which improve the cardiorespiratory system.

AEROBICS CLASSES

This is continuous training usually done to music, and involves the use of legs, arms and whole-body movements. Variations of this include:

- **step classes:** similar routines are carried out, but a step is used to maximise body effort. Steps can be varied in height for different fitness levels
- **aquaerobics** is performed in water. The resistance of the water to movement is a useful way of increasing the work rate, while the buoyancy of the water relieves stress on the joints
- **chair** aerobics: this is an effective way of maintaining fitness for older people and wheelchair users.

Effects of aerobics classes

- the heart becomes more efficient
- the stroke volume is increased, and as a result the heart rate becomes lower
- recovery to normal becomes faster
- blood volume, red cells and haemoglobin increase
- arteries grow larger
- diaphragm grows stronger
- lungs are more expandable increasing in volume
- alveoli become more efficient.

Imagine you are a wheelchair user. Devise some activities you might be able to do in a sitting position to improve your cardiovascular fitness. Test your programme to make sure it is feasible.

Step aerobics

INTERVAL TRAINING

This is intermittent training with periods of high-intensity work interspersed with rest or very low-activity periods. Distances above 30 metres or times of 30 seconds–5 minutes are used to decide the work rate. After each activity a set time or distance is allotted for the rest or very light-activity period. During this rest period, the oxygen debt which will have occurred during the work phase can be repaid (see Chapter 2). The activity is restarted and the process continues for a number of repetitions and sets. Interval training needs careful planning, as the duration, intensity of work and rest phases need to be carefully matched to the level of fitness of the athlete. Interval training can be used for most team games and is an effective and accurate method for aerobic training in athletics and swimming.

Advantages

- distances and times can be adjusted to suit individual sportsmen and women and it is suitable for a variety of sports
- sets targets to be reached
- can be used for aerobic and anaerobic training or a mixture of both.

Disadavantages

- needs careful and accurate planning
- can be boring.

CONTINUOUS TRAINING/LONG SLOW-DISTANCE

Working without a rest can only be done at moderate intensity, about 75 per cent of maximum. Fitter sportspeople can work at a higher rate than this. Continuous activity such as running, swimming and aerobics classes mean that the heart rate and breathing are maintained at a high level over a sustained period of time. In fitness gyms, the same effect can be achieved by skipping, running on a treadmill, or using rowing machines and exercise cycles.

Activity needs to be maintained at the correct level for at least 15 minutes. Long slow-distance running is another way of continuous training.

Advantages

- may not require much equipment
- training levels easily controlled by the sportsman or woman
- easy to organise.

Disadvantages

- does not develop anaerobic fitness and change of pace required for many sporting activities
- difficult to measure training amounts
- can be monotonous.

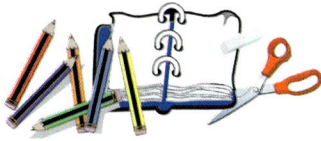

In pairs, work out detailed plans of an interval training session in a sport. Then, do the training as you have detailed. Evaluate how well or badly you did. Was it too hard or too easy? Modify your plan accordingly.

Including this in a Fartlek session would be beneficial

FARTLEK

Based on Swedish training methods, the word means 'speed play'. Athletes can vary their pace and style of running and walking as they wish. There are no fixed amounts of each activity, and much depends on how the athlete feels during training, which could take place on a track, or cross country. Because of its flexibility, both aerobic and anaerobic systems can be improved. It is both enjoyable and a valuable method of training, giving variety and maintaining motivation. Athletes need to have a planned session however, to make the best use of this training. A typical session might be:

- 5-minute slow jog
- 3-minute normal jog
- 3-minute fast walk
- 5-minute fast jog
- 2-minute hopping alternate legs
- 5-minute 30-metres sprint/30 metre walk
- 3-minute fast jog
- 2-minute fast walk
- 2-minute cool down.

Advantages

- range of both aerobic and anaerobic training
- can be adapted for different sports
- variety in pace.

Disadvantages

- difficult to measure training amounts
- needs self-discipline to maintain work rates
- not sport specific.

WEIGHT TRAINING

Dynamic, explosive and static strength are all dependent on the force exerted by the muscles. Weight training is an effective way to improve muscle strength, but the type of strength which will be developed determines how this is applied. The general principles of developing strength are as follows:

- a light weight moved many times increases muscular endurance
- a medium weight moved very fast will increase explosive strength
- a heavy weight moved a few times will increase static strength.

Weight training can be done with barbells (a bar with weights at each end) and dumbbells (similar to barbells but with a very short bar). These are often referred to as free weights. Weight-training machines have now replaced barbells and dumbbells in schools, colleges, fitness gyms and sports centres. Although there are many ways of using loose weights, some machines are able to exercise muscle groups which could not be achieved previously with loose weights. There are many advantages of weight machines over free weights. Weight machines

- are safer, easier and more comfortable to use
- work specific muscles or groups of muscles
- have results which are easy to see
- can be fitted into a small space safely
- can help with motivation.

But, they are more expensive!

Repetitions (reps) and sets

When devising a weight-training programme, the number of repetitions and sets must be determined:

- **repetitions** are the number of times an activity is repeated. This might vary from 3/4 up to 30. High repetitions will assist in the development of muscular endurance; low repetitions are aimed at static strength improvement
- **sets** are the number of times an activity is taken in a training session. Often three sets of activity are done in weight-training sessions.

An example of the above system would be a person doing 15 bench presses (repetitions) and taking this activity three times (sets) in a training session.

A typical fitness gym

Training for muscle action

The three types of muscle action, isometric, isokinetic and isotonic (see Chapter 2 for further details) require special weight-training methods:

Work out a weight-training programme for yourself for either strength or endurance. Make sure you list all the activities, the exact weights to be used and the repetitions and sets. Try the programme.

Working with a partner, can you find examples in sport of isometric, isotonic and isokinetic actions, which might be included in a training programme?

- **isometric** training (where the muscle remains at the same length throughout the exercise) can be practised with **heavy** immovable weights
- **isokinetic** training requires the use of weights which provide **resistance** through the full range of movement. In a simple curl with a free-weight bar, the amount of muscular force is reduced as the arms become more flexed. If using a curl machine, however, the resistance of the weight continues for longer during the movement
- **isotonic** training involves the same resistance or weight but the muscle either shortens (**concentric** contraction) or lengthens (**eccentric** contraction). The biceps curl is again a good example: as the bar is lifted towards the chest the biceps, which are the prime movers, shorten as they contract. Lowering the bar to the starting position means that the biceps are still under tension, but this time they are being lengthened throughout the action.

Advantages

- specific muscle groups can be targeted
- can be adapted for most sports
- muscles' strength and endurance can be quickly increased.

Disadvantages

- special equipment needed, which can be expensive, as well as needing a suitable location
- needs to be well planned, so that the correct training of isometric, isotonic and isokinetic exercises are used.

CIRCUIT TRAINING

Circuit training was originally devised to improve fitness levels with large numbers of people in a small space during a relatively short session. A minimum amount of equipment is needed, as the performer's body provides the 'weight'. It is a highly adaptable form of training suitable for different aspects of fitness and skills or both at the same time.

Areas or equipment in the gym or hall (or outside) have specified activities. These locations are known as **stations**. After completing the activities at one station, the subject then moves to the next station in the correct order. Activities at each station differ, so that different muscle groups can recover while other muscles are working. There may be five to fifteen stations, and the activities will be determined by the type of circuit planned. Activities at each station will be repeated a specified number of times or for a fixed period of time. There may be rest intervals between activities, or better still a range of low-intensity activities interspersed, allowing oxygen debt to be repaid.

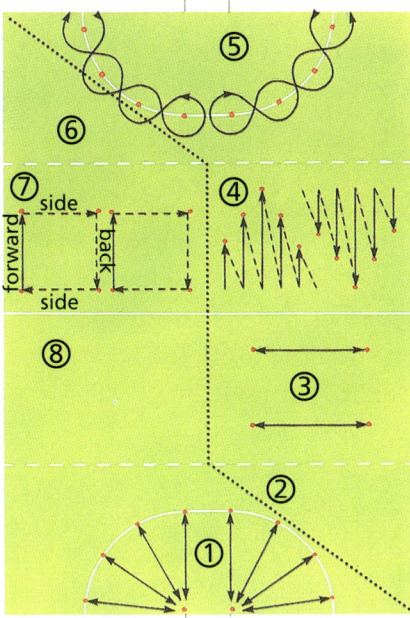

Activities
1. Circle shuttle
2. Burpees
3. Partner pull (10 m)
4. Pyramid run
5. Swerve the curve
6. Squat thrusts
7. Square bash
8. Press ups

Organisation
After warm-up:
- work in pairs
- complete either number/circuits or time

NB All warm-up and circuits done *with* a hockey stick

A simple fitness circuit using a hockey field

Design a small card to use in circuit training described above. Include maximum score, training dose and time taken.

Factors of circuit training design

- the purpose of the circuit – skills and/or fitness
- type of activities to achieve purpose
- number of stations in circuit
- number of repetitions of each activity
- time for each activity
- rest or recovery time
- number of circuits
- total length of training time.

Intensity and overload

If everyone in the group does exactly the same number of repetitions or works for the same length of time, no account is taken of individual levels of fitness or skill. Some may be working well below their fitness level, while the activities may be too hard for others to complete.

Performers can be tested on each activity to determine their maximum score, or how much they can do in a fixed period of time (30–45–60 seconds). Their maximum score is recorded, and the total is halved. These half scores become their **training amounts**. Three circuits are completed, with each performer working at their own level. A time is recorded when the three circuits have been completed, and an improvement on this time serves as a target for the next circuit training session. Using this method, the performer is overloading by 50 per cent on each activity.

Maximum score	= 20 sit ups
Half score for training dose	= 10 sit ups
Three circuits 3×10	= 30 sit ups

A nine-station circuit to improve cardiovascular and strength fitness could be:

1. sit ups – abdominals
2. bench dips – arms
3. step-ups – legs
4. squat thrusts – abdominals and legs
5. press ups – arms
6. shuttle runs – legs
7. burpees – abdominals
8. pull-ups – arms
9. star jumps – legs.

Range and performance of fitness activities

The above circuit includes a small number of the activities which can be used to develop fitness. Any activity using large muscle groups in a repetitive way can be included in a circuit. The space and equipment may be a determining factor as to the number of stations and the range of activities.

Guidelines to the correct movement patterns need to be clear: how far down to dip on a bench? How much flexion at the knee on squat thrusts? This means that the same activities are performed when circuits are repeated, allowing results to be compared.

Skill circuits

Circuit training in games such as netball, basketball, hockey and soccer can be easily planned, but will probably take up more space than fitness circuits. Basic skills of passing, dribbling and shooting are performed at the various stations. Outdoor areas can be used for skill circuits in the major outdoor games. For example see the hockey circuit on the previous page.

Advantages

- variety of activities keep motivation levels high
- adaptable for fitness and skills for a variety of sports
- can be done with little specialist equipment
- can incorporate aerobic, anaerobic and weight-training exercises
- can accommodate large numbers of people in a small area.

Disadvantages

- needs considerable organisation and planning
- may need some specialist equipment.

ALTITUDE TRAINING

In preparation for the Olympic Games in Mexico City many countries organised training camps at a high altitude, because Mexico City is at 3,000 metres (10,000 ft) above sea level. Training at altitude is particularly important for distance runners, as at a high altitude there is less oxygen available, and the body increases the mass of red blood cells as well as levels of haemoglobin to cope with this. When the athlete returns to sea level there are normal amounts of oxygen and the athlete is able to make better use of this and so increase his or her performance in endurance events. Athletes who live at high altitude and train at sea level are able to increase the oxygen-carrying capacity of the blood.

Advantages

- very effective for training for events which require good aerobic levels
- good preparation for events to be held at both high altitude and at lower levels.

Disadvantages

- expensive, particularly for countries which do not have high mountains, such as the UK and the Netherlands.

Work out a skill circuit for your favourite sport. Describe the area you are using and the equipment needed for a group of 20 players.

PLYOMETRICS

This is an effective way of improving explosive strength. It involves rapidly stretching a muscle, and using the energy generated in the elastic part of the muscle. The muscle then contracts using the stored energy. An example of this type of training is a simple jumping exercise. On landing there is little flexion at the knee and ankle joints. As soon as the feet touch the ground, the next jump should be made, minimising the time in contact with the ground.

The principal effects of plyometrics for **endurance** strength training:

- muscles work harder and for longer as a result of improved efficiency
- energy obtained from fat rather than glycogen is effectively used
- increased capillary growth enables more efficient transfer of oxygen to the muscles.

Effects for **explosive** strength training:

- muscles contract more strongly
- the tendons increase in size, enabling larger forces to be transferred from muscle action.

Effects for **static** strength:

- muscles increase in size as fibres grow thicker.

Advantages

- little specialist equipment required
- can be used for different sports
- develops.

Disadvantages

- not suitable for inexperienced sportsmen and women
- training levels not easily measured.

FLEXIBILITY TRAINING

Maintaining and improving flexibility, the range of movement about the joints, is an essential part of fitness. There are four methods of improving flexibility, which are explained below.

Static stretching

A muscle is held in a stretched position for a short time. As flexibility increases the time can be extended, but should be at least ten seconds. After a short rest the exercise can be repeated.

Performing passive stretching on someone is a careful task

Passive stretching

An external force is applied to a limb or joint, and held for a number of seconds. This is usually done by a partner or coach, who knows the flexibility of the athlete. Care must be taken in this activity so as not to damage the athlete.

Active stretching

Sometimes known as ballistic stretching, the limbs and body are moved vigorously, stretching the appropriate muscles. Extensive muscle warm-up should take place before using this active method of improving flexibility, and even then care must be taken not to make movements too violent.

PNF stretching

Immediately after contracting, muscles can be more easily stretched. The muscle being worked on is strongly contracted against a high resistance. Immediately, the muscle is stretched to the end of its range. The exercise is then repeated.

Effects of flexibility training

🔍 the muscles and tendons can be stretched more easily, thus increasing the range of movement at the joint.

DANGER: TOO MUCH TRAINING!

Many dedicated athletes train at a level which is detrimental to their health. Often training takes place too early after injury or even when injured, causing even further problems. Overtraining in skills can lead to boredom and mental staleness which reduces performance levels in competitions.

Hurdlers need to work at their flexibility during training and before an event

Hand/eye coordination skills need to be learned

AGILITY TRAINING

Strength, speed and balance are important elements of agility, and any training of these will result in improved agility. In many games, agility is a necessary skill and can be developed in a skill coaching session.

Effects of training

- body movements can be made quicker
- more unpredictable movements in games to beat opposition.

BALANCE TRAINING

Balance requires delicate control and often good static strength in relation to body weight. Balance in gymnastics (both static and dynamic) is practised during the training. Performing a handstand on the floor requires use of large body movements, followed by small movements in body shape and hands. In the initial stages of learning to balance, a very low beam is used in gymnastics and beginners in wind surfing can practise on a simulator.

Effects of training

- **static** balance – fine muscle control and stability in balance
- **dynamic** balance – better control in more extreme conditions (eg staying on surfboard in high waves).

COORDINATION TRAINING

Many movements in sport are a series of coordinated events and muscle actions. Very young children are unable to coordinate hand and eye movements when catching a ball. Teaching and training from a young age leads to increasing control in eye-and-limb coordination, leading to the correct order of events, and muscle responses. In events such as triple jump, each phase needs coordination, as well as the joining of the phases themselves. Hitting the ball in hockey requires not only hand – eye coordination, but correct foot placement, and movement of hands on the stick.

Effects of coordination training

- movements appear smooth with no jerkiness
- movements become more effective.

REACTION TRAINING

Although it is unlikely that reactions can be improved, response time *can* be improved. The speed of reactions governed by the speed of transmission from the input to the brain (a tiny electrical impulse), shows little variation. The response, however, is dependent on the recognition of what is required and the physical response. Training and playing sport means a considerable amount is experienced and learned. As players improve they are able to think and act more quickly in game situations. They therefore *respond* more quickly.

Effects of training

- faster muscle responses
- less errors in movement
- improved performance in choice reaction situations
- more time to make decisions.

TRAINING FOR TIMING

Training for improving timing involves repetition of activities until the person learns to judge speed and distances. Learning to jump in a rugby line-out requires practice in that situation; timing the jump to be at maximum height as the ball is above the head.

Questions on training

1 The training method which involves a variety of different speeds such as jogging, sprinting etc is
   a interval training
   b Fartlek
   c continuous training
   d plyometrics.

2 In the FITT principle of training, F stands for
   a full
   b fast
   c frequency
   d fitness

3 What is meant by a threshold level in training?

4 Name four parts of a single training session.

5 Give two activities in a circuit training session.

6 Name one sporting activity where anaerobic training might be useful.

7 Give the four main principles of training.

8 Name two types of flexibility training.

9 What is meant by continuous training?

10 What is altitude training?

Exam-style questions

1 Name five methods of training. (5 marks)

2 a What is meant by threshold? (1 mark)
  b Overload is one of the principles of training. Give the three (3 marks)
    ways overload can be increased.
  c Name the other three principles of training with a brief (6 marks)
    explanation of each.

3 a To improve cardiovascular endurance should a person (1 mark)
    use aerobic or anaerobic training?
  b Why is it important to start a training session with a time (3 marks)
    for warm-up, and how does this affect the body
  c For a hockey player during the season describe a typical (5 marks)
    training session.
  d A hockey player needs to plan their training over the whole
    year. Give two examples of activities they might do during their
    training in
    i   pre-season. (2 marks)
    ii main season. (2 marks)
    iii off season. (2 marks)

4 a Name five activities in a circuit training session for (5 marks)
    general fitness.
  b Give two advantages for using the circuit training method. (2 marks)
  c Give two disadvantages for using Fartlek training. (2 marks)
  d What is meant by a training zone, and how does it depend (6 marks)
    on a person's age?

Quality of written communication. (5 marks)

8

Drugs and Sport

Most people have a range of drugs in their house

Drugs are chemical substances which can affect the working of the body. Most drugs have a beneficial effect in relieving pain, illness or disease. When used in sporting activities, drugs can affect the performance of an athlete, and drug taking is known as 'doping'.

The use of drugs in sport is not a new problem; it is possible that competitors in the ancient games in Greece took stimulants. However, the first reported use of drugs in sport was in 1879 when a group of cyclists were found to have taken substances to improve their performance at a cycling event.

There are many types of drugs; some can be legally bought at a pharmacist, others are only available on prescription from a doctor, and it is illegal to possess some of the more powerful drugs.

LEARNING OBJECTIVES

🔍 categories of drugs
🔍 doping methods
🔍 other drugs
🔍 controlling drugs in sport

Categories of drugs

In order to control the use of drugs in the 1968 Olympic Games, the International Olympic Committee (IOC) became the first world organisation in 1967 to establish a medical commission. As new drugs develop, the IOC continues to fight against the use of drugs in sport. In 1994 the IOC categorised drugs into the following types:

- stimulants
- narcotic analgesics
- anabolic agents
- beta blockers
- diuretics
- peptide hormones and analogues
- other substances.

STIMULANTS

These raise the heart rate and *stimulate* the nervous system. Reactions are improved and the person feels more alert with increased confidence in their abilities. High levels of work can be maintained without the feeling of pain and fatigue. Increased confidence may, however, lead to misjudgement of abilities, and cause accidents. In the 1967 Tour de France the successful UK cyclist, Tommy Simpson, died as a result of the effects of taking stimulants.

Caffeine – 'an illegal substance'

Examples of stimulants

- **caffeine**, which is found in coffee and tea
- **amphetamines** such as ephedrine, dexedrine, benzedrine and 'speed'.

Possible side effects

- increase in hostility
- high blood pressure
- irregular heart beats
- overheating of body as pain and fatigue signals are suppressed
- mental depression after the immediate effects of the drug have passed
- addiction.

NARCOTIC ANALGESICS

These *suppress* pain and enable athletes to perform when injured. After a hard physical performance they encourage sleep, enabling the body to recover. Cyclists who have to perform at high level for a number of days have been found using these drugs. Narcotics cause drowsiness and analgesics are painkillers.

Examples of narcotic analgesics

- **morphine** – medical pain killer
- **heroin** – medical pain killer
- **codeine** – available over the counter as a pain killer, and is sometimes found in medicines for diarrhoea.

Possible side effects

- highly addictive (illegal in most countries for this reason)
- constipation
- mental apathy

Check any pain killers,
cough medicines or
diarrhoea preventatives for
the chemicals they contain.
Can these affect an athlete's
performance, and if so,
how?

Steroids help to increase muscle growth

Can you think of some team
games where the players
might be tempted to use
anabolic steroids illegally,
to improve performances?
Give specific examples.

- low blood pressure
- over-training when injured.

ANABOLIC AGENTS

More commonly known as anabolic steroids, these drugs were developed in the 1940s to help *build up* patients suffering from muscle and soft tissue loss. Hormones are naturally produced in the body to repair damaged tissue, and steroids were developed artificially to perform the same function as hormones. The male hormone, **testosterone**, is responsible for the *androgenic* effect of developing male characteristics such as a deep voice, hair on the chin, and the *anabolic* effect of stimulating muscle growth.

In most sports, muscular power and endurance are important. First used by body builders in the 1950s, other athletes realised that by taking steroids they were able to increase the rate of muscle growth. These drugs also raised competitive levels of performance in most events; throwing events in athletics could be particularly improved.

In 1999/2000 many sportsmen and women were tested positive for nandrolone; in the UK alone 24 competitors from ten different sports. Many said that this was because they had taken food supplements which were converted into nandrolone by the body.

Examples of anabolic steroids

- **nandrolone**
- **stanozolol**
- **artificial testosterone**
- **clenbuterol.**

Possible side effects

- heart disease
- high blood pressure
- bone, tendon and ligament weakness
- infertility
- growth of facial hair in females
- deepening of voice in females
- liver disorders
- balding in females
- acne
- stunted growth in children
- aggressive behaviour.

BETA BLOCKERS

To perform some sports well, it is necessary to lower anxiety levels either before or during the event. Rifle shooting and snooker are two examples of these sports. Beta blockers slow down heart and breathing rates, counteracting the adrenaline release which occurs before an event, and speeds up heart and breathing rates.

Example of beta blockers
🔍 **propranolol.**

Possible side effects
🔍 drowsiness
🔍 insomnia
🔍 depression.

Tranquillisers such as **diazepam** (valium) are also used to reduce anxiety levels. They cause muscle relaxation and are addictive.

DIURETICS

In events such as boxing, wrestling and judo, getting the right body weight at the weigh-in just before the event is important. Diuretics increase the amount of water in the urine which not only reduces body weight quickly, but may also disguise traces of drug in the urine by diluting it.

Example
🔍 fruscmide probenecid.

Possible side effects
🔍 rashes
🔍 nausea
🔍 loss of sodium and potassium salts
🔍 muscle weakness and numbness.

PEPTIDE HORMONES AND ANALOGUES

These are growth hormones, which control pain and increase the amount of red blood cells. They balance the effects of anabolic steroids and help to increase body weight, protein and cellular growth.

Can you think of other sports in which it is useful to be calm and steady throughout? Can you think of events which are very active and then need steadiness and high levels of concentration, which might tempt an athlete to take drugs illegally?

The correct body weight is important at the start of a competition

Argue the case for and against using drugs to enhance performance.

Examples of peptide hormones and analogues

🔍 **corticotrophin**
🔍 **gonadotrophin**
🔍 **erythropoietin.**

Possible side effects

🔍 increased risk of strokes
🔍 abnormal growth.

OTHER SUBSTANCES

Sportspeople may be allowed certain levels of other substances in their bodies when taking part in an event, such as local **anaesthetics** and **corticosteroids**. Athletes often wish to take part even though they may be suffering from an injury. A decathlete may suffer an injury during the first day but may want to continue in the competition. Drug treatment of such injuries is permissible, eg a local anaesthetic to reduce the pain, or an injection of a corticosteroid (hydrocortisone) to reduce severe swelling of a joint.

Possible side effects

🔍 competing when injured can often cause further damage.

Doping methods

The IOC list the following methods of doping:

🔍 blood doping
🔍 pharmacological, chemical and physical manipulation.

BLOOD DOPING

Increasing the number of red blood cells enables more oxygen to be carried to the muscles. In blood doping, extra red cells (either the performer's own or taken from someone else) are injected into the bloodstream. In extreme cases, blood transfusions take place where larger amounts of treated blood are put into the performer.

Possible side effects

🔍 allergic reactions
🔍 kidney damage if blood is not correctly matched
🔍 transmission of diseases such as HIV, hepatitis and AIDS.

PHARMACOLOGICAL, CHEMICAL AND PHYSICAL MANIPULATION

Athletes who have taken drugs try a number of ways to avoid being detected. A common way is to use clean urine from another person. This might be hidden in a bag and released into the sample bottle through a tube. In extreme cases athletes have clean urine put through a ureter (a small tube) into the bladder, so that the sample is clean. The tests are very precise and often the smallest trace of drugs are picked up even with clean urine from the bladder. Some athletes may have others take their place at a drugs test, but obviously only if the athlete is not well known.

Other drugs

'No smoking' signs in public places aim to prevent passive smoking

SMOKING

Nicotine is taken into the bloodstream through smoking. It is an addictive drug which raises the heart rate and blood pressure. There are other reasons why smoking can damage health:

- lung cancer – tars are deposited in the lungs, making them less efficient; this can lead to cancer
- increased risk of heart disease – nicotine causes higher adrenaline output, which increases the heart rate and raises the blood pressure as blood vessels in the skin contract
- carbon monoxide reduces the effectiveness of the oxygen-carrying capacity of haemoglobin – haemoglobin absorbs carbon monoxide before oxygen, and so less oxygen can be taken to the muscles
- throat cancer – irritant gases and tar passing down the throat
- reduced levels of fitness
- less resistance to illness, such as bronchitis
- loss of smell, taste and appetite.

Smoking also affects other people, who may develop these side effects by inhaling cigarette smoke in the air. This is called passive smoking.

ALCOHOL

Small quantities of alcohol are not harmful to general health, but it does affect performance in sport. Alcohol contains the chemical **ethanol** which acts on the brain to affect balance, speech and coordination. Side effects include

- loss of balance, coordination and reactions
- dehydration – alcohol is a diuretic, and can increase water levels in urine

- loss of body heat because of increased blood flow to skin (see Chapter 3)
- reduction of glycogen levels and slower lactic acid removal (see Chapter 2)
- affected judgement, leading to possible accidents
- aggressive behaviour.

RECREATIONAL DRUGS

Although most of these drugs have been produced for medical purposes, they are often taken illegally. Many are addictive and some long-term effects are fatal. They have no place in sport.

Amphetamines

These are a stimulant as mentioned earlier, and can increase energy and lift depression. Their common names are 'speed' or 'uppers'. If used over long periods, they can cause psychological problems. **Ecstasy** is an hallucinogenic amphetamine which affects temperature and appetite control. Because it causes dehydration and overheating of the body, use of this drug can lead to death.

Barbiturates

A type of sleeping pill, such as valium. Common names are 'downers' or 'sleepers', and these drugs are psychologically addictive.

Cocaine

Produced from cocoa leaves, cocaine gives a feeling of exhilaration and energy. It was used by native Indians in South America to help them run long distances when hunting. It is a very addictive drug and can be fatal if taken in large doses. Possession of cocaine is illegal.

Cannabis

This drug is called by many names, such as marijuana, grass or hashish. It is made from the Indian hemp plant, produces mild intoxication and can be addictive. It is considerably more likely to cause cancer than tobacco. Possession of cannabis and growing the plant is illegal.

Heroin

Derived from the opium poppy, heroin produces intense intoxication. It is extremely addictive, and hard to stop taking. Large amounts can prove fatal. It is illegal to possess heroin in the UK.

Lysergic Acid Diethylamide (LSD)

LSD is a chemical which causes hallucinations. Behaviour becomes extreme and can cause death or serious injury. A long-term effect can be mental disorder.

> **All recreational drugs are dangerous. Name and describe in detail two types of recreational drugs, their effects on the body and reasons why they are dangerous.**

Solvents

Sniffing the fumes of solvents such as glue and dry cleaning fluid leads to hallucinations. They can cause suffocation and damage to the heart, brain and liver.

Controlling drugs in sport

International governing bodies want to stop the use of drugs in their sport. Apart from the fact that it is cheating, many drugs are illegal and the side effects are harmful. Sportspeople are important role models, and their illegal behaviour could influence their fans and supporters to follow suit.

CHECKING FOR DRUGS

In most sporting events, there are procedures for checking athletes for drugs.

1 Competitors chosen for testing

Rules in each sport vary considerably. Competitors can be tested in training, or after their event. Perhaps the first three in a race and a random selection of other runners would be required to attend the doping control centre immediately after the race. To avoid any confusion, competitors are usually notified in writing that they will be tested.

2 Reporting to the doping control centre

The doping control centre will be near to where the event has taken place. The competitor may be accompanied by an official to the centre. The identification of the competitor is made, who will then declare any medication s/he is using.

3 Providing a urine sample

The competitor selects a sample bottle which is numbered. A sample is given under strict supervision, and enough clothing has to be removed to observe the sample being given. Only the competitor is allowed to handle the sample bottle. Sealed drinks are available for competitors who may be dehydrated.

4 Using sealed containers

The competitor then selects two sealed containers, breaks the seals on these and divides the sample equally between these containers. The competitor then seals the containers and one bottle is marked A, the other B.

5 Recording information

The bottle code numbers are recorded and checked by the competitor. The competitor then certifies that the procedure has been carried out correctly.

6 Laboratory analysis

Both samples are sent to an approved laboratory. The technicians at the lab are not told who the samples belong to.

7 Testing

Sample A is tested. If there is no indication of drugs, samples A and B are destroyed. The governing body of the sport is informed, but not the competitor. If sample A gives a result showing drugs have been used, the governing body of the sport is informed and the competitor is usually suspended. The competitor is allowed to give an explanation, and if requested, sample B is tested.

8 Arranging a hearing

If there is no doubt that drugs have been used, the governing body arranges a hearing where the competitor may present their case with the help of others. The governing body will then decide what the punishment should be. It could be a short ban or even a lifetime suspension. The competitor may appeal against this.

The Doping Control Laboratory for the Olympic Winter Games in Nagano, 1998

Diane Modahl

FUTURE OF DRUG TESTING

Drug testing is not a foolproof method: mistakes can be made, so that an innocent competitor is charged with using drugs, while some drugs are difficult to detect, so the guilty competitor is not found out.

Mistakes in testing can be made at a laboratory: samples may become mixed up, or they may not be stored at the correct temperature. The tester may make a mistake during the test, producing a mistaken result. Many competitors will not appeal if their result is positive and they know they are guilty of taking drugs. Professional athletes who are clean (ie they do not take drugs) will contest positive results, as sport is their living. Diane Mohdahl tested positive in an event before the Commonwealth Games in 1994. The results became known when she was at these games and she was suspended. After a year of appeals, she was proved innocent of having a testosterone level of over 40 times the normal limit. However, by then she was no longer at the peak of her fitness and has competed in few events since.

As drug testing becomes more precise, cheating competitors are continually seeking new ways to avoid being caught. Manufacturers produce drugs which are more and more difficult to detect. As drugs are made to resemble natural body hormones, detection becomes nearly impossible. Competitors will continue to take drugs to improve their performances for many reasons because

- they want to win at all costs
- by winning they can earn more money
- there is pressure on them to win.

TESTING AND PUNISHMENT

Although the availability of accurate drugs testing is open to the governing body of every sport, it is not always used. Testing may often only take place at competitions or in season. In 1996, the UK was one of only 30 countries of the 197 competing in the Atlanta Games to hold drug tests outside of competitions. Competitors can train throughout the year using drugs, and then stop taking drugs in enough time before the competition to avoid detection.

Punishment for taking drugs is left up to the governing bodies of sport. Some may pay little regard to recreational drugs, but react strongly to performance-enhancing drugs. Drug-enhanced performances by Ben Johnson in the Seoul Olympics 1988 contributed to the growing concern over use of drugs in sport on the world stage. The IOC have been at the forefront of establishing accurate and fair methods of drug detection, and unlike other governing bodies, have been prepared to ban athletes from future games when they have been found guilty of drug abuse. Testing may not always be accurate, but the threat of testing is a significant factor. In Sydney Olympics 27 Chinese athletes withdrew eight days before the games began.

Do you think that there should be a difference in the punishment imposed for the use of recreational and performance-enhancing drugs? What do you think is a suitable punishment for taking these drugs?

Questions on drugs and sport

1 Which of the following is found in tea or coffee?
   a ethanol
   b heroin
   c caffeine
   d codeine.

2 Which is not an anabolic steroid?
   a nandrolone
   b cocaine
   c clenbutorol
   d stanozolol.

3 Name two stimulant drugs.

4 Which organisation controls drugs in sport?

5 Name two sports where competitors might be taking beta blockers.

6 What type of drugs might a long-distance cyclist take and why?

7 List two recreational drugs.

8 Name two side effects of anabolic steroids.

9 What physical advantages might a 100-metre sprinter gain from taking steroids?

10 What is meant by blood doping?

Exam-style questions

1 Name five categories of drugs identified by the IOC.   (5 marks)

2 Drugs can affect a sportsman's or woman's performance. Give examples of this, naming the substance and its effect on performance.
   a a stimulant   (2 marks)
   b a narcotic analgesic   (2 marks)
   c a beta blocker   (2 marks)
   d smoking   (2 marks)
   e a recreational drug.   (2 marks)

3 a Describe the procedure taken for drug testing at an athletic event in the UK.   (10 marks)
   b Apart from testing competitors at events, in what other ways might drug testing be used to reduce the numbers of athletes taking drugs?   (5 marks)

4 Technological advances with equipment such as fibre glass vaulting poles and better running surfaces, have helped athletes to improve their performances. Over the last few years more and more athletes have been found taking drugs to improve their performances. In the light of this discuss:
   a What are the benefits from taking drugs? Give examples taken from sporting events.   (5 marks)
   b What are the disadvantages in taking drugs?   (5 marks)
   c Should there be different punishments for competitors who take performance-enhancing drugs, as opposed to those who take 'social' drugs?   (5 marks)

Quality of written communication.   (5 marks)

9

Diet and Exercise

Diet is important not only to maintain healthy body systems, but also to provide energy for exercise.

LEARNING OBJECTIVES

- food
- balanced diet
- diet and energy
- diet problems
- diet for sport

Food

Food is the body's source of energy, enabling muscle movement, growth and repair. The food we eat should contain a number of essential items:

1. carbohydrates
2. fats
3. protein
4. vitamins
5. minerals
6. fibre
7. water.

CARBOHYDRATES

The body breaks down carbohydrates to give glucose and glycogen, the main sources of energy. Although energy can be gained from other sources, the speed and efficiency of getting energy from carbohydrates is important. Carbohydrates can be split into two types:

Crossing the Channel will use up energy from fat

① **simple** carbohydrates – these are sugars. Jam, honey, cakes, chocolate, fruit, milk and sugar itself are some of the foods which are part of this group

② **complex** carbohydrates – these are starches. Vegetables, cereals, rice, pasta and bread are in this group.

During digestion, carbohydrates are broken down into glucose. Simple carbohydrates have a high level of glucose and are readily absorbed into the bloodstream. As the amounts of glucose build up, and if there is little activity, it is converted to glycogen and stored in the liver and muscles. If the digestive system is unable to break down all the carbohydrate, then this is stored as fat.

FATS

Energy can be provided by fats but is not as readily available; the body releases it slowly. Higher levels of oxygen are needed to release the energy from fats. Fats are essential in providing

🎾 an energy source when resting or sleeping
🎾 a layer below the skin keeping the body warm
🎾 protection to vital organs.

Fats contain three types of fatty acids:

① **saturates:** in animal products, milk, meat, cheese, cream and butter

② **polyunsaturates:** in fish oils and products made from vegetable seeds such as sunflower and corn

③ **cholesterol** is found in the blood, and the level of cholesterol is increased when eating certain foods. Fatty animal products

Healthy foods – low levels of saturated fat

contain cholesterol, and eating these increases the amount in the body. Too much cholesterol leads to a clogging of the artery walls, increasing blood pressure and causing circulatory problems. It is therefore important that the intake of saturated fats should be reduced.

PROTEINS

Proteins are made from amino acids and are essential in building cells, making blood and regenerating muscle tissue. There are two types of amino acids:

① **essential amino acids** cannot be produced by the body and therefore these have to be taken as food. There are eight essential amino acids, which are contained in meat, fish, eggs and cheese

② **non-essential amino acids** are produced by the body.

Most body tissue is made up of protein, so the intake and the production of amino acids is essential.

Proteins are used to

- make tissue, bones and skin
- repair damaged tissue
- enable growth.

Protein only supplies energy when there is a deficiency of carbohydrate and fats, and this is only when intense activity is maintained over a long period.

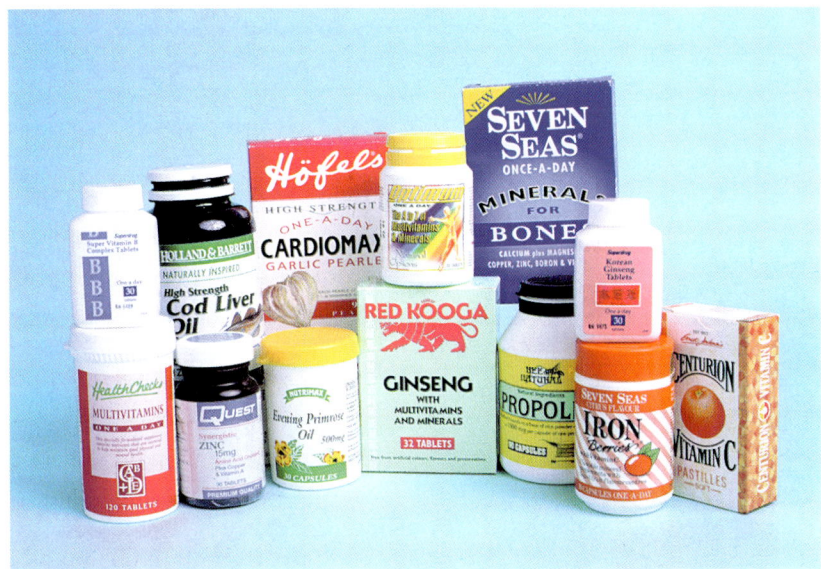

A balanced diet should provide sufficient vitamins

VITAMINS

Vitamins are trace substances in food which are necessary for the normal efficient functioning of the body. There are two groups of vitamins:

① **water-soluble vitamins** cannot be stored in the body and therefore must be taken in the diet daily (vitamins B and C)
② **fat-soluble vitamins** can be stored in the body (vitamins A, D, E, K).

Vitamins serve a number of functions:

- regulating chemical reactions in the body
- releasing energy from food
- helping with growth and repair of tissue
- maintaining resistance against disease.

Vitamin	Source	Purpose
A (retinol)	milk, butter, eggs, fish, liver	healthy skin, good vision
B (thiamin, riboflavin, niacin)	as above, plus cereals and vegetables	helps energy production
C (ascorbic acid)	citrus fruit, vegetables	healthy skin, gums, heals wounds
D (calciferol)	oily fish, eggs, butter	builds up bones and teeth
E (tocopheral)	green vegetables, wheatgerm	protects cells from damage
K (phytomenadione)	green vegetables, liver	prevents blood clotting

Table 9.1 Major vitamins

MINERALS

These are very small quantities of chemical substances in food. Calcium in milk, iron in meat, liver and green vegetables are examples of minerals. The body uses minerals in specific ways – see table 9.2.

FIBRE

Fibre does not contain nutrients, but it is essential in the digestive system. It is found in wholemeal bread, vegetables, fruit and cereals:

- it provides bulk for food
- it encourages slower, even release of sugars
- it prevents constipation.

Some evidence shows that fibre may help to prevent bowel cancer.

Mineral	Source	Purpose
calcium	milk, sardines, vegetables	hardening of bones and teeth
iron	liver, meat, green vegetables	production of haemoglobin in red blood cells
iodine	dairy products, seafood	healthy thyroid gland
sodium	salt, cheese, bread	muscle contraction and maintenance of body fluid
potassium	milk, bananas, oranges	muscle contraction

Table 9.2 Major minerals

Rehydration during activity

WATER

Water makes up two-thirds of the body contents. It is taken into the body through fluids and food, and lost by the body through sweat, urine, faeces and breath. As there is a constant loss of water throughout the day (over two litres), this must be replaced to stop dehydration. As activity levels increase, more water is lost; hot weather conditions increase this loss even further.

Balanced diet

Ask a partner about the last main meal s/he had, and write it down. Can you decide if it was a balanced meal?

The body needs to take in food in the correct proportions, so that the essential elements are included. A good balanced diet will be

- 10–15 per cent protein – white meat such as chicken is better than red meat
- 25–30 per cent fat – polyunsaturated fats rather than animal fats
- 50–60 per cent carbohydrate – starch rather than simple sugar carbohydrates.

This will also give the necessary amounts of vitamins, minerals and fibre.

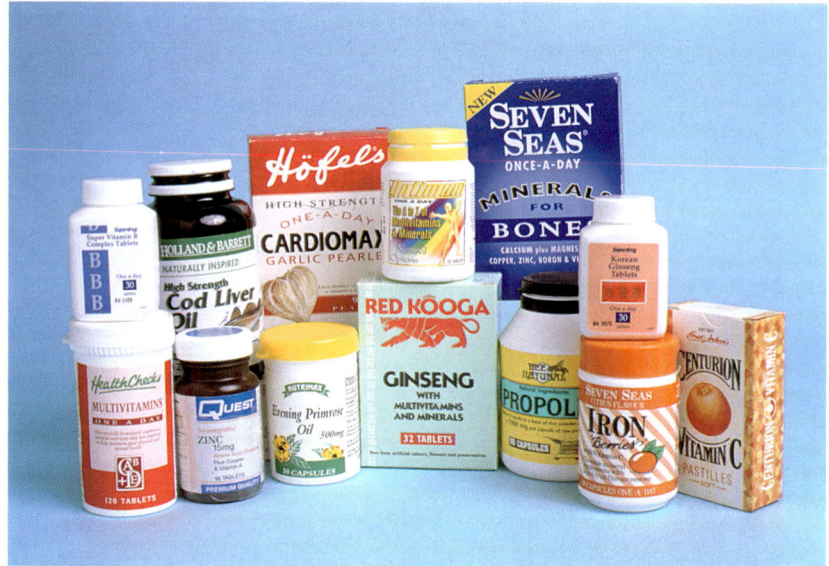

ADDITIVES

Most packaged food contains additives, which enhance flavours and give colouring to foods. They have no nutritional value and some people are allergic to some of the additives. The food packaging indicates what additives are included, and usually E numbers are used to identify them.

Diet and energy

Energy levels differ between people, due to

- age – during growth, more energy is needed
- sex – males tend to use more energy than females
- lifestyle – active people need more energy.

Basal metabolic rate (BMR)

This is the lowest level of energy required by the body for normal healthy living. Age, sex, body size and body composition determine BMR.

Physical activity (PAL)

Any activity requires a further amount of energy. The higher the activity level, the higher the energy input and output needed.

The total energy needed = BMR + PAL

MEASURING ENERGY

Energy is measured in joules or kilojoules. Typical examples of energy needed each day are shown in table 9.3.

The exact amount of energy available in food is marked on the packet. This is usually given as the number of kilojoules per gram of the food constituent. Some common foods are listed in table 9.4.

> Look at the packaging of quick snacks such as crisps, nuts and chocolate. Identify the constituents and the energy they provide. Which snack is the healthiest, if any?

Age and activity	Male	Female
8 yrs	8,200	7,300
15 yrs	11,500	8,800
adult office worker	10,500	9,000
adult manual worker	14,000	10,500
retired adult	9,000	7,000

Table 9.3   Energy needed everyday, in kilojoules

Food	Kilojoule/gram	Food	Kilojoule/gram
butter	31.2	white bread	10.6
low-fat spread	28.0	chips	9.9
peanuts	24.5	roast chicken	7.7
chocolate (milk)	24.2	eggs	6.6
cake	18.0	boiled potatoes	3.3
sugar	16.5	milk	2.7
pork sausages	15.5	apple	1.9
cornflakes	15.3	beer	1.2
rice	15.0	cabbage	0.34

Table 9.4   Constituents of energy in food

By weighing all the food eaten and identifying the constituents of the food and their energy values, the total number of kilojoules taken in during a day can be worked out.

Activities require different levels of energy: golf needs less energy (560 kjs) than playing squash (1,254 kjs). Unfortunately it is not always easy to work out exactly how much energy is needed in an activity, as it is affected by factors such as how long the activity lasts, and how hard the player works. If the input equals the output then there is no body change (weight loss or gain). A male office worker using 10,500 kjs each day needs to have an input equal to that. If the input of food is worth 12,000 kjs, then 1,500 kjs are left over.

> Keep a diary of your day, the activities you take part in and the food you eat. Does your energy equation balance?

At this age high levels of energy are needed

Activity	Energy used in kilojoules	Activity	Energy used in kilojoules
walking	380	rugby	1,130
golf	560	squash	1,254
housework	560	jogging	1,320
badminton	710	cycling	1,380
gardening	880	swimming	1,500
tennis	1,000		

Table 9.5   Energy needed for activities

This does not disappear, but is stored as *fat*. If the same worker feels unwell and does not have much to eat on one day and their intake of food only provides 9,500 kjs, then the body has to find the missing amount, 1,000 kjs, from somewhere. This is taken from the *stored fat*.

Diet problems

Many people find it hard to match their diet with the amount of energy they expend in normal everyday tasks as well as in sporting activities. Young children and teenagers rarely have this problem as their intake of food is not only needed for activity but also for growth. As people get older they become less active; it may be their job requiring little physical effort, it may be their lifestyle where there is little time for exercise. As the body does not need as much energy when this occurs, does the diet match this? Eating more than required for our daily energy needs causes the body to store this excess, usually in the form of fat. If this continues to increase, **obesity** occurs. When the body becomes extremely fat and the person becomes overweight there are serious health risks to the heart, joints and muscles. The reverse can also occur, where insufficient food is taken in to maintain health. **Anorexia** is a mental illness where the person refuses to eat regularly, and as weight is lost it can lead to a serious condition, and can result in death. Many people follow a dieting routine to lose weight. It is important, whatever the diet, that there is a correct balance of food, and that there is sufficient to maintain a normal lifestyle.

Diet for sport

Carbohydrate loading?

Sports with high-activity levels need considerable amounts of energy. Much of this energy will come from glycogen stores in the muscles. This is a limited amount, but can be increased by eating extra carbohydrates which can then be converted into glycogen (remember Chapter 2). Energy is also taken from the fat stores in the body during aerobic exercise, where there is plenty of oxygen available to release energy from fat.

BEFORE EXERCISE

A planned diet is essential for top sportspeople, and it is part of their planned programme of training for their event. In events such as boxing or judo where weight is critical, diet must be exact. In some sports, particularly endurance, diet planning is often refined and timed to coincide exactly with the event. Sportspeople involved in long distance events such as cross country, marathon running and cycling will increase the amount of carbohydrate they eat. This is known as **carbohydrate loading**, and will increase the amount of glycogen available.

Eating immediately before an event is unwise as the digestive system requires increased blood supply, and the stomach will be full putting further strain on the abdominal muscles. A light meal two hours before the event should include starches, and not simple sugars which increase insulin level and can lead to tiredness.

DURING EXERCISE

Fluids need to be taken during extended activities such as marathon running and long-distance cycling, to prevent dehydration. Drinks containing glucose are beneficial as they help conserve glycogen stores.

> **Compare the contents of a fizzy drink bottle with a high-energy sports drink, by looking at the label on the bottle. Is the sports drink worth the money?**

> **Plan a diet for a cross country runner three days before the event and on the day itself.**

AFTER EXERCISE

Energy deficiencies need to be replaced. Liquids help replace lost fluid shortly after events, and carbohydrates restore glycogen levels. At the end of many sporting events competitors are given **isotonic** drinks. These often contain glucose, and the combined effect is to help with both rehydration and restoration of glycogen levels.

Isotonic drinks help to rehydrate and restore glycogen levels

Questions on diet and exercise

1 Fibre is essential to
   a aid digestion
   b provide energy
   c increase muscle growth
   d repair damaged tissue.

2 Which of the following activities needs the most energy?
   a swimming
   b walking
   c gardening
   d golf.

3 What are vitamins?

4 Why is iron an important mineral in food?

5 Name two types of carbohydrate and give an example of each.

6 What are amino acids and why are they important in a diet?

7 What occurs when the input in kilojoules from food eaten exceeds the person's energy output?

8 When is fat used as an energy source?

9 What is meant by the BMR?

10 What is an isotonic drink and why is it useful after exercise?

Exam-style questions

1 Fibre and water are two essential items of the food we should eat, name the other five. (5 marks)

2 a Give an example of a simple and a complex carbohydrate. (2 marks)
   b From where are polyunsaturated fats obtained? (2 marks)
   c Why are polyunsaturated fats better than saturated fats? (2 marks)
   d What are essential amino-acids? (2 marks)
   e Name two vitamins and their purpose. (2 marks)

3 a What happens when energy input in food falls below energy output of a person? (3 marks)
   b Name two foods, one with high and one with low kilojoules per gram. (2 marks)
   c Which are the main food groups needed in the following activities?
      i Sprinting (2 marks)
      ii Jogging (2 marks)
      iii Circuit training. (2 marks)
   d What is meant by carbohydrate loading and in which sporting activity would it be useful? (4 marks)

4 People have different lifestyles. Using the examples of a sportsman or woman, and a person who does not take part in any sport, compare their typical energy requirements, their diets and the effects on their bodies. (15 marks)
   Quality of written communication. (5 marks)

Facilities for Sport and Leisure

All sports and leisure activities need some indoor or outdoor area. It may be a small room for judo or several acres for a golf course, or access to rivers, lakes and the countryside for outdoor activities.

> **LEARNING OBJECTIVES**
>
> ⊕ local authorities
> ⊕ national authorities and organisations
> ⊕ private and commercial organisations
> ⊕ councils, colleges and universities
> ⊕ voluntary organisations
> ⊕ company sports clubs
> ⊕ outdoor activities
> ⊕ hosting international events

Local authorities

Local authorities are local government administrative areas, such as a town, city, district or county council. These authorities control two important aspects which provide sporting and recreational facilities; education and leisure departments.

Education departments

Schools and community colleges, which come under the control of education departments, are required to provide facilities for physical education. These may range from a simple gym and grass playing fields, to a complex with swimming pool, sports hall, gym and floodlit pitches. Although the majority of schools are owned by their county council, they have considerable control over the use of their facilities. Schools often hire their facilities to sports clubs in the evening when

Can you find out who uses your school's sports facilities at night, at weekends and during school holidays?

not used by their pupils, or they may be the centre for scouts, youth clubs or adult education. Schools with very good sporting facilities often operate under a **dual use** system, where the school has full use of the facility during the day and the local council controls the facilities for the community in the evening. Sometimes new sports facilities are built specifically for a school and its community. Often this is supported by the Sports Council who might provide staffing for the management of the facility. This is known as **joint provision**.

Leisure departments

These control and maintain a wide range of sport and leisure facilities more accessible to the public than schools and colleges. These include leisure centres, sports halls, playing fields, athletic tracks, golf courses, bowling greens, swimming pools and tennis courts.

Where there is a big capital expense, such as a new swimming pool or leisure complex, the local authority may well receive a grant from the Sports Council/ National Lottery. The council may often work with a school or college under joint provision or dual use.

The running costs of sports facilities are high, particularly swimming pools. Many councils have helped with the running costs of these facilities by **subsidising** them. This means that facilities remain open even though there may be very few users. Imagine the cost of operating a swimming pool:

- heating the water
- lighting
- reception
- lifeguards.

If there are only a few people swimming, they will not pay enough admission to cover even the lifeguards' wages. Because councils think that provision of sports facilities are important, they will see that some of the money collected through local taxes is used in this way.

What is the name of your local council, and what sporting facilities do they provide?

National authorities and organisations

Although the UK Sports Council (see Chapter 15) work alongside schools, colleges and local authorities in the provision of sporting facilities, they do not own these. They do, however, provide for high-level sport development at a number of specialist centres around the country.

Centres of excellence

The **UK Sports Institute** will be based on some of these centres, with additional ones, with the object of providing

- expert advice
- personal development training
- coaching
- support staff
- specialist facilities
- resources
- scientific and medical services.

Location and name	Specialist activities
Crystal Palace* Norwood, ENGLAND	swimming, badminton, **athletics**
Holme Pierpoint* Nottingham, ENGLAND	rowing, **sailing**, canoeing and other water sports
Bisham Abbey* Marlow, ENGLAND	**tennis**, weightlifting, rugby and hockey
Lilleshall* Newport, ENGLAND	**soccer**, gymnastics, squash, volleyball and golf
Plas y Brenin* Capel Curig, WALES	outdoor activities, **mountaineering**
Scottish National Water Sports Centre Cumbrae, SCOTLAND	all water sports and related activities
Inverclyde National Sports Centre Largs, SCOTLAND	gymnastics, squash, golf and hockey
Glenmore Lodge Aviemore, SCOTLAND	**skiing** and other outdoor activities
National Sports Centre for Wales Cardiff, WALES	basketball, gymnastics, badminton, swimming and tennis
Plas Menai National Watersports Centre Caernarfon, WALES	water sports
The Northern Ireland Centre for Outdoor Activities Tollymore, N. IRELAND	all outdoor activities

* Formerly controlled by the Sports Council

Table 10.1 The National Sports Centres

The ten centres of excellence are:

Location
Bath University
Bedford
Bisham Abbey
Crystal Palace
Gateshead
Holme Pierpoint/Loughborough University
Lilleshall
Manchester
Southampton University
Sheffield

Table 10.2

In Wales, Scotland and Northern Ireland there are similar centres in

- Cymru Network Wales
- Scottish Institute of Sport – Stirling University
- University of Ulster, Northern Ireland

Private and commercial organisations

Providing sporting facilities for competition and recreation is an established and expanding business

HOTELS

Can you find a hotel with a leisure club? What facilities does it have, and what is the membership cost?

Many hotels now have leisure suites, with a swimming pool and fitness room with weights and aerobic machines. Some larger hotels may have tennis and squash courts and even small golf courses in the hotel grounds. Usually these facilities are available free or for a small charge for hotel residents. However, as few hotels are fully booked throughout the year, local residents are able to join the hotel leisure clubs through some kind of membership.

Holiday complexes based around leisure activities are now established in this country, where a large leisure pool is the centre of focus, and people can take part in a range of sports and outdoor activities.

Center Parc, a private-sector holiday complex

COMMERCIAL SPORTS CLUBS

Providing a venue for a sporting event has long been seen as the chance to make money. The village inn, in the past, was often the centre for sports such as bowling, cricket and football, and staging such events meant increased takings at the bar: there was *profit* to be made from sport.

Commercial sports clubs have grown due to the demand of the public and the investment of business money. Many commercial clubs provide a facility which would otherwise not be available, but they exist primarily to make money for their owners. Squash, tennis and golf are some of the sports where private developments have taken place. These facilities require a considerable capital investment for construction, and often need to operate for many years before the owners see any profit.

Can you find examples of small gym and fitness clubs in your area? What activities are held there and what was the building originally used for?

A wing of Cambridge Labour Club has been turned into a sports facility

On a smaller scale, there has been considerable growth in fitness, weight and aerobic gyms. Requiring little space to accommodate weights and other fitness machines, and occasionally a small floor area for some type of aerobic work, these clubs are to be found in high street locations. Disused church halls, old cinemas, vacant shops are all some of the venues for these clubs. Often they have a small membership, allowing maximum use of machines without undue queuing.

Not all of these gyms are purely for fitness; some are dedicated to martial arts such as boxing and judo or even line dancing.

Colleges and universities

Is there a college or university near where you live? What sports facilities do they have? Can the public use any of these facilities?

Very similar to grant maintained and public schools, colleges and universities often have excellent facilities which are usually accessible to the public when not in use by their students. During the term there may be little free time, but during holidays they often become the centre for some kind of summer school or sports festival. They often provide very good facilities such as artificial grass playing surfaces, sports halls and swimming pools.

Facilities at Loughborough University

Council sports facilities at
Sheepmount, Carlisle

Voluntary organisations

There are many voluntary organisations both small and large, some
of whom own their facilities which are available to their members.
Small groups might use a village hall for their badminton club and
often the church and village hall might be the centre of many
activities in a small village.

A village hall used by a badminton club

Sports clubs provide specialist facilities for their members. Many
long-established sports clubs, often cricket, golf and tennis, may own
their facilities, but new clubs often have to hire their facilities because

of the cost of land and buildings. However, new clubs are helped by the Sports Council with building costs. Few if any swimming clubs can afford their own swimming pool, or athletics clubs their own track.

As clubs led to the development of national governing bodies (Chapter 15), so some of these developed their own national centres, such as the RFU at Twickenham and more recently the Hockey Association's centre at Milton Keynes. Although most major soccer events in this country were held at Wembley, the FA did not own this but had to hire it from a private company. At the present time the plans for the 'New Wembley' are being reviewed, and many major events are being transferred to the Millennium Stadium in Cardiff until the new stadium at Wembley becomes available in 2004.

Company sports clubs

One of the first company sports club was created by Robert Owen, a mill owner in Scotland in 1850. He believed that his workers ought to be able to participate in leisure and physical activities, and made arrangements for his employees to take part in some physical activity.

Today, many companies have sports and social clubs, where employees can take part in sporting and leisure activities. Sometimes they are near the factory or plant, or perhaps some distance away, but invariably funded by the company who will maintain the facility. Usually the workers have free access to these facilities, and a range of activities might well be organised. Many companies believe that by providing these facilities, their workers might stay fit and be happy at work, just as Robert Owen thought.

Outdoor activities

To take part in a range of outdoor activities such as water sports, climbing and walking people need to be able to gain access to the natural environment. Many local authorities own centres in areas such as the Lake District where they can provide a range of activities for children and adults. Access to the outdoor environment is often not restricted, people are able to walk in hills, and climb, pothole without charge. Sometimes access to water is more difficult as there may be launching fees on some rivers and lakes. The **Outward Bound Association** has four centres: Ullswater and Eskdale in the Lake District, Loch Eil in Scotland and Aberdovey in Wales. As the numbers of walkers increase in some of our national parks there are increasing concerns about damage to the environment. Many popular paths to mountains such as Skiddaw and ScaFell are being worn away, and there is increased traffic and car parking in the valleys.

Hosting international events

When a city or country hosts an international event, its competitors will have some advantage. Crowd support, less travel and positive media coverage are all important factors. The costs and potential rewards in staging international events are also considerable. However, as the events become bigger, with more sports and competitors, the organisation becomes more difficult. Even staging an international match with another country can be costly and needs to be planned well in advance of the date. Questions which organisers need to ask are

- are the facilities good enough for the competition?
- where will all the competitors stay?
- can spectators get to see the competitions?
- who will provide the funding for the competition?
- what security arrangements need to be made?
- what television coverage will there be?

Many cities and countries try to win top international events. There are advantages and disadvantages in staging large-scale events.

ADVANTAGES

- more and better sports facilities – Ponds Forge swimming pool was built in Sheffield for the World Student Games, 1991
- access, transport and hotels improved – new roads and hotels were built at Mangy Coers in France for the French Grand Prix
- increased tourism and business – the European Soccer Championships in 1996 brought increased business to the UK.
- more jobs created for building facilities and staffing the events
- the city or country will become well known – only 20 cities have hosted the Olympics
- it might help national unity – the 1995 World Rugby Championships in South Africa were important in bringing black and white South Africans together under one flag.

Sheffield Supertrams

Public transport developed as a result of hosting the World Student Games in 1991

Select any sport and work out what you would need to organise an international event.

DISADVANTAGES

- the increased number of people visiting the area can cause a major disruption to the everyday life of the residents. Anyone living near a major sports ground will be aware of the access and car parking problems
- finance needed to build new or improve old facilities might be taken from areas such as education or healthcare. Both local and national governments are criticised if money is spent on sport when people are homeless – this happened when Mexico City hosted the Olympics in 1968
- security to control crowds and prevent terrorists is expensive – the extra cost of security at the Montreal Games was one of the factors contributing to the financial loss of these games
- extra staff may be unfamiliar with the city – in the 1996 Atlanta Games, many of the bus drivers did not know the way to some of the venues.

Questions on facilities for sport and leisure

1 The main public providers for sport and recreation are
   a   private clubs
   b   commercial organisations
   c   local authorities
   d   the Sports Council.

2 Which of the following is owned by a national governing body?
   a   Twickenham
   b   Wembley
   c   Wimbledon (tennis)
   d   the Millennium Stadium.

3 What is dual provision?

4 Name two facilities for sporting activities you might find in a small village.

5 What are the advantages of joint provision?

6 Give examples of two commercial facilities for sports.

7 Name two centres of excellence and the **major** activity held there.

8 What is meant by a company sports club? Give one example.

9 What two problems might there be to the environment with the increase in hill walking?

10 Give one advantage and one disadvantage to a city hosting a major international competition.

Exam-style questions

1 a Give two examples of public provision of sports facilities in your area. (2 marks)

b Give two examples of private or commercial sports facilities in your area. (2 marks)

c Give one example of a company sports club. (1 mark)

2 a What is meant by joint provision? (2 marks)

b What are the two main ways in which local authority can provide sporting facilities? (2 marks)

c What is meant by a subsidy? How might it benefit users of local authority sports facilities? (3 marks)

d Why do some sports clubs have to hire facilities? Give one example. (3 marks)

3 a Name two centres of excellence, and the main sport held there. (4 marks)

b Give five major functions of a centre of excellence. (5 marks)

c Give three reasons for and against centres of excellence. (6 marks)

4 Staging a major international event has both advantages and disadvantages.

a Give three advantages. (3 marks)

b Give three disadvantages. (3 marks)

c Some national governing bodies have their own stadiums, such as Twickenham. Argue the case for a national stadium. (9 marks)

Quality of written communication. (5 marks)

11

Factors Affecting Participation

There are a number of factors which affect participation; we have seen how the provision of facilities is essential, but even when they are available there are many reasons why people do and do not participate. The following factors influence participation:

LEARNING OBJECTIVES

- age
- ability
- disability
- gender
- physique
- access
- education
- family
- peer groups
- environment
- media
- role models
- tradition and culture
- ethnic background
- politics

Age

The sport and leisure which people take part in is often closely related to their age and local traditions. As people get older, not only do they take less part in sport, but the nature of that sport changes. Taking part in gymnastics when young is ideal, when the body is flexible. In contact sports such as soccer and particularly rugby, recovery time after an injury takes longer as people age. Swimming competitively is more associated with young people, but this does not stop older people from enjoying swimming.

As the body ages, there is reduced flexibility at the joints; sprains and other minor injuries become more frequent; it is recommended that less explosive events and activities are played. Some activities are suitable for all ages because skill rather than strength, speed and power is more important. Golf is a good example, and while top players can hit huge distances (Tiger Woods' average length drive in 1997 was in excess of 300 metres), older players can still compete in this game for many years. For example, Jack Nicklaus still competes at a high level.

Walking, green bowling and swimming are some of the activities enjoyed by all ages, but particularly older people. Some older people do still take part in active and explosive sports, such as athletics. There are veteran championships each year, with some creditable performances.

> **Can you think of two team games which are unsuitable for most older people, and two games which might be suitable for them? Give reasons for your decisions.**

A veteran athlete running the London Marathon

Ability

Most sports require certain physical and mental abilities to perform well. Your ability can determine both the sport and the level at which it is played. Age and ability are interrelated, particularly in activities where mental ability is as important as the physical. Having the physical ability to run through forests and up mountain sides is important in orienteering, but route planning and map reading is an essential skill in the sport.

Martina Hingis, a young player of high ability who started on the professional circuit at the age of 14

Having a high ability in any sport means that there could be increased participation, which in itself can lead to improvement in performance. However good a young participant in sport is, there may be restrictions on them playing with older players, even though they may be better. Many clubs have age groupings with junior and senior sections. The usual rules at golf clubs require junior players to allow other members to 'play through' – juniors have to let other players get past them on the course by standing aside. Being good at a sport is not the only factor in participation, as your age and size and the nature of the sport all have to be taken into account.

Think of two sports which are suitable for players of high ability, but are not dependent on age, size or other factors. Can players of different abilities play together successfully?

Disability

Name four activities in which sportspeople with disabilities can take part. What provisions are there in your area for these people to take part in sport?

Take one sport and consider what provisions would be needed to enable people with disabilities to play.

Sport for people with disabilities has changed considerably, with governing bodies devising rules and activities suitable for all disabilities. The Sports Council published an action plan in 1993 to help people with disabilities take part in sport. The seven main objectives were

1. to raise the profile of disability in sport
2. to ensure that plans for sport include people with disabilities
3. to provide sporting opportunities for people with disabilities
4. to improve access to sport
5. to encourage people with disabilities in international sport
6. to ensure the best use of resources and increase finance
7. to make sure that the sporting needs of people with disabilities are met.

Each year more and more sport is being made available to people with disabilities. The televising of wheelchair basketball has helped to raise public awareness, and the media coverage of the Paralympics has done much to support this cause. Most sports centres now make provision for people with disabilities.

Gender

Fewer females take part in sport than males. Every year 33 per cent of men take part in some sporting activity, but only 10 per cent of women are involved in sport. This is not a new phenomenon, as shown below.

A SHORT HISTORY

At the **ancient Olympic Games**, women were not even allowed to watch the activities, let alone compete. In England by the end of the **nineteenth century**, women were taking part in sport, but they tended to come from the middle classes. Working women from the lower classes did not have the time, energy or money to participate. For those middle-class women, there were opportunities to take part in tennis, badminton, croquet, cycling and golf. The **Victorian** attitudes of the time, however, meant that they often played in cumbersome dresses, making any kind of movement difficult.

In the 1900s, the national **governing bodies** of many sports were formed and there were organised competitions for women, but usually separate from the men's competitions.

There are few sports where men and women compete in the same events. Can you name three sports where this happens? Why is it possible in these sports but not in others?

Sportswear for women in the 1900s

Acceptance at the **Olympic Games** proved harder for women. They did not compete in the 1896 (Paris) Olympics, and competed for the first time in 1904, but only in archery. From then on, the number of events open to women continued to increase, although even in the 1996 Atlanta Games, there were 163 men's events and only 97 women's events.

The turning point in women's sports came during and after the **First World War**. Although many women had worked hard for long hours in mills before the war, they had not worked in heavy industry. During the war, they were employed in heavy engineering, making guns, ammunition and machinery for the war. The myth that women were weak, had little energy and were unable to cope with 'men's' work was exploded. If they could do this sort of work, they could cope with men's sport as well. This was the **golden age** for the emergence of women's sport and sporting heroines. Captain Webb was the first person to swim the English Channel in 1875, and Gertrude Ederle swam it in 1926. Not only was she the first woman to do so, but by taking two hours off the existing male record, she proved that women could compete with men.

The Wimbledon Tennis Championships were restarted in 1919, after the war. Suzanne Lenglen beat the existing champion Mrs Lambert Chambers, who had been unbeaten for 11 years. While the win was impressive, the clothes worn by Miss Lenglen shocked many of the older players, spectators and club officials. A pleated skirt and stockings to the knee broke away from the traditional dresses. No doubt her increased mobility around the court gave her some considerable advantage.

Although more and more women were taking part in sporting activities, working class women did not have the same opportunity as those from the middle classes. The women's place was still considered to be at home with their children.

During the **Second World War**, women worked in heavy industry again. However, there was a significant change in their status. After the war, more women continued to work. They had more money to spend, and more freedom to participate in sport and leisure activities.

At national and international level, women competitors were becoming well known.

- Russian and East German women dominated athletics, swimming and gymnastics
- American women won many of the Wimbledon Championships.

Women such as Olga Korbut, Nadia Commaneci, Martina Navratilova, Merlene Ottey, Sally Gunnell and Liz McColgan became well known as the media continued to cover their sporting events.

REASONS FOR LOW PARTICIPATION LEVELS

Even though participation levels continue to increase as well as the prize money for professional sportswomen, there are still reasons why they will continue to fall short of men's participation levels.

> **In some sports, the equipment or the rules are different for men and women. Name one of these sports and describe two differences. Why do you think different rules are necessary?**

Ashia Hansen

Ladies' triple jump is now an accepted event in the Olympics

Name three sports or events in which women are not able to participate.

Using a broadsheet paper over the period of a week, record references, match reports, comments and news about male and female sports. What did you find?

Physique

Some sports have been thought too dangerous for women. The collapse of a number of women competitors in the 1928 Olympic 800-metre race cast some doubt as to whether women could compete over this distance. The event was removed and not reinstated until the Rome Olympics in 1960. Four athletic events remained closed to women until quite recently: 3,000 metre steeplechase, hammer throwing, pole vault and triple jump; of these, only the triple jump appeared in the Atlanta Olympics. Women are physically able to compete at these events, but often the opportunity does not exist.

Social attitudes

Can women commit time to sport when they have 'home' responsibilities? Fanny Blankers-Koen proved this to be true when she won four gold track medals in the London Olympics in 1948, being the mother of two children. To be a top sportswoman, you need to train for long hours, be psychologically tough, muscular and competitive. These characteristics are often seen as acceptable for men but not for women.

Role models

For boys there are many role models in a wide range of sports from athletics, to soccer and rugby. There are fewer female role models (some of these top performers have been mentioned earlier).

Finance

Sportswomen do not receive as much sponsorship as some sportsmen. The top prizes in events are often less. In 1997, the prize money for the Men's Singles Championship at Wimbledon was £415,000, whereas the prize money for the Women's Singles Championship was £373,500.

Media coverage

Linked with sponsorship, less media coverage of women in sports means a lower profile. There are fewer women involved in the media itself – newspaper sports reporters and television presenters are predominantly male.

Coaching

Many men coach women's sports teams and individuals. Specialist training for physical education teaching for women happened 40 years earlier than for men. One might expect to find men coaching women in traditional men's sports such as soccer and rugby, but there are many men involved in the coaching of ladies' gymnastics and hockey.

Two organisations which continue to work towards increasing the participation of women in sport are the **Women's Sports Foundation** (WSF) and the Sports Council.

Physique

People's size, weight and shape may help them to participate in some sports but not in others. In the 1950s, an American, W.H. Sheldon, classified people into three different types:

① **meso**morph
② **ecto**morph
③ **endo**morph.

This is known as **somatotyping**, and is a way of describing body types. Very few people can be classified as one particular type; most people are a mixture of types. A person's **build** is inherited, and little can be done about **height**. **Muscle** can be built up and fat reduced by training and diet.

Measurements can be taken which classify people on a score from 1 to 7, in how much they are mesomorphic, ectomorphic and endomorphic.

> **Think of three events in athletics where different body types might be important.**

Mesomorph
Broad shoulders, narrow hips, square head, muscular arms and legs, small amounts of body fat

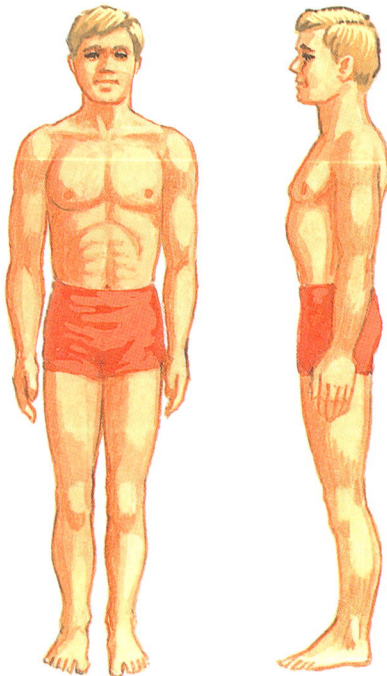

Ectomorph
Narrow shoulders and hips, thin face, high forehead, thin arms and legs, little muscle, small amounts of body fat

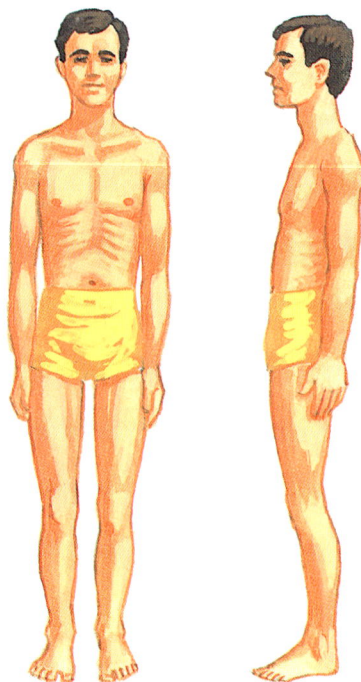

Endomorph
Narrow shoulders, wide hips, large head, fat on arms and legs, lots of body fat

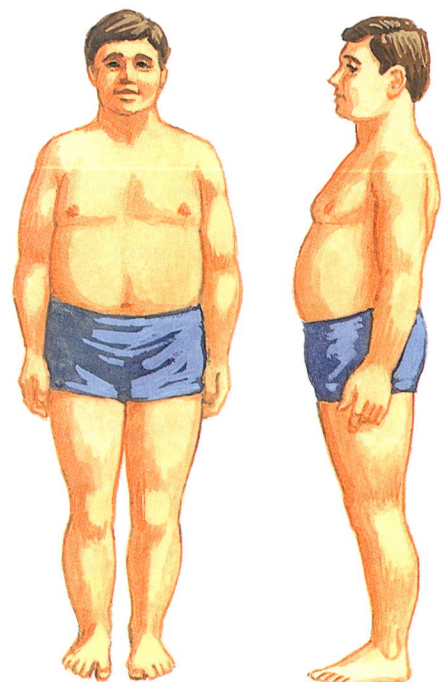

A somatochart

Somatotyping of athletes

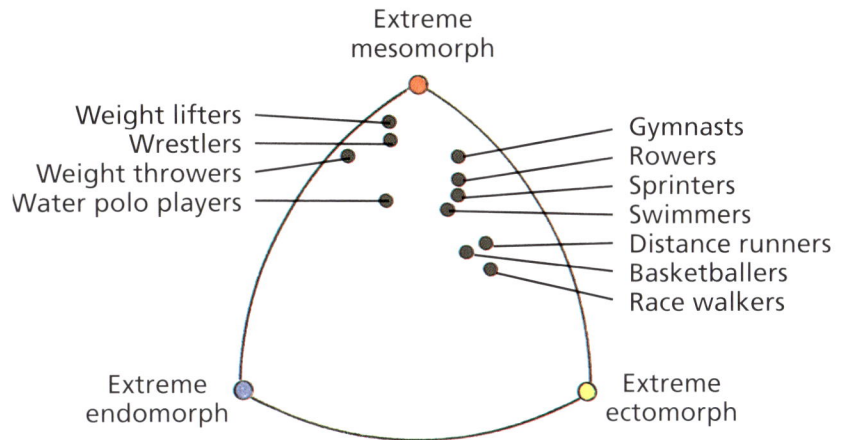

BODY TYPE AND SPORT

Most sportspeople are between the mesomorphic and ectomorphic extremes, with a greater tendency towards the mesomorphic. In sports such as gymnastics and wrestling, it is an advantage to have good muscular strength in relation to size. In events where objects have to be thrown such as shot, hammer and javelin, muscular strength and speed are important, as is bulk for stability. These sportspeople tend to be a mesomorph and endomorph mixture. Sumo wrestlers need to have considerable weight and strength to force their opponents out of the circle.

HEIGHT AND WEIGHT

Being tall is important for basketball and volleyball players, but a disadvantage to gymnasts. Being tall and heavy is ideal for many positions in rugby, but particularly in scrummaging and line-outs. Many leading backs in rugby are big, and when moving fast, they are difficult to stop.

BODY COMPOSITION

Two people of the same weight might differ in the ratio of fat, muscle, bone and connective tissue in their bodies. Weight can be a misleading measurement, particularly for slimmers, who may be unaware that they could be losing muscle and not fat! As mesomorphy is common to most sportsmen and women, they tend to have a low percentage of body fat. This can be measured by using **skin fold callipers**, which measure the amount of fat in different parts of the body. Special tables are used to work out the percentage of body fat for different age groups.

In the following sports, state the physique which is best suited for becoming a successful performer. Give reasons for your decisions:

- jockey
- marathon runner
- long-distance swimmer
- hockey player.

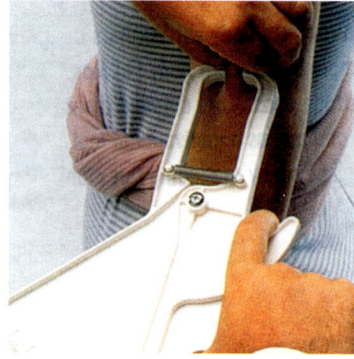

Skin fold callipers

Access

Access can be thought of in two ways:

- are the sporting facilities available?
- how easy is it to get to them?

In the previous chapter we have seen that there are many providers of sporting facilities, but not all are conveniently located. In rural areas a car is often necessary to access sporting facilities. In towns and cities, sports and leisure centres are often, but not always, located close to the town or city centre, and may be accessible by public transport. Sometimes for less popular sports, perhaps fencing, participants might have to travel some considerable distance to the nearest club.

Education

Select two activities from Key Stage 3 or Key Stage 4. Justify why one should be included and why one should be removed.

Schools play a major part in developing attitudes towards participation in sport. Since 1902 the government have passed Acts for the inclusion of physical education in the syllabus. The present National Curriculum for physical education came into force in September 2000.

Pupils in different school years are allocated to **key stages**: see table 11.1. The PE programme of every school will have some similarities, but because each school has different facilities, they are allowed some choice in the activities which they provide for their pupils.

Key Stage	Pupil's age	Year group	Activities in physical education
1	5–7 yrs	1–2	games, gymnastic activities, dance (swimming optional)
2	7–11 yrs	3–6	games, gymnastic activities, dance ⎤ all athletic activities, outdoor and adventurous activities, swimming. Pupils to be taught the six areas of activity ⎦ 2 from these
3	11–14 yrs	7–9	pupils taught four of the above activities
4	14–16 yrs	10–11	pupils taught a minimum of two of above activities.

Table 11.1   PE in the National Curriculum

For many sportsmen and women it is their school that has started them on and helped them develop their sport. Building on physical education lessons schools provide for all pupils with inter-house and inter-form events, clubs and inter-school competitions.

Family

The family is a major influence in determining sport and leisure activities, not only in early life, but from one generation to the next. Parents, brothers and sisters provide role models, and sometimes families take part in events together, perhaps in

Henry and James Redknapp

orienteering or in other outdoor activities. Even when parents do not take part in a sport themselves they provide financial support, buying clothes and equipment as well as transporting their children to sporting events. The sons and daughters of famous sportsmen and women do not always follow in their parents' footsteps, but occasionally they do. A good example of this would be Henry and James Redknapp.

Peer groups

People are often influenced by others of the same age; this is known as **peer group pressure**. Friends may have the same interests, playing on the same team at school or in a club. They may enjoy taking part in recreational activities together such as mountain biking or swimming. Unfortunately not all peer pressure is positive, and people could be discouraged from taking part in sport because of friends' influence.

Environment

The environment is a contributing factor to participation and might be sport specific. Living in Cornwall may offer the chance to take part in surfing; in the Lake District there are opportunities for many outdoor activities, in East Anglia there is no mountain walking, but plenty of water-sport activities.

Media

Although the media has an influence on professional and international sport, it also affects individual's participation. Events on the television in particular can create the growth of an activity. The coverage of the London Marathon inspired many people to run in this and events such as the Great North run, not to win, but for health and social reasons to raise money for charity.

Role models

There are many role models in sport, many sportsmen and women have been influenced to not only take up a sport, but to reach the top as the result of seeing a top performer. The **Sporting Ambassadors Scheme** involves sports stars visiting both primary and secondary schools.

Tradition and culture

Tradition and culture can have both a positive and negative influence on participation. Countries may have strong traditions in a particular sport; the West Indies and Sri Lanka in cricket, and rugby in New Zealand. In the UK there are regional strengths in certain sports, such as rugby league in Yorkshire and Lancashire, rugby union in Wales, shinty in the north of Scotland and hurling in Northern Ireland. Certain sports might only occur in small geographical areas, such as lacrosse in and around Manchester.

Ethnic background

Ethnic background may influence people's participation in sport. In cultures which have strict dress codes, people may be prevented from wearing the appropriate sports kit, and so may not take part. In other cultures, female participation in sport is frowned upon. On the other hand, ethnic groups might be discriminated against by the majority group, and prevented from taking part in activities for no reason. Some people think that certain ethnic groups are unsuitable for certain sports, and this is often reflected in the participants of these sports. There are many more Afro-Caribbean players in mainstream games such as soccer and rugby; many Asians play in first-class cricket and hockey teams, but very few in league football teams. Many Premiership soccer teams include players from different ethnic backgrounds, but there can be discrimination against certain ethnic groups.

Treating people differently because they come from different races is called **racism**. In sport this might be done by not allowing certain groups to play, practise or even join a club. It might also occur at

Are there any special schemes in your area to help ethnic minority groups to take part in sport?

major sporting events with verbal abuse of players from ethnic minorities. The Professional Football Association (PFA) were concerned about the increasing amount of racial abuse at football matches and set up a campaign in 1993 with the Commission for Racial Equality to *Kick Racism out of Football*. In certain areas of the country with larger ethnic minorities, special events and initiatives have been launched. Leicester City Council working with Leicester City Football Club, are running the Leicester Asian Sports Initiative to encourage young Asians to take part in soccer.

Leicester City Football Club's initiative with young Asians

Politics

The government can influence participation in a number of ways, some of which have been mentioned elsewhere. Briefly their areas of influence are

- providing funding for facilities
- ensuring time for physical education in schools
- promoting sport and leisure activities as being beneficial to health.

Questions on Factors affecting participation

1 Which of the following sports is suitable for people of all ages?
   a   rugby
   b   golf
   c   soccer
   d   gymnastics.

2 Peer group pressure is when you are influenced by
   a   family
   b   friends
   c   the media
   d   tradition.

3 Name two sports which are suitable for young children.

4 What is the WSF and what is its purpose?

5 What is meant by 'access' to sport?

6 Name two sports where skill is the most important factor.

7 Give two examples of how the environment might affect sport.

8 What is the Sporting Ambassadors Scheme?

9 Give two examples of how tradition affects sporting participation.

10 Give an example of how the media has increased participation in a sporting activity.

Exam-style questions

1 Name five factors which influence participation in sporting activities.   (5 marks)

2 a State two sporting activities which were popular with women in 1900.   (4 marks)
   b Why were women thought to be able to take part in sporting activities after the First World War?   (4 marks)
   c Name two female role models, who might influence girls to participate in a sporting activity.   (2 marks)

3 a Age is an important factor when participating in sporting activities. Give an example of a sport which is suitable for
   i   young children   (2 marks)
   ii older people   (2 marks)
   iii families.   (2 marks)
   b What part does a family play in supporting children's participation in sport?   (4 marks)
   c What is meant by peer pressure and how does it influence participation?   (5 marks)

4 a Politics can influence sporting participation. Explain how government becomes involved.   (5 marks)
   b Tradition and culture can have both a positive and negative effect on participation in sport. Discuss these issues and give examples to illustrate.   (10 marks)

Quality of written communication.   (5 marks)

12

Reasons for Participation

There are a number of social factors which influence people's participation in sport and leisure facilities. Obviously personal reasons for participation in the previous chapter are significant, but there are other social factors which have an impact on sport and leisure participation.

> **LEARNING OBJECTIVES**
>
> - leisure time
> - work
> - cost
> - technology
> - health
> - leisure activities
> - vocational factors

Leisure time

The time when you are not working at school, at home or at a work place, is often known as **leisure time**: you can do what you want and when you want. For many people, sporting activity is an essential part of their leisure time, either taking part or watching. For others, reading a book or watching television is equally important. Everyone has different amounts of leisure time and there are some important factors that have arisen as people's leisure time has increased, but at the core of this is the pattern and type of work for most people. If leisure time is non-work time, then the less work time, the more leisure time.

There was little time to participate in sport for the mill workers of the nineteenth century

Mark on a pie chart how you spend a particular day during term time. Include time at school or college, time for homework, time taken for meals and sleeping. Indicate on the chart your leisure time, and what you do during that time.

CHANGES IN LEISURE TIME

When people moved from the country to towns during the **Industrial Revolution** of the eighteenth century, they lost much of their leisure time. People working in the country would work long hours at certain times of the year (eg getting in the harvest), but they could take part in sport and leisure activities during saints' days, festivals and public holidays. When people started to work in factories and mills, they had much less non-working time. Twelve hours a day and six days a week was the usual pattern of work. Monday, not Saturday, was the day for sport and recreation. Gradually workers gained more free time as technology developed so that the same amount of goods could be produced in less time, and without the highly intensive labour force.

Work

Patterns and types of work have undergone considerable change and this affects participation in sport and leisure.

WORKING WEEK

For many people the working week is shorter than it used to be, and it is also more flexible. Not everyone starts work and finishes at the same time. In offices where there is 'flexi' working, employers work the necessary hours, but may start and finish early or later, with perhaps an extended lunch break. Many more people are working from home, which enables them to take part in leisure activities during the day.

You're never too old!

What advantage might there be in flexible working hours and taking part in physical recreation and sporting activities?

The following factors help to create more leisure time:

- fewer people have full-time jobs
- there are not sufficient jobs for those who wish to work
- many people now finish their working life by the age of 50
- some people choose to work at home through computer links to their offices and so reduce travel time
- labour-saving devices in the home have reduced the amount of time needed for doing domestic chores
- continued and improving healthcare means that more and more elderly people are fit enough to take part in recreational activities.

UNEMPLOYMENT

Many people are unemployed, or perhaps work part-time, or have seasonal work. This means that they have more time to take part in leisure activities, although the cost of taking part may prevent them.

CarlisleCARD

LEISURE ACCESS

A discount leisure card.

Some local authorities **subsidise** the costs for unemployed people to encourage them to take part in leisure activities.

RETIREMENT

Increasing numbers of people retire early, many by the age of 50. At this age people still enjoy an active lifestyle and often at this age take up new sports and leisure activities such as golf.

Cost

Taking part in sport and physical recreation costs money:

- basic equipment such as sports clothes and shoes are needed
- admission charges to sports centres may be subsidised by the local authority, but costs can mount up for weekly participation.

Some activities are much more expensive than others: to play golf even on many municipal courses might be expensive, and even then you will need to hire or take your own golf clubs.

Private members clubs can be even more expensive. Joining a tennis club, or taking out membership at a hotel leisure club can cost hundreds of pounds a year. To become a member of some private golf clubs, players have to put their names on a five-year waiting list, pay a joining fee and also an annual subscription. This could easily cost over £1,000 in a big city.

Find out the charge of hiring a badminton court at your local sports centre. Are there different prices for different times or days?

Does your local authority have special arrangements to help unemployed people take part in sport and leisure activities?

The home of golf and a public course at St Andrews

Many local authorities have special rates for children and clubs may often have a junior membership section with a reduced subscription. Some local authorities run day-time sessions for unemployed people, or allow them a special discount card for other local authority sports facilities.

Technology

Technology has had a significant impact on the world of work. Machines have replaced muscle power in the western world; many factories and production lines are controlled by fewer and fewer people. More people are now able to work from home instead of travelling to 'the office' every day with the advent of computer links. At home there are more labour-saving devices thus reducing the amount of time spent on domestic chores. All this means that people have more time to spend on leisure activities.

Health

More and more people are aware of health issues and the importance of exercise. The government both nationally and locally are active in stressing the importance of exercise to maintain good health. Also with good healthcare more and more elderly people are fit enough to take part in recreational activities.

Leisure activities

Leisure and physical recreation are closely linked. There is now a leisure industry but not all recreation is physical or a sport. Bingo, theatres and cinema are just some of the non-physical recreational activities. In the USA caravans and campers are known as RVs (recreational vehicles). Physical recreation is important for a number of reasons:

- health is important. It has been proved that physical activity is good for maintaining a level of fitness for everyday life. Weight control, body shape, flexibility and prevention of coronary heart disease are all physical benefits. In a world of increasingly stressful occupations, taking part in physical activity is an important issue for mental health as well
- enjoyment is often the main reason that people take part in recreational activities. No matter how good an activity might be for your health, you need to enjoy it to keep taking part. Some people prefer to work in large groups and are happy to follow instructions such as in aerobics. Others enjoy the challenge of individual sports such as rock climbing or sailing
- social aspects such as working in teams are a part of everyday life for some people. Many people enjoy working with groups and playing as part of a team, such as an orchestra or rugby team. Just going to a sports centre with a friend may be valued for the social contact.

> **What are your favourite physical and non-physical leisure activities?**

Vocational Factors

Many people work in the leisure industry; for them sport and leisure activities are more than recreation, it is their work. For others involved in team games such as soccer and rugby there is now a fine line between amateur and professional (see Chapter 19). Semi-professional and professional players may enjoy their sport, but it may cease to be recreational as it is a way of earning money. Sometimes professional players in one sport may take part in another sport as a recreational activity, perhaps in the close season. Rugby union is a good example of how an amateur game, played for recreation by the majority of people, has changed significantly with retaining fees being paid to players in lower divisions of national leagues.

Questions on reasons for participation

1 Leisure time is
   a   playing a sport professionally
   b   working in the leisure industry
   c   taking part in an activity in your own time
   d   taking part in a physical education lesson at school.

2 Flexible working is
   a   working the same time every day
   b   doing stretching in a warm-up
   c   being able to decide the start and finish time of work yourself
   d   being retired.

3 Give a definition of leisure time.

4 Give two reasons why people have more leisure time now than in the past.

5 What is meant by a subsidy and how does this help unemployed people to take part in leisure activities?

6 Give two reasons why retired people might take part in leisure activities.

7 Name two sport and leisure activities a fit retired person might take part in.

8 What two pieces of technological equipment in a home have reduced time spent on **domestic** tasks?

9 Name one specific health reason for taking part in a recreational activity.

10 Name two recreational activities which help develop teamwork.

Exam-style questions

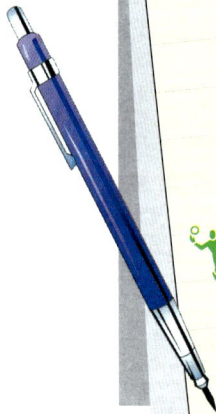

1 Give five reasons for increased leisure time.   (5 marks)

2 a How have patterns of work changed over the last 50 years   (4 marks)
   b What effect has this had on the leisure **industry**?   (6 marks)

3 a State two ways to help the unemployed get involved in sport and give examples   (4 marks)
   b Many people now retire early. What activities are they likely to continue or start to play? (4 marks)
   c More people have flexible working hours. What is meant by this and how does it create opportunities to take part in a sport or leisure activity? (7 marks)

4 a Give two examples of technological changes, one in the home and one in the work place, which affect leisure time. (2 marks)
   b How does a person's vocation affect their involvement in recreational activities? (5 marks)
   c The government encourage people to take part in sport and exercise for health reasons. Give examples from a range of activities, and describe how these are beneficial to health. (8 marks)

Quality of written communication.   (5 marks)

13

School and Club Sport

The public schools in Great Britain played a major part in the organisation and development of sports and games in the nineteenth century. Schools continue to be one of the most influential factors, both positive and negative, in the participation levels of young people in sport. The link between school and club sport is an important issue in keeping young people involved in sport towards the end of their compulsory schooling and afterwards.

LEARNING OBJECTIVES

- public school sport
- Education Acts and the National Curriculum
- extracurricular activities
- physical education and sport
- school and club links
- developing excellence

Public school sport

The foundations of most of our sports rest in the history of the British public school. Sports and games in the eighteenth and nineteenth centuries were not developed for what they were, but how they could influence pupils' behaviour at school: as a channel for youthful energy, for toughening the body and for building the character. Many public school pupils went to the universities of Oxford and Cambridge, where sports developed further. As graduates, they would often return to teach at public or grammar schools, bringing their knowledge of new sports with them. Their influence and enthusiasm was considerable:

Drill was an essential part of early physical education

they encouraged their pupils to participate through organised games in school and against other schools. However, for the lower classes in state schools, few pupils, if any, experienced games. Their physical education consisted of Swedish drill in the school playground.

Education Acts and the National Curriculum

EDUCATION ACTS

In 1902 the War Department drew up a syllabus for physical education in school based on military drill, to improve the fitness of the pupils. A series of new **syllabuses** were produced by the Board of Education, each one reducing the military content a little. The 1933 syllabus contained some gymnastics which you would recognise today.

At the end of the Second World War, the **1944 Education Act** brought in free education for all. Physical education changed considerably, with state schools including many more team games. Swimming, cross country and athletics became popular. While most schools taught a very similar programme of physical education and games, there were often significant differences, usually determined by the facilities and local traditions.

The **Education Reform Act** in **1988** reinforced the position of physical education in schools, making it a compulsory subject. However, only in 1992 were the exact details of what should be included decided by the government. This was further revised in 1995 with the issue of the Dearing Report. In September 2000 a new National Curriculum was introduced.

THE NATIONAL CURRICULUM 2000

The National Curriculum in schools means that pupils should have similar experiences in physical education irrespective of where they live. See P151.

During Key Stage 3 pupils are expected to become more expert in their skills and techniques and how to apply them in different activities. They start to identify the types of activities they prefer to be involved with and to take a variety of roles such as leader and official. In Key Stage 4 pupils are expected to become involved in different roles, and not just performers. They need to understand and take on the role of coaches, choreographers, leaders and officials.

There are wider issues for physical education in schools, and these are often known as **cross curricular**.

Spiritual, moral, social and cultural issues

Spiritual development – a positive attitude towards themselves and gain a sense of achievement.

Moral development – a sense of fair play, accepting decisions, good sporting behaviour and **etiquette**.

Social development – team cooperation and collaboration, personal commitment, loyalty and teamwork.

Cultural development – understanding of their own and others' cultures, perhaps in dance and in national games of other cultures.

Key skills

Communication – verbal and non-verbal communication, by giving instructions and coaching verbally, and non-verbally through expressive movement in gymnastics and dance.

Application of number – collecting and analysing data in health and fitness, measuring and calculating in athletics, using maps and compasses in orienteering.

Information and communication technology – making use of technology such as digital video and interactive white boards. Using computers to store and model data with databases and spreadsheets. Using the internet to search for information. Use of word processing and desk-top publishing to present information.

Working with others – adopting roles in groups and teams, cooperating with others and observing rules when competing against others. Improving learning and performance – recognising what is being done well and knowing how to improve.

Problem solving – recognising the challenge and adopting a variety of ways to approach the task, using effective strategies.

Other aspects

Thinking skills – through critical evaluation of performances and to generate and express their own ideas and opinions.

Work-related learning – through learning about organisation of sporting events and adopting different roles. To work alongside teachers with younger pupils.

Education for sustainable development – increasing understanding of healthy lifestyles and challenging environments.

Extracurricular activities

Design a poster for a new or existing sports club at your school or college.

For most children, physical education at school is their first contact with organised sport, although some will have learned to swim before starting school. Throughout their time at school they will have the opportunity not only to take part in a range of physical activities during lessons, but also in organised games during lunchtime, after school and against other schools. These are known as **extracurricular activities** because they take place outside normal school time.

Sally Gunnell: A schoolgirl champion and world record holder

Inter-school competition is important in developing high standards of play, but the activities are dependent on a number of factors:

- which activities are included in the school physical education programme
- the facilities which are available to the school. (Some schools may be able to use facilities which do not belong to them. Schools without swimming pools may have swimming teams; their training might take place in the public baths or at another school's pool)
- the interests and skills of the staff
- coaches and parents might be involved in physical education, school teams and matches. Site managers, technicians, cleaners and groundstaff might have the skills needed to help with school teams. These people provide valuable assistance to physical education staff in schools.

In many sports there is a natural progression from school sport to international sport. There are many well-known schools governing bodies, such as the English Schools Football Association and the English Schools Athletics Association. These governing bodies are usually affiliated to national governing bodies, who lay down rules, organise championships and arrange international matches.

Can you find more information about other national schools-governing bodies?

Physical education and sport

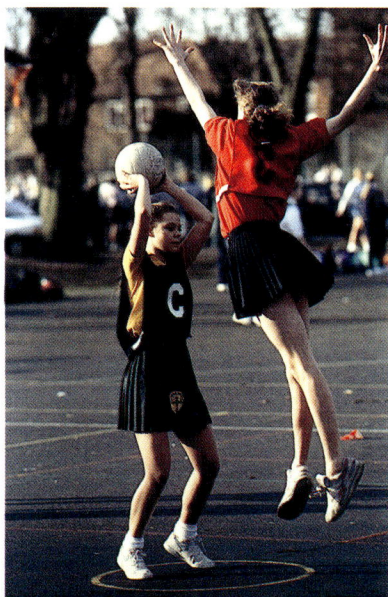

At the centre of all physical education are sports activities. Physical education is a school subject, like history, English and art. In physical education pupils learn not only the way to *perform* in sports activities such as swimming strokes, dribbling in hockey and other skills, but they also learn through *taking part* in physical activity. Look again at the section on public school sport, and the reasons for taking part.

Many physical education teachers will have had a high involvement in sport when they were at school. They may have been international performers at school level and moved to full international either at college or in their first years of teaching. Most physical education teachers will have experienced many sports during their time at school and during their training. Some may hold coaching qualifications in specific sports and be either players or coaches at their local clubs. Therefore physical education teachers will not only want pupils to have good experiences in the subject, but will also want to encourage excellence in performance. However, there is a difference between physical education teachers and coaches. In coaching:

Sports activities are at the centre of physical education

- more time is spent on an activity
- the participants are usually there by choice
- groups being coached are often of the same ability.

Physical education is also an examination subject. Many of you reading this book will be working towards an exam qualification in PE. In 2000 over 100,000 pupils took GCSE PE and increasing numbers are taking A level PE and associated GNVQs.

School and club links

Think of ways you might develop links between your school or college and local sports teams.

In recent years, there have been many schemes to link school sport and local clubs. The Sports Colleges, Youth Sports Trust (YST), National Coaching Foundation (NCF) and the Sports Council (see Chapter 15) all regard the link between schools and clubs as a very important part of their work. Often links between schools and clubs exist, but these may be informal. A local sports club may use the school facilities in the evening or at a weekend. Teachers from the school may be members of a local sports club and so encourage pupils to join that club. In the past, many schools had Old Boys Associations who organised sports fixtures, but this might have been limited to the major games of soccer, rugby and cricket.

The range of sports clubs has increased, and the age of participants has reduced. No longer do pupils join clubs after they leave school; many are club members throughout their school life. Swimming and gymnastics are two activities where very young children might be club members.

A gym club for young children

Developing excellence

Governments and other organisations realise that developing sporting activities in schools, can lead to a better and bigger base for national teams. The Department for Education and Employment are responsible for schools and the curriculum; other organisations such as Sport England, NCF and YST have a significant input in schools. The role and functions of these organisations are shown in more detail in Chapter 15.

In 1995 the Conservative government announced a policy 'Raising the Game' which had four central aims:

- to put sport back into the heart of the weekly life of every school
- to bring every child in every school within reach of adequate sporting facilities by the year 2000, and to protect our nation's playing fields
- to enable sporting opportunities to continue after school in college and university and to provide a better link between school and club sport
- to develop excellence among the most talented of British sportspeople by creating a new British Academy of Sport.

A report one year later showed that £20 million had been spent on schools sports facilities, and two initiatives which would raise the standards in school sport and physical education were announced, Sportsmark and sports colleges.

SPORTSMARK AND SPORTSMARK GOLD

Secondary schools throughout the country were able to bid for these awards. The awards are made to schools on the quality of physical education and sport provision. Schools with exceptional provision are awarded Sportsmark gold. The awards last for three years after which the schools must reapply. By September 2000, 1,477 schools achieved Sportsmark, with a further 136 gaining Sportsmark Gold. Schools have to make a decision for which award they are applying; when the form has been sent in a panel decide to make the award. The following information is used to decide whether a school or college deserves Sportsmark or Sportsmark Gold:

- curriculum – does the school curriculum meet the National Curriculum? Also curriculum activities must be of 12 hours in length (ie six hours' athletics in Year 7 and six hours' in Year 8)
- extracurricular activities – 12 opportunities for activity for *all* pupils – four recreational or clubs and eight competitive activities such as inter-form or inter-school events

- Sportsmark – 35 per cent of pupils to take part in extracurricular
- Sportsmark Gold – 50 per cent of pupils to take part in extracurricular
- leadership – pupils should experience leadership inside and outside of lessons
- sporting partnerships – with sports clubs, leisure centres, other schools, youth groups
- professional development for teachers – evidence of teachers continuing training in all aspects of physical education.

Activemark and activemark gold

This is an award similar to Sportsmark but for primary schools, and was started in 2000.

SPORTS COLLEGES

In 1996 the Conservative government launched the sports colleges initiative. Schools could apply to become sports colleges if they met certain criteria. Some of the objectives behind this scheme are

- students to gain a sports qualification such as GCSE PE, or equivalent
- to increase the range and participation of sports, courses and qualifications for students
- to maintain physical education and sports courses for post-16 students
- to increase the time available for PE by increasing the length of the school day
- to identify and develop sporting potential for gifted children
- to develop links with governing bodies of sport
- to expand the school's facilities and encourage wider community use
- to improve participation and achievement in PE and community sport
- to develop stronger links with feeder primary schools and local communities
- to share their resources, enhancing the total pattern of provision for pupils, families and the wider community.

Schools applying for the scheme would have to prove their ability to meet these demands, but also they would be expected to:

- have good sporting facilities
- able to meet the criteria for Sportsmark award
- have raised £50,000, the government will then award £100,000.

It is the government's intention to have 1500 specialist colleges by 2006, teaching in sports, technology, languages and performing arts. By September 2001 there will be 85 sport colleges in the U.K. This number will be increased considerably over the next four years.

Sports college logo

The National Curriculum for physical education, and the work by the YST, the NCF and the Sports Council are all aimed at improving the quality of pupils' experiences and performances in physical education and sport. Schools and clubs have an important part to play in the development of their pupils and members. The National Lottery has provided extra funding for sports facilities throughout the country. Many schools have benefited from this, not only strengthening and increasing school–club links, but also raising standards of play. Although raised in 1995 the plans for the proposed British Academy for Sport have undergone considerable changes. In 1997 the Labour government proposed a UK Sports Institute to be based in Sheffield. These plans were superseded and the UK Sports Institute Network established in 2000 will comprise

- English Sports Institute
- Northern Ireland Network Centre
- Scotland
- Wales.

The English Institute for Sport will not be based at one centre, but will have regional centres, some based on Sport England National Centres, others being created with new developments or based on existing high-class facilities. The Scottish Institute uses three centres, Inverclyde, Cumbrae and Glenmore Lodge, whilst the Welsh Institute have a central base in Cardiff and the Plas Menai for Water Sports.

Questions on school and club sports

1 Which of the following activities are in the National Curriculum in Key Stage 3?
   a   archery
   b   horse riding
   c   gymnastics
   d   sky diving.

2 Sportsmark is an award made to
   a   primary schools
   b   youth clubs
   c   secondary schools
   d   universities.

3 Name one sport and a public school with the same name.

4 Name two activities which are in the National Curriculum in Key Stage 4.

5 Give two moral issues in sport.

6 Give two examples of the use of information and communication technology in sport in a school.

7 What are extracurricular activities?

8 Give two differences between teachers and coaches.

9 Give two important reasons why a school might not be awarded Sportsmark.

10 How is the English Institute of Sport organised?

Exam-style questions

1 Gymnastics is one area of the National Curriculum, name the other five. **(5 marks)**

2 **a** Give three factors which affect extracurricular activities in a school. **(3 marks)**
   b How might extracurricular activities develop excellence? **(3 marks)**
   c Suggest two ways in which a school might promote links with a local sporting club. **(4 marks)**

3 **a** What is meant by cross-curricular issues? **(2 marks)**
   b Physical education helps a pupil to develop skills and understanding of sporting activities, but give four examples of how it can help personal development. **(4 marks)**
   c Give four factors which are important in a school's bid for a Sportsmark award. **(4 marks)**
   d What is a sports college? **(1 mark)**
   e Give five factors for a school to gain sport college status. **(5 marks)**

4 The original plan to have a British Sports Academy has been abandoned in favour of having regional centres. Both of these have advantages and disadvantages. Argue points for and against having regional centres. **(15 marks)**

Quality of written communication. **(5 marks)**

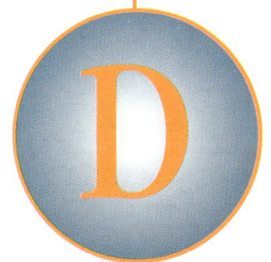

Organisation of Sport

14

Local Sports Organisation

A local sports club is the basic unit of any sport. Clubs are formed when like-minded people come together to play the game. Sports clubs, small and large, have similar structures and functions.

LEARNING OBJECTIVES

🏆 **how clubs work**
🏆 **finance**

How clubs work

The structure of any sports club (such as cricket, rugby or archery) is very similar.

MEMBERS

People who belong to a club are its members. In most clubs the members take part in the club activity, although members may not always be very active. Golf clubs have lots of members who may make little use of the golf course, but prefer to be in the clubhouse. Local soccer clubs will have more playing members and fewer social members. Club members are the lifeblood of the club: they pay subscriptions, take part in activities, organise matches and training, and participate in fundraising events.

A local cricket club

COMMITTEES

Even in the smallest clubs, it would be difficult for every member to be involved in making decisions about the club. Therefore members usually elect a smaller number of people to look after the club's affairs. This is usually known as a committee, and these are the **officials** of the club (not to be confused with match officials who control the games). Members of the committee tend to have special jobs in running the club.

Chairperson

This is usually the most important official in the club. S/he controls committee meetings and represents the club at special events.

Vice-chairperson

If the chairperson is ill or unable to attend a meeting, then the vice-chair will stand in.

Secretary

Secretaries arrange committee meetings, and carry out club correspondence. During a meeting they will take notes, which are known as **minutes**. After meetings, the secretary will let the rest of the members know what the committee has decided.

Treasurer

The treasurer is responsible for the club's finances, for collecting subscriptions from members and for paying club bills. Each year the treasurer will have to produce a set of accounts showing how money was raised and spent throughout the year.

A soccer club boardroom

Can you find the names and positions of the officials at a local sports club? If possible, interview one of the officials, or write to them to find out how they work for the club.

Design a poster for a local sports club of your choice. Include the facilities available and the cost of membership.

Other officials

In larger clubs there may be more officials:

- a fixtures secretary
- a member responsible for team selection
- a coach
- a trainer
- a physiotherapist.

President/vice-president/patron

These people are not usually involved with the running of a club. They are often appointed to this special position because they are well-known people in the community who might raise the profile and improve the image of the club. They may or may not have been club members; in some cases they may not have even played the sport.

In most clubs the officials are voluntary (they do not get paid for the work they do for the club). They are usually club players or former players, and have a commitment to their sport or club. Quite often they have specialist skills which are useful in running the club. The treasurer may be an accountant, or the coach might be a PE teacher with special skills in a particular sport.

As clubs get larger, officials might be paid for the work they do. They then become **officers** rather than officials, although they still work for the club members. As rugby union was an amateur game until recently, there were very few paid club officials. To coach a team was an honour and no payment was made. As clubs expand into professionalism, many coaches will be paid substantial amounts.

Finance

For any club to be successful, there must be adequate finance. There are a number of sources:

- members who pay subscriptions
- grants from local authorities, governing bodies, the National Lottery, the Foundation for Sport and the Arts
- sponsorship either gained locally or through the national governing body
- fundraising through raffles, car boot sales and other charity events
- donations from wealthy patrons.

How much is the membership fee of your local sports club? Give details of different categories of membership, such as juniors and adults.

Questions on local sports organisation

1 The treasurer of a club is responsible for
   a   organising fixtures
   b   taking charge of meetings
   c   looking after the club's finances
   d   coaching the players.

2 Junior members are important to clubs because

   a   they help to organise the club
   b   they ensure that the club will build up its numbers
   c   they coach other players
   d   they take charge of fixtures.

3 Give two functions of a sports club.

4 What does the president of a club do?

5 Why is the secretary of a club an important position?

6 What is the difference between an officer and an official?

7 What advantages are there in having a committee to run a club?

8 In what ways might a club raise money?

9 Give an example of two sports where you must be a club member to play.

10 Give two ways in which a club might encourage junior players.

Exam-style questions

1 Sports clubs often provide social facilities for their members. (5 marks)
  Give five other functions of a sports club.

2 Sports clubs are the base unit for many of our national games
  and they need to have good links with schools.
  a Give two ways in which a club might develop links with (2 marks)
    a school.
  b Give two ways in which a school might develop links with (2 marks)
    a club. (2 marks)
  c Why is it important that all clubs have coaches? (4 marks)
  d Describe four ways in which a club finances itself.

3 a Some club members might have special non-sporting skills.
    Give three examples and a brief description of how this might (6 marks)
    benefit the club. (3 marks)
  b How might a club attract new members not from schools? (6 marks)
  c Name and describe the role of three club officials.

4 Many small clubs are run by a few dedicated members, who do lots
  of jobs in the club, from marking out pitches to running the bar. As
  clubs get larger many officials get paid. Give the advantages and
  disadvantages of a club growing large in size. What benefits might (15 marks)
  there be to its members both young and old? (5 marks)

  Quality of written communication.

15

National Organisation of Sport

There are a number of organisations involved in the organisation of sport at a national level, and of course this has an impact on club and school sport at a local level.

LEARNING OBJECTIVES

- governing bodies of sport
- Central Council for Physical Recreation (CCPR)
- British Sport Trust
- Sports Councils
- Youth Sport Trust (YST)
- Sports Aid Foundation (SAF)
- Countryside Commission (CC)
- National Trust
- National Coaching Foundation (NCF)
- British Sports Association for the Disabled (BSAD)
- Women's Sports Foundation (WSF)
- National Playing Fields Association (NPFA)
- British Olympic Association (BOA)
- Outward Bound

Governing bodies of sport

The governing bodies of sport, sometimes known as national associations, were formed when sports were being developed in the ninteenth century. As more and more teams travelled further to play matches there was a need to standardise the rules of games. International governing bodies were formed when international matches started. There are over 300 governing bodies in the UK; most governing bodies are organised on two levels, regional and national. Clubs belong to their regional (county) associations, and each region will have a representative on the national association. The governing bodies have wide responsibility for their sport. These are

- rules – usually rule changes require the international governing body to agree, but national governing bodies might be allowed to have experimental rule changes. If these are successful then international rules might then be changed
- competitions – local and national, and international competitions are organised by governing bodies. Often a national cup is organised on a regional basis, with regional winners moving on to the next round of the competition
- team selection – committees or selectors are responsible for regional and national teams, usually done by having trials
- clubs and players – if there is a dispute between a club and a player, perhaps over a contract, the governing body might help resolve the problem. Also governing bodies are often responsible for disciplining of clubs and players
- finance – members and clubs have to pay an affiliation fee to their regional or national governing body. Other finance comes from grants from the sports councils, National Lottery, sponsorship and TV deals made by the governing body. This is then distributed to the clubs to develop the sport
- promotion – by promoting their sport governing bodies can improve the standard, increase its popularity and bring in more revenue
- coaching – governing bodies provide coaching at all levels of the sport from school to national teams
- technical advice – governing bodies are able to give advice to clubs about equipment and facilities.

RAISING FINANCE

Clubs pay fees either to their local or national governing body, and by doing this become affiliated. This allows them to take part in competitions and vote on issues in their sport.

The governing bodies are funded in a number of ways:

- affiliation fees
- grants – from Sports Council, Foundation for Sport and the Arts, National Lottery
- sponsorship – from deals with companies
- television deals for the right to televise certain matches or competitions.

DISTRIBUTING FINANCE

Clubs and players benefit from this as they receive money from their governing body to support their club. New buildings, the development of youth policies or financial support for overseas competitions are some of the ways in which a club benefits from its governing body.

PROMOTION

Governing bodies need to promote their sport to increase participation, which can bring in increased revenue and a larger foundation on which to build excellence. Media coverage, particularly through television, not only brings in finance but increases public awareness of a sport.

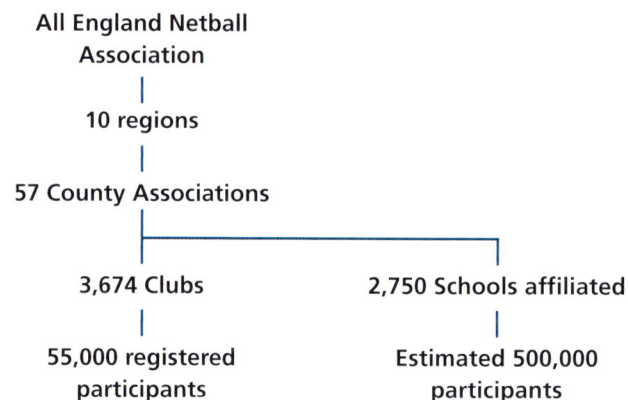

All England Netball Association

|
10 regions

|
57 County Associations

3,674 Clubs   **2,750 Schools affiliated**

55,000 registered participants   **Estimated 500,000 participants**

The structure of the All England Netball Association

COACHING

All governing bodies are concerned with improving the standards of their sport through coaching. Through the Champion Coaching Scheme, governing bodies are able to develop their work in the coaching of junior players.

TECHNICAL ADVICE

Many governing bodies are able to offer technical advice to clubs on facilities or equipment. Installing an artificial pitch is costly, and therefore it is important that the pitch meets with the requirements of sports governing bodies if future high-level matches are to be played there.

Can you find the full name of three different national governing bodies?

Central Council for Physical Recreation (CCPR)

The CCPR is a non-governmental body, which is made up of all the national governing bodies. It was first set up in 1935 when there were 82 governing bodies; there are now over 300. Because of the variety of games and sporting activities, the CCPR is split into six divisions:

- games and sports
- major spectator sports
- movement and dance
- outdoor pursuits
- water recreation
- interested organisations.

The Central Council of Physical Recreation has two main objectives:

1. to encourage as many people as possible to participate in all forms of sport and physical recreation
2. to provide the separate governing bodies of the individual sports with a central organisation that represents and promotes their individual and collective interests.

For further information refer to www.ccpr.org.uk

British Sport Trust

Find as much information as possible about the JSLA. Do you think that this is a useful qualification to have?

Administers four awards: fifty thousand young people took these awards last year.

1. Junior Sports Leader Award
2. Community Sports Leader Award
3. Higher Sports Leader Award
4. Basic Expedition Leader Award.

For further information see www.thebritishsportstrust.org.uk/

Sports Councils

The UK Sports Council, now known as UK Sport, was set up in 1997. It is responsible for the development of high-performance sport and has four aims:

1. to provide UK world-class performers with world-class support
2. to extend the UK's profile and influence on the international sporting stage
3. to promote ethical standards and manage anti-doping programmes
4. to create a framework for attracting and running the world's major sporting events.

To achieve these aims costs considerable amounts of money; in 2000 the government provided £12.6 million and the National Lottery £20.5 million.

For further information see www.uksport.gov.uk

The countries in the UK have their own sports councils:

- Sport England
- Sportscotland
- Sports Council for Wales
- Sports Council for Northern Ireland

Sport England's three aims are:

- More people!
- More places!
- More medals!

More people
To achieve this aim there are three new programmes:

1. Active schools – to support physical education and school sport and to stimulate participation by all young people
2. Active sports – this involves local clubs, local authorities, schools and governing bodies, working in partnership. The 45 partnership areas will be led by an Active Sports Manager
3. Active communities – this programme is designed to increase and sustain lifelong participation in sport and recreation. Its intention is to build on the Sports Council's first ever campaign, 'Sport for All'. As part of the active communities programme there will be 30 Sport Action Zones to bring the benefits of sport to deprived communities.

More places
Sport England plays a central role in the strategic development of sporting facilities and awarding of National Lottery money.

More medals
Through its support of the UK Sports Institute and the World Class programme Sport England is making a commitment to improve the standard of performance of English sportsmen and women.

Sport England have had a major role in the distribution of National Lottery money to develop many aspects of sport. To date over 3,300 capital awards have been made with over £1.2 billion being allocated.

Previous Sports Council Campaigns

'SPORT FOR ALL' (1972)

This campaign was to encourage all members of the community to participate in sport. Although partially successful the following campaigns become more focussed with particular groups of people being targeted.

'SPORT FOR ALL – DISABLED PEOPLE' (1981)

During the International Year of the Disabled in 1981, the Sports Council launched this campaign. Its aims were

The Sport England logo

Look at the sports facilities in your school or college. Have special arrangements been made to help people with disabilities use the facilities? If nothing has been done, suggest ways to help wheelchair users to take part in sport in your school or college.

- to make people aware of the needs of people with disabilities
- to encourage people with disabilities to take part in physical activities
- to integrate people with and without disabilities through sport
- to make sure that people with disabilities have suitable facilities and coaching.

Wheelchair abseiling organised by The Back-Up Trust

Can you find out whether there are any special sessions for people over 50 in your area?

Draw a poster to attract a 13–14-year-old to take part in a particular sport.

'FIFTY PLUS – ALL TO PLAY FOR' (1983)

This was aimed at older people, particularly the 50–60-years age group. The campaign stressed that not only were there health benefits in taking part in sport, but there were social advantages in meeting people. Special sessions were arranged throughout the country by local and regional sports councils.

'EVER THOUGHT OF SPORT?' (1985)

Figures showed that young people, particularly school leavers, were not taking part in sport, although the age group targeted was 13–24-year-olds. This campaign coincided with the International Year of Youth. The campaign was jointly sponsored by Weetabix, and there was considerable media coverage on television and radio.

'WHAT'S YOUR SPORT?' (1987)

The Milk Marketing Board sponsored a big campaign to increase awareness of where and how to take part in sport. Television coverage encouraged people to send for a sports pack, containing this essential information. As a result, over 100,000 enquiries were made and 1,200 information points were set up.

Write down four items of information which you think someone would need to start a new sport of your choice.

'MILK IN ACTION FOR WOMEN' (1989)

This was launched to encourage more women to take part in sporting activities. During the campaign, sports centres around the country provided taster courses in a range of activities, targeting women.

YEAR OF SPORT (1991)

The World Student Games, one of the largest events next to the Olympic Games, was staged in Sheffield during 1991. This was an ideal opportunity for the Sports Council to make further promotions. There were many events held throughout the country with a range of sporting and social activities such as sports festivals and fitness roadshows, in which people were encouraged to participate.

FACILITIES

To participate at any level in sport, facilities are the most essential element. Sport England has had a central role in the development of new facilities and the upgrading of older ones. Their role has been not only to distribute grant aid, but to give advice on buildings, research into new materials and offer advice on management and finance in the operating of sports facilities. The provision of sports facilities showed remarkable growth over a ten-year period from 1982 to 1992.

Youth Sport Trust (YST)

YST logo

This is not a government organisation, even though it works with government departments. The Youth Sport Trust is a registered charity, set up in 1994 to improve sporting provision for all children in the UK. The YST wants all children to have

- fun and success in sport
- sports suited to children's own level
- an opportunity to develop a range of sports skills
- top coaching and top resources
- a chance to develop good sporting attitudes
- positive competition
- a sound foundation for lifelong physical activity.

The YST operates a range of programmes:

① **Top Tots:** introduces simple games at home to children aged 18 months to 3 years.
② **Top Start:** develops basic movement and ball skills with children aged 3 to 5 years.

③ **Top Play:** for 4–9-year-olds which includes core skills and fun sports.

④ **Top Sport:** for 7–11-year-olds. This includes specific sports of basketball, cricket, football, hockey, netball, rugby, squash, table tennis and tennis.

⑤ **Top skill:** challenging 11–14 year olds to extend their sporting skills and knowledge.

⑥ **TOP Link:** provides training for secondary school pupils (Key Stage 4 and post-16) to enable them to run TOP festivals for primary schools in their area.

Sports Colleges: The Youth Sport Trust has a contract with the Department of Education and Employment to help secondary schools with their applications to become sports colleges (part of the specialist schools initiative).

⑦ **Millennium volunteers:** building opportunities for 16–19 year olds to volunteer through sport.

⑧ **SportSability:** creating opportunities for young disabled people to enjoy, participate and perform in PE and Sport.

In England, TOP Play and TOP Sport are joint ventures between the Youth Sport Trust and Sport England.

Sports Aid Foundation (SAF)

Although many top athletes are professional and receive substantial appearance money, the majority of athletes still struggle to find the funds to compete at top level. In a survey of young athletes in 1997, it was found that on average athletes spend £5,200 per year on their sport for travel, equipment, training and medical costs.

The SAF was set up in 1976 to raise money for sport through sponsorship from companies and local authorities. The SAF gives money to the governing bodies who administer the funds.

For further information see www.Sportsaid.org.uk

> **Imagine you are a young athlete. Write a letter to the SAF saying why you should receive a grant from them in the coming year, and how you intend to spend the money.**

Countryside Agency

Established in 1968, the Countryside Agency is a public agency which looks after the English countryside. Countryside in Scotland, Wales and Northern Ireland is looked after by Scottish National Heritage, the Countryside Agency for Wales and the Department of the Environment Northern Ireland. The Countryside Agency is funded by the Department of the Environment, Transport and the Regions, and is an important organisation for all those who enjoy outdoor recreation. It has a number of key roles:

- the maintenance of the countryside
- running the National Parks of England
- developing and maintaining national trails for walkers, hikers and cyclists
- advising the government about countryside matters
- enabling access for those taking part in outdoor pursuits.

The **Country Code** was an initiative set up by the Countryside Agency to teach people how to use and respect the countryside.

Find more details about the Country Code for walkers and cyclists.

Mountain biking

National Trust

Although the National Trust is responsible for many historic houses, it is also the largest landowner in the UK. It owns 570,000 acres of field, coastline, forest, lake and moorland. Perhaps one of the most important areas for sport and recreation owned by the Trust is the Lake District, where climbing, sailing, walking, canoeing and skiing are possible. The National Trust for Scotland owns vast amounts of Scottish countryside, making it available for many forms of outdoor activities.

What is the nearest National Trust property to your school or college that has recreational pursuits? Name the activities.

Part of the Lake District which is owned by the National Trust

National Coaching Foundation (NCF)

Established by the Sports Council in 1983, the NCF has two main aims:

1. to promote education through its coaching courses and awards
2. to increase knowledge through information centres, a magazine *Supercoach*, videos and its subsidiary company (Coachwise Ltd) which provides a service for its coaches to purchase books and resources on coaching matters.

The NCF is an independent charity funded by its members and by the Sports Council. The standard of coach education in the UK has improved greatly as the NCF has developed.

Look through a copy of *Supercoach*. In the news section, find one topic which you find interesting. Describe how this might help develop a particular sport.

British Sports Association for the Disabled (BSAD)

The BSAD is a national voluntary body which works for people with disabilities in sport. Since it was established in 1961, it has helped thousands of sportspeople with disabilities to take part in sport, from recreational participation to national championships. Funding for the BSAD comes from the Sports Council, sponsorship, local authorities and various charities.

People with disabilities can take part in many sports

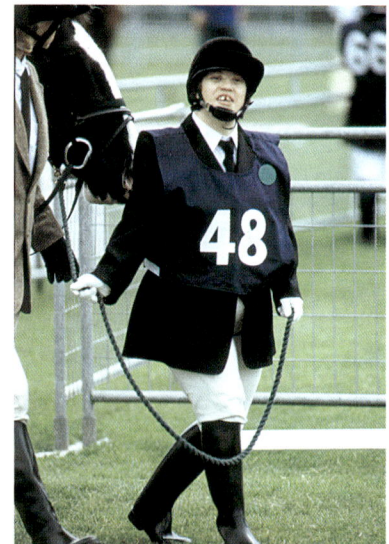

Women's Sports Foundation (WSF)

This association was formed in 1984 to help women become involved in sport at all levels. This is done by raising public awareness about women in sport, by promoting their achievements and enabling better access to sport for women. Financial support comes from the Sports Council and members' subscriptions.

National Playing Fields Association (NPFA)

This is a long-established charity founded in 1925. It is an important organisation which acquires and develops all kinds of play areas, playing fields and playgrounds. There has been much public concern over the number of playing fields sold to private developers for housing and commerce. The NPFA continues to fight to save playing fields in the country.

British Olympic Association (BOA)

British Olympic Association logo

The BOA is responsible for the Great Britain Team at the Olympic Games, winter and summer. It also has an obligation to develop and protect the Olympic movement and its ideals in the UK. There are a number of key functions of the BOA; these include:

- overall organisation and administration of the Olympic teams' logistics, travel, clothing, accreditation, etc, for an Olympic Games
- to provide support services to Olympic sports-governing bodies in the areas of team management, coaching, psychology, physiology, sports medicine and sport science, amongst others
- to provide support to athletes in their careers, education, employment and lifestyle
- to spread the Olympic ideals and encourage mass participation in sport.

FINANCE

The BOA is one of the very few national olympic committees which receives no funding from the government. This means that it has to raise money to send UK sportsmen and women to the Olympic Games. Money is raised in three ways:

- nationwide appeals
- sponsorship programmes
- licensing.

Appeals

The BOA makes appeals throughout the UK for funds well before an Olympic year. Often, top sportspeople will travel around the country to raise awareness and funds.

Sponsorship

Only a limited number of quality sponsors are used. In return for their financial support, the sponsors are allowed to use the official BOA logo. There are different categories such as clothing, soft drinks, technical equipment. These are created so that only one company in each category has exclusive rights of sponsorship and the marketing value.

Licensing

Specific merchandise such as sports goods carry the official BOA logo. For each item sold the BOA receives a **royalty**, which is a percentage of the price of the item.

POLITICS

Because the BOA is given no money from the government, the government has no control over the activities of the BOA, including who represents the UK at the Olympics. The government may try to put pressure on the BOA not to attend an event because of the reactions of other countries. The BOA is able to resist this pressure, and the UK is one of only five countries never to have missed an Olympic Games. In 1980, the government did not want the BOA to send a team to the Moscow Olympics, as many western nations (including the USA) boycotted these games. The BOA stood firm against the government and gave sportspeople the choice of going to the games.

Can you find the names of two UK gold medal winners who decided to compete in the Moscow Olympics?

Outward Bound

The Outward Bound is primarily concerned with the provision of a range of outdoor and adventurous activities at its four centres, for all ages (see Chapter 10 for details).

Questions on national organisation of sport

1 Governing bodies were first set up to
   a control drugs in sport
   b to decide on the rules
   c to provide coaching
   d to provide funding.

2 The Sports Council has had a number of campaigns over the last 30 years. Which of the following was not a Sports Council Campaign?
   a Sport for some
   b Fifty plus – all to play for
   c What's your sport?
   d Ever thought of sport?

3 Name one national governing body.

4 Name one international governing body.

5 What does CCPR stand for and what is its function?

6 What are the four aims of Sport England?

7 What is the National Coaching Foundation?

8 Why is the National Playing Fields Association important for sport?

9 Give two important functions of the British Olympic Association?

10 Name two activities which are helped by the work of the Countryside Commission.

Exam-style questions

1 National governing bodies decide on the rules of their games. Give five other ways in which they support their sport. (5 marks)

2 a Name four of the six divisions of the CCPR. (4 marks)
   b What are the two main objectives of the CCPR? (2 marks)
   c The CCPR have two awards which can be taken by pupils in school. Name one of these, and why you think it might be a useful qualification? (4 marks)

3 a UK Sport supports high-level performance in four ways. Name three of these. (3 marks)
   b The Sports Council ran a number of campaigns to encourage people to take part in sporting activities. Name and describe two of these campaigns. (6 marks)
   c The Youth Sport Trust have a number of TOP programmes. Name two of these and say why they might be valuable in schools. (6 marks)

Exam Style Questions (continued)

4 a Name one national organisation and describe how it helps people to take part in outdoor activities.   (5 marks)

b There are plenty of open spaces, countryside, hills and moorland for people to take part in outdoor activities. Discuss whether the next campaign to get people to take part in a sporting or recreational activity should be to encourage people to take part in an outdoor activity.   (10 marks)

Quality of written communication.   (5 marks)

16

International Sport and Politics

Success in international sport is the ambition of most sportsmen and women. Competing at the highest level possible, for one's country and against the best in the world is perhaps the greatest honour they can achieve. World-class sportsmen, women and teams bring recognition of their country to the rest of the world. Governments are well aware of how successful teams can raise the image of their country, and international competition and politics often come together.

> **LEARNING OBJECTIVES**
>
> - Olympic Games
> - International Olympic Committee
> - Winter Olympics
> - international competitions
> - World championships
> - Olympic-style competitions
> - politics in international and national sport

Olympic Games

Held every four years the Olympic Games are the largest multi-sporting event on the calendar. The ancient games, first started in Greece, were abolished in AD 393. Pierre de Coubertin was responsible for re-establishing the games in Athens in 1896.

The most important thing in the Olympic Games is not to win but to take part. Just as the most important thing in life is not to triumph but to struggle. The essential thing is not to have conquered but to have fought well.

Not the words of Baron de Coubertin but a US preacher in 1908, and still used today.

International Olympic Committee (IOC)

The games are organised by the IOC who are responsible for

- selecting the venue for both summer and winter games
- deciding which sports should be included in the games
- working with the city and country hosting the games.

The IOC is made up of members from each country which has an Olympic committee.

The IOC receives funding from marketing and television rights. For the Atlanta Games in 1996, the US television company NBC paid $456 million for the rights to broadcast the games, and also paid a further $705 million for the rights of the winter games in Nagano and the summer games in Sydney in 1998 and 2000 respectively. Sponsorship from multinational companies is another source of funding.

All the revenue gained by the IOC is distributed to international sports federations, national olympic committees and the organising committee for each of the games.

Do you think some sports ought to be taken out of the games? Why?

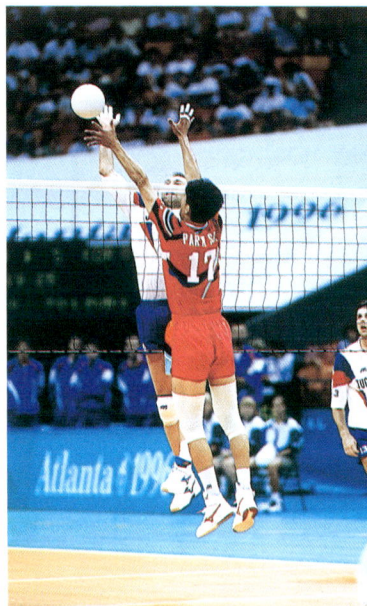

Indoor and outdoor volleyball were in the Atlanta Olympic Games for the first time

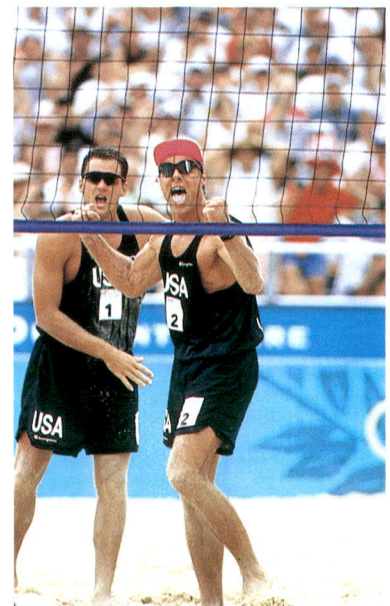

Since the modern Olympics began there have been controversial incidents involving sportsmen and women and governments. The original intention to have games for amateurs with only medals and not money seems to have been lost in the most recent games.

The oath taken by the athletes at the start of the games –

We swear that we will take part in these Olympic Games in the true spirit of sportsmanship and that we will abide by the rules that govern them, for the glory of sport and the honour of our country

– has not always been followed by some of the competitors. Significant events of the modern summer Olympics are:

1896 ATHENS

The first of the modern games was opened by the King of Greece. There were only nine sports in these games, with a total of 311 competitors. Many competitors made their own way to these games and entered the events they wished to. One Englishman, who happened to be in Athens at the time, played in the Olympic tennis competition. Even the first games became a problem for the organisers with the cost being much higher than expected. Only the intervention of a wealthy businessman saved the Greek government from financial embarrassment. However, it was fitting that the first marathon to be run in the modern games was won by a Greek.

1900 PARIS

The games were held at the same time as the Paris Universal Exhibition. Even though there were 13 new sports, the games did not attract public attention due to other attractions and poor organisation.

1904 ST LOUIS

Only 12 countries took part in these games. The time and cost of transatlantic travel at the time was probably a contributing factor to the poor response to the games. As was to be expected, the majority of the winners were Americans. The World Fair was held in St Louis at the same time as the Olympics, and the games became just another attraction. The marathon winner, Horz, took a lift in a car and was disqualified. Hicks was the eventual winner but needed injections and brandy for medicinal purposes to complete the course.

1908 LONDON

Sets of rules were drawn up for these games and metric measurements were used. National pride in teams and competitors was apparent, with national flags being prominently displayed. There was a dispute between the British and Americans, and a race had to be re-run; an Italian athlete, Dorando Pietri, was disqualified after crossing the line first because he had been helped after collapsing in the stadium.

The Olympic flag, first seen in Antwerp, 1920

1912 STOCKHOLM

There were increased numbers of competitors with women taking part in swimming for the first time. The decathlon and pentathlon were won by an American, Jim Thorpe. After the games it was discovered that he had played baseball for money, and was then disqualified because he was a professional – only amateurs could compete in the Olympics. Electronic timing was used for the first time.

1914 AND 1918

There were no games during the First World War.

1920 ANTWERP

As a result of the First World War, there was a notable lack of competitors, although 29 countries took part. However, Germany, Austria, Hungary, Bulgaria and Turkey were banned from these games because of their involvement in the war. The Olympic flag which Pierre de Coubertin had introduced in 1914 flew for the first time at the Antwerp Games.

1924 PARIS

The number of countries taking part increased to 44, and there were many more competitors (3,092) than there had been in the previous games. The banned teams (apart from Germany) were again allowed to compete. The first summer games were held in Chamonix.

1928 AMSTERDAM

There was a further increase in the number of participating countries, with a total of 48. Additional events allowed women to take part in athletics and gymnastics. The Olympic flame, lit by the sun's rays on Mount Olympus in Greece, was kept burning in the stadium throughout the games.

1932 LOS ANGELES

There was a reduction in the number of competitors, probably due to the location on the West Coast of the USA. However, the games were popular, with high spectator numbers and 100,000 attending the opening ceremony. For the first time, a dedicated village was available for the competitors. Photo finish was installed for track events.

This stadium was used for the 1932 and 1984 Olympic Games in Los Angeles

Jesse Owens at the 1936 Olympic Games

1936 BERLIN

By 1936 Hitler had risen to power and the rest of the world were becoming aware of the situation in Germany. It was too late to cancel the games, and some countries were reluctant to send teams. The Americans were aware of Hitler's views on Jews and black athletes. He believed that true Germans were the master race, known as Aryans: blond and fair-skinned. Even at the time of the games, Jews were being persecuted in Germany: the German ladies high-jump champion and record holder was unable to compete for Germany as she was Jewish.

When a German athlete, Hans Woellke, won the shot, Hitler was delighted to present the medal and show the world the greatness of the Aryan race. However, the Nazi propaganda image was destroyed when a black athlete from the USA, Jesse Owens, won four gold medals. Hitler refused to present any of these medals, leaving the stadium before the presentations.

The Olympic flame was brought by torch relay for the first time and the events were televised.

1940 AND 1944

There were no games during the Second World War.

1948 LONDON

Germany, Japan and the former Soviet Union did not take part; however, there were 59 countries and 4,500 competitors. On home ground, the UK won only three events probably as a result of the disruption caused by the war.

The 1948 Olympic Games in London

1952 HELSINKI

Although these are referred to as the 'Friendly Games', the East–West rivalry began with the Soviet Union competing for the first time for 40 years. Germany were still excluded from the games.

1956 MELBOURNE

These were the first games where teams withdrew because of political and national reasons. Just before the games, the UK and France were involved in the Suez crisis; as a result of this, Egypt, Lebanon and Iran withdrew from the games. Spain, Holland and Switzerland withdrew because of the former Soviet Union's invasion of Hungary. China withdrew because Taiwan, previously part of China, entered a team. Germany were readmitted and entered a combined East and West German team.

1960 ROME

These games were the first to be broadcast worldwide on television. A Danish cyclist died after using drugs. South Africa had an all-white team.

1964 TOKYO

The IOC banned Indonesia and North Korea because they had been involved in a disputed competition prior to the games. South Africa was also banned because of the apartheid situation in the country and for the selection of an all-white team. The games continued to grow, with 94 countries taking part, but the cost of staging the games increased, with $200 million being spent.

- **can you find out more about apartheid?**
- **how has it affected international sport?**

1968 MEXICO CITY

At an altitude of over 3,000 metres (10,000 ft), it was a controversial decision to award the games to Mexico. It was a country with great problems of poverty and homelessness, and the prospect of spending many millions of dollars on sport caused riots in Mexico City. The Army were called in to restore the peace, but sadly over 200 demonstrators were killed.

The games are remembered for three events in the athletics arena:

- Tommie Smith and John Carlos raised black-gloved fists during the medal ceremony to protest about the treatment of black people in the USA. They and others who joined in with this salute were sent home from the games by the US Olympic Committee
- Dick Fosbury became the Olympic high-jump champion with his unusual style of jumping which became known as the 'Fosbury Flop'
- Bob Beamon broke the world long-jump record to set a new distance of 8 m 90 cm, which stood for 23 years.

1972 MUNICH

Further 'black power' salutes during the medal ceremonies by two black Americans were overshadowed by events outside the stadium. The continuing trouble between Palestinians and Israelis spilled over to the Olympics. Palestinian terrorists broke into the Olympic village, taking nine hostages and leaving two Israelis dead. The German police attempts to rescue the hostages failed and all the hostages, the five terrorists and one policeman lost their lives.

1976 MONTREAL

Security was increased for these games after what had happened at Munich. The cost of the games continued to rise, and after a bad winter and labour disputes, the opening ceremony took place in an unfinished stadium. Although the South African team remained banned because of apartheid, they were still at the centre of a dispute. New Zealand had sent a rugby team to South Africa prior to the games. The other African countries objected to this and demanded that New Zealand withdraw their team. In the event they refused to withdraw and many African countries did not attend the games.

1980 MOSCOW

As a very successful country in previous games, the Soviet Union were delighted to be awarded the games by the IOC. However, in 1979 the Soviet Union invaded Afghanistan, and even during the games they still had troops in that country. Although 81 countries took part, a further 52 nations including the USA and Canada refused to attend. The UK government at the time did not support the UK team at these games, although many UK athletes did attend.

1984 LOS ANGELES

The USA commercialised these games from the start, with major sponsorship and marketing deals. The Hollywood-style opening ceremony was spectacular. The Soviet Union and other Eastern Bloc Communist countries boycotted the games, not because they were in the USA but because of security arrangements. They expressed concern over the safety of their competitors and also over the commercialism of the games. However, there were 140 countries competing, and for the first time an Olympic Games made a substantial profit.

1988 SEOUL

South Korea was awarded the Olympic Games even though the IOC were aware of the continuing dispute with North Korea. The IOC refused permission for some events to take place in North Korea and therefore the country boycotted the games.

Tennis was reintroduced to the games, and as it had become open, professionals took part in the games for the first time. However, they competed for medals, not prize money. On the track the major talking point was the performance of Ben Johnson in the 100 metres. Two days later, as a result of drugs tests, he was disqualified and lost his gold medal.

1992 BARCELONA

South Africa competed in these games after a 30-year ban from the Olympics. The break-up of the Soviet Union into different states and the reunification of East and West Germany brought a new look to the games. Instead of the massive Soviet Union team, there were 12 separate teams. New events included badminton and baseball and there were 257 different events with a total of over 12,000 competitors and officials taking part. As the rules on professionalism were relaxed, the USA fielded a fully professional basketball team, referred to by the media as the 'dream team'. Naturally they won all their matches, to take the gold medal.

1996 ATLANTA

Described as the Coca Cola games, the USA had considerable sponsorship from this company whose headquarters are based in Atlanta (see page 227). The growth of the games was shown by the

Germany has been excluded from some Olympic Games. East and West Germany have sometimes competed separately, sometimes as one team. Trace the involvement of Germany in the modern games.

197 countries participating and over 10,000 competitors. These games were perhaps the most commercialised since Los Angeles, and even the purpose-built stadium was designed to be converted to a baseball stadium after the games. Security was high but even this did not prevent a bomb in a park near the stadium.

2000 SYDNEY

The Olympic Games continue to grow in size and cost. Building work was started soon after the games were awarded to Australia for the second time. A $(Australian) 40 million scheme to create an Olympic village for the 1,300 officials was undertaken. The athletes' village housed 15,000 athletes and a media village for 6,000 people was situated nearby. Ten major sponsors paid over $A 50 million for the rights to be associated with the games. The indoor arena for gymnastics and basketball alone cost $A 197 million, providing spectator accommodation for 15,000 for these events. Even the car park for 3,500 cars is estimated to have cost $A 63 million. As can be seen the cost of staging the games was colossal and is estimated at $A 2.4 billion. The Sydney Organising Committee for the Olympic Games (SOCOG) raised $A 1.6 billion from television rights, and with guaranteed sponsorship and funding by the Australian Government the games may not have run at a loss.

Kathy Freeman, an Aboriginal, won the 400 metres and raised the profile of the Aboriginal culture.

2004 ATHENS

Athens had made a bid for the Centennial Olympics and was extremely disappointed not to be awarded these games. In 1997, in a close contest between Rome and Stockholm, Athens was awarded the games even though there were doubts about its organisation. The Chairman of the International Athletics Federation was less than happy at the organisation of the World Athletics Championships held in Athens in 1997. Also, the level of air pollution in Athens has been a cause of concern for many years.

The year is 2004 and the summer Olympic Games in Athens have just finished. You have been to the games. Write a short report, about 100 words, on important events at the games.

Winter Olympics

Begun in 1924 in Chamonix (France), the winter Olympics follow the same four-year cycle (or **Olympiad**) as the summer games. These games are for traditional winter activities based on skiing, skating and tobogganing. The location is critical in that there must be the

Aerial skiing, now an Olympic sport

right conditions especially for the skiing events. Even though some countries have little or no snowfall and lack facilities for tobogganing, they are keen to enter teams in the winter games. The UK always enters competitors in these games, particularly in the bobsleigh competition; although the most unusual entry in this competition was the Jamaican team in the 1994 games in Norway.

As the numbers of teams and competitors continued to increase in both summer and winter games, the IOC decided that these games should not be held in the same year. Therefore the 1994 games in Norway were only two years after the 1992 games in France. Following the four-year cycle from now on, the winter and summer games will be separated by a two-year interval.

The popularity of the winter games continues to grow. Nagano, Japan hosted the 1998 games. There were seven sports with a total of 64 events. Aerials were added to the freestyle skiing; curling and women's ice hockey made their first appearance at the games.

International competitions

Competitions between countries have a long history. An England cricket team played against the USA and Canada in 1844; the first England v Scotland soccer match was in 1870, and rugby union in 1871. As more and more sports spread throughout the world so there was an increase in international fixtures. Those sports which were not included in the Olympics staged their own international events. Sometimes these were restricted to a particular continent, such as the European Athletics Championships; or the African Soccer Championships; sometimes they became world championships.

In prize fighting, there were many international events with fighters coming from all over Britain and Ireland, parts of Europe and America. The black American Tom Molyneux fought Tom Cribb for the World Championship in 1810.

During the latter part of the nineteenth century, sports spread throughout the world. In the days of the British Empire, the spread of ideas and the increasing trade between Britain and the rest of the world meant that sports and games were exported as well as goods. The rules for badminton were devised by British Army officers in India in 1873.

By 1890, tennis was being played not only throughout Europe, but in Australia, South Africa and in the USSR. Netball was introduced to England from America by a Dr Toles on a visit to Madam Osterberg's

English football players in 1881

Have any international sports events been held recently, or will soon be held in your area? Name the venue and the sport.

Physical Training College (Dartford) in 1895. (Madame Osterberg was Principal of the first physical training college for women.) Volleyball spread from the USA to Canada, then India in 1900, and within the next ten years it was being played in South America, China and Japan.

As countries developed their abilities in these new sports, so the development of international competition took place. No longer were the Olympics the only opportunity to compete against other countries. Also, many sports were *not* included in the Olympics and therefore had to stage their own international events

World championships

World championships in some sports are relatively new. One hundred years after their first international between England and Scotland, rugby union held its first World Cup in New Zealand, in 1987. However, many competitions have been regarded as world championships for a long time. The All England Badminton Championships held in 1899 would have been seen as the top world competition, although there were very few countries playing the game at the time.

Where are the other Grand Slam tennis events held each year?

In tennis there are no world championships. The rankings of the top players are worked out by computer, using their results throughout the season. Although the Wimbledon Tennis Championships is only one of the **Grand Slam** tennis events (one of the four top tennis competitions), it is perhaps still regarded as the most prestigious to win.

The national competitions for American football and baseball are seen as their world championships. In the Lake District, the 'World Championship in Cumberland and Westmorland Wrestling' is decided each year at the Ambleside Games. This type of wrestling is thought to have been introduced by Norse settlers over 1,000 years ago. It became popular all over the country, but now competitions are restricted to Cumbria and parts of Northumberland and north Lancashire.

Westmorland wrestling – a world championship event?

One of the oldest world competitions is for the **Jules Rimet Trophy** (Soccer World Cup). The first World Cup soccer competition was held in Uruguay in 1930. Uruguay were the reigning Olympic champions, having won in Paris (1924) and Amsterdam (1928). FIFA, whose president was called Jules Rimet, awarded the tournament to Uruguay. The offer by their government to meet the competing teams' travelling expenses and provide a new 100,000 – spectator stadium must have been a deciding factor.

See Table 16.1 on the next page for details of world competitions.

Sport	Founded	World championships
rugby union	1871	1977
cricket	1787	1983
tennis	1875	none
badminton	1893	1949 men 1956 women
soccer	1863	1930
hockey	1886	1975 women 1980 men
squash	1928	1979 women 1981 men
table tennis	1901	1926

Table 16.1 Details of world competitions

Olympic-style competitions

Working with a partner devise an Olympic-style competition to be held in your school or college. You may be able to carry out your plan.

The format of the Olympic Games has been copied by other organisations. The **Commonwealth Games** (formerly the Empire Games) is similar to the Olympic Games. Only Commonwealth countries such as Australia, New Zealand, India, Canada and many other smaller countries which were formerly part of the British Empire, can take part in the competition. It is held every four years, two years after each Olympic Games. It was first held in 1930 in Hamilton, Canada.

The World Student Games is one of the largest competitions outside the Olympics, and has very similar events to the Olympics. Sheffield hosted these games in 1991.

Politics in international and national sport

Politics and sport are often linked.

- leading up to the ancient games in Greece, a truce was declared between the independent states who were often at war with each other
- the continuing hostility between Honduras and El Salvador became a war after a World Cup qualifying match when Honduras lost on the soccer field in 1981.

The England soccer team giving the Nazi salute before a game against Germany in 1938

A memorable example of sports and politics mixing

The Olympics and other international sporting events often become the target for protests. Even 'friendly' matches can be used by countries to take political advantage. The English soccer team were advised by the British Ambassador to give the Nazi salute before their match with Germany in 1938 in Berlin.

However, the link between politics and sport is not always negative. The USA sent a table tennis team to China in the early 1970s as a means of restoring diplomatic relationships. A marathon held in Berlin on New Year's Day in 1990 followed a route through East and West Berlin, reflecting the unification of the country (after the collapse of the Berlin Wall in 1989).

The performance of national teams and individual sportspeople in international and national competitions is important to the government. Successful national teams provide a positive focus for the public, and raise the country's profile abroad:

- the success of the Cameroon soccer team in the 1990 World Cup gave the country more publicity than they had received at any other time during their history
- Harold Wilson, prime minister during the 1960s, gave the first public receptions for successful sporting teams and individuals, bestowing **honours**, such as the Commander of the British Empire (CBE) or Order of the British Empire (OBE) on some of the players.

Only very special sportspeople are **knighted** for their services to sport (this means they can be called 'Sir'/'Dame'). This is awarded when someone has made a special contribution to their sport and their country.

Can you find three sportspeople who have received such an award? List their names, their award and the sport they play.

Find the name of one sportsperson who has been knighted.

Can you find the name of the present minister for sport? Which government department is responsible for sport?

When teams fail at international level, whose fault is it: The players, the coach, the organisations of the sport, or the government? Discuss this in small groups.

Other prime ministers (including Tony Blair) have done the same, inviting both winning and losing sportspeople to Number 10, Downing Street. The success of UK teams in 1997, such as the British Lions in South Africa, the efforts of Greg Rusedski and Tim Henman at Wimbledon and the winning UK athletics team in the Europa Cup are examples of achievements that have been recognised by Blair.

POLITICAL ATTITUDES

It was under the Labour government in 1964 that moves were made to raise the status of sport within the government. Dennis Howell MP, who had been a football referee of international status, became responsible for sport as part of the Ministry of Education. In 1974 he became the first minister for sport, and since then governments have appointed ministers with that responsibility.

Most countries treat their successful sportspeople with considerable respect, often rewarding them in some way. In the former USSR and East Germany, top athletes were granted special privileges by the State: special accommodation, top coaches, high positions in the armed forces, unlimited training time and free travel.

Losing teams of course do little to enhance a country's reputation in the world. While in the UK, the public does not like the national teams to lose, it is unlikely that players will suffer the same fate as the losing Iraq soccer team. In June 1997 the Iraq soccer team lost at home to Kazakhstan. It was alleged that the team were taken to a local prison in Baghdad, where they were whipped and beaten because they had lost. Three weeks later they lost to the same team playing away, and further beatings followed. FIFA have investigated the incident, although there are no FIFA rules about torturing players.

Questions on international sport and politics

1 The Olympic Games are held
  a every two years
  b every three years
  c every four years
  d every five years.

2 Which of the following is not an award made to a sportsman or woman by the prime minister?
  a CBE
  b DCM
  c MBE
  d OBE

3 When and where were the first modern Olympics?

4 Russia and the USA each boycotted Olympic Games in the 1980s. Which games were they and when?

5 Two athletes were outstanding at the Mexico Olympics. Who were they and what did they achieve?

6 Name two of the first international events.

7 What are the similarities between the Olympic and Commonwealth Games?

8 Name two events where world championships are not what they seem.

9 Who is the present minister for sport?

10 Give three special privileges East German athletes received from their government.

Exam-style questions

1 a What does IOC stand for? (2 marks)
  b What three things is it responsible for? (3 marks)

2 a A number of countries have been barred from taking part in certain Olympic Games. Name three of these countries and why they were barred. (6 marks)
  b New events are introduced to most Olympic Games. Suggest a new event and the reason why you think it should be included. (4 marks)

3 a Politics have an important part in international sport. State two international sporting events (not Olympic Games) where a political issue has had some effect on participation. (6 marks)
  b When a national team loses in a competition, who should accept the blame and why? Should it be the fault of the government, the governing body for that sport or schools? (9 marks)

4 a How might a good team performance in an international event help a country? (3 marks)
  b How might a government reward an individual or team for winning a world championship? (3 marks)
  c There has been considerable discussion about the appointment of a foreign coach for the English soccer team. Argue for and against a foreigner taking charge of a national team. (9 marks)

Quality of written communication. (5 marks)

17

Media

Sports coverage in the media is an important issue. Newspapers sell because of good sports coverage; people expect to be able to listen to and see sport on the radio and TV. There are many ways of finding out more about sport, with the internet now being a significant source:

LEARNING OBJECTIVES

- newspapers
- magazines
- books
- CD ROMS
- radio
- television
- video
- cinema
- internet
- relationship between media and sport

Newspapers

Sport has been reported in UK newspapers for nearly 300 years. As early as 1700, some London newspapers had advertisements for games of cricket. Today newspapers continue to contain information about individuals, teams and sporting events. They also contain articles about well-known sportspeople, popular events and previous winners. Sensational headlines are often used to encourage people to buy the paper.

Most newspapers have sports pages, and some have whole sections just for sport in a supplement (a minipaper inside the main paper). Newspapers employ reporters whose main job is to collect local and national sporting news. Some of the larger newspapers also have photographers who specialise in sports photography.

These are some of the things reported on after a Premier League soccer match:

- who scored the winning goal
- the teams and substitutes
- the size of the crowd
- the current league position
- next week's match
- crowd behaviour
- the state of the pitch.

There will always be a time delay between the end of the match and the sports paper with the match report. Sometimes, an evening paper can publish a report very soon after the match has finished, and new technology helps speed this process up. In daily newspapers, results appear the next day or later; people are still interested in reading sports reports long after the result is known.

	P	W	D	L	F	A	W	D	L	F	A	GD	Pts
Man Utd	23	9	1	1	31	6	7	4	1	23	10	38	53
Sunderland	23	8	3	0	16	5	4	3	5	15	17	9	42
Arsenal	23	9	3	0	31	8	2	4	5	8	15	16	40
Ipswich	23	6	4	2	19	10	6	0	5	16	16	9	40
Liverpool	22	9	1	1	25	8	3	2	6	17	18	16	39
Leicester	22	6	3	2	16	12	4	2	5	8	13	−1	35
Newcastle	23	7	2	3	18	12	3	2	6	10	19	−3	34
Charlton	23	7	3	1	18	7	2	2	8	13	29	−5	32
Chelsea	22	8	2	1	29	10	0	5	6	10	18	11	31
Tottenham	23	8	3	0	22	9	0	3	9	8	25	−4	30
West Ham	22	4	4	3	17	11	3	4	4	14	15	5	29
Leeds	21	6	1	4	20	15	2	4	4	11	13	3	29
Aston Villa	21	4	4	2	14	10	3	4	4	9	12	1	29
Southampton	23	6	2	4	18	15	1	5	5	10	19	−6	28
Middlesbro	23	3	4	5	14	16	2	4	5	13	14	−3	23
Everton	22	3	4	4	13	14	3	1	7	8	19	−12	23
Derby	23	4	5	2	14	15	1	−3	8	10	25	−16	23
Coventry	23	2	4	5	8	15	3	2	7	14	25	−18	21
Man City	23	3	2	7	16	19	2	3	6	11	23	−15	20
Bradford	22	2	4	5	10	17	1	2	8	6	24	−25	15

THE INFLUENCE OF NEWSPAPERS

Newspapers can have a considerable influence on the popularity of an individual, a team or even a sporting event. They

---

Use two newspapers for the same day: one tabloid (such as the *Mirror*, the *Sun*) and a broadsheet (such as The *Telegraph*, *The Times*). How many sports are mentioned in each paper? Compare the sports headlines and photographs in each paper. Which do you find most interesting and why? What percentage of each paper covers sport?

Read the match report of one of your local teams in a local paper, then read about your team in a national paper. Are the reports different? How do they differ? Why do you think they should differ?

Example of a football league table

- analyse a team performance over a relatively long period of time
- speculate about future managerial appointments, the effect of injuries to an individual and how this might influence a result
- promote discussion and debate amongst fans.

Newspapers can build up the image of an individual sports personality, but they can also spoil that image.

NON-BRITISH NEWSPAPERS

There are no national daily sports newspapers in the UK, but in other parts of Europe sports papers are more common. The best known in France is *L'Équipe*.

Can you find out the name of one other European sports paper? Think of a title for a national sports paper for this country: do you think it would be popular?

Magazines

There are many specialist sports magazines, ranging from mountain biking to judo. For example

- *The Runner*
- *Serve & Volley*
- *The Climber*
- *The Cricketer*
- *Athletics Weekly*.

Some of these can be easily bought in newspaper shops, whereas others are only available to members of sports associations or by subscription.

They often contain

- information to help the reader develop their own skills
- information about personalities, and forthcoming events
- game plans and performance statistics.

They are often good sources of reference about a particular sport. However they do not often contain *current* news about events, particularly if they are only published monthly.

How many sports magazines can you find at a large newsagents? Which sports have more than one magazine?

Check to see if your local library has bound copies of some sports magazines. Compare old issues with present-day ones. How have they changed?

Some specialist magazines

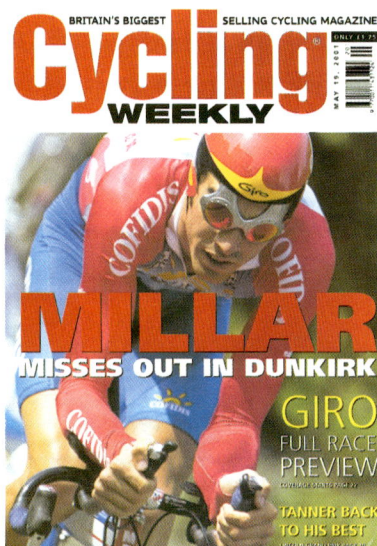

Books

There are many books about sports, and these fall into two main categories:

① biographies and autobiographies give the life story of famous sporting personalities, from either team or individual sports
② other books are about a sport or a particular sporting event; eg the history of a sport, or something to do with the technical aspects of a sport such as a coaching manual.

Select a sports book and write a review of about 150 words on it, to appear in a sports magazine. What is the book about? Who would read it?

In your local library, select two different sports and find how many books there are on each.

I was talking about the drugs business with a few of our female athletes, including Diane Modahl. She was asking questions which were so naive it was quite clear she didn't know anything about the subject. We were exchanging rumours. I was telling them the stories I had heard about me, that I was big and old in athletics terms, and there was no way I could be running so fast unless I was on drugs!

Excerpt from *To Be Honest With You*, Linford Christie's autobiography (Penguin, 1996)

CD ROMS

A CD ROM is a special computer disk which stores large amounts of information: not only text, but also video clips and sounds. There are now many encyclopaedias on CD ROM, and these often contain information about sports, sporting events and sports personalities.

If possible, in your school/college library explore a sports-related CD ROM and make notes about it.

Radio

Most sports are covered by the radio both at a local and a national level. Radio sports broadcasting began in the early 1930s, long before regular television sports coverage. Its main appeal was its 'live' aspect – radio allowed people to follow an event as it was happening.

Radio broadcasters became very popular personalities and were often associated with certain events. These broadcasters were skilled at setting the scene, describing in detail the location, competitors and events as they happened. Radio broadcasters need to be able to entertain the listener when there is no action, such as in between races, when rain interrupts play or at half-time in a soccer or rugby match. Some listeners enjoy the detail these commentators can give so much that they might watch cricket on the television but listen to

Using a *Radio Times* or a similar magazine, work out how many hours of sport are broadcast on Radio 5 each week.

the radio commentary. This is particularly true for Radio 3's programme 'Test Match Special', which gives live coverage of five-day test cricket matches. The late Brian Johnston was a popular commentator on this programme.

Radio 5 (BBC) has more sports coverage than other radio channels, with both commentary on matches and in-depth discussions about sporting issues.

Local radio plays an important part in many communities, giving information and match commentary on local teams.

Radio 5 Schedule	
0500	Morning /Reports – news, sports, and business
0600	Brief lives – 5 Live's obituary column
0630	Breakfast show with Nick Robinson and Sheila Fogarty
0830	London Marathon – coverage of the cpital's 21st annual extravaganza.
1200	Five Live Report – Current affairs
1230	Sport on Five – coverage of the FA Carling Premiership and the Nationwide League.
1800	Sunday 6-0-6 – football phone-in with Alan Green
1900	Sport on five – Rugby League coverage
2000	News Extra – news and sport round up with Susan Bookbinder
2030	Brief lives – 5 Live's obituary column
2100	Global – news from around the world
2200	Late Night Currie – late night debate with Edwina Currie
0100	Up All Night – Richard Dallyn presents stories from around the world

A typical schedule for Radio 5

Television

TERRESTRIAL TELEVISION

The first live televised soccer match in the UK was part of the 1937 FA Cup Final between Sunderland and Preston North End, with the full match being televised the following year. Only a few people were able

Using a television guide, make a list of the different sports screened on both Channel 4 and Channel 5. Work out how many hours are devoted to sport broadcasting on terrestrial channels in a week.

As more and more sports are shown on satellite television, how do you think this will affect these sports?

to watch as television sets were rare, and the broadcasting range was only a few miles in the London area.

The growth of televised sport since that time has been enormous. When satellite links which relay television pictures around the world were developed, sport became a live global event. Today all major events are shown on television.

Some events are organised just for television. In 1970 when BBC 2 first started, limited-over cricket in which matches are finished in one day, was introduced specifically to be screened.

From 1954, commercial television made successful bids for sporting events, although the first league soccer match to be screened by ITV was not until 1960 (Blackpool v Bolton). Sport has benefited financially as ITV and BBC have to bid against each other for the rights to screen the most popular events, usually paying huge sums of money. Channel 4 does not compete for mainstream events due to the huge cost, but has shown and popularised many minority sports such as

- wheelchair basketball
- American football
- netball
- cycling.

Television however, can have other significant effects on sport and associated activities:

- programmes can be dedicated to sports and issues affecting sport
- programmes about coaching can provide up-to-date strategies and tactics
- issues such as drugs, fitness and children in sport can be brought to the public's attention
- sports quizzes have large television audiences and the BBC's review of the year's sport in their annual programme 'BBC Sports Personality of the Year' continues to prove very popular.

Television has raised the public's awareness of this sport

Analyse the amount of time allocated to different sports on all Sky sports channels for one week. Draw a table showing this data in detail.

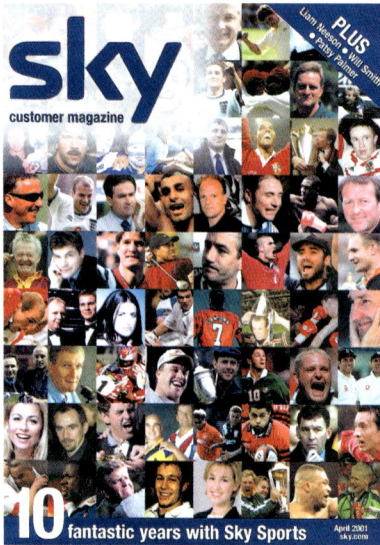

Will all sports be shown on satellite television in the future?

SATELLITE TELEVISION

In 1992, satellite television was launched. People pay to receive broadcasts in their homes, via a satellite dish on their roof. The number of channels available to the public has increased dramatically, and whole channels are devoted entirely to sporting events.

Sky Television (the largest UK satellite company) secured a deal in 1992 with the Premier League, which meant that £214 million pounds would be available to the Premier League clubs for exclusive live coverage on Sky. In the 1997/98 season, Sky Television signed contract with the Premier League for a four-year period worth £670 million. Over the same period, the BBC paid the Premier League a further £73 million to screen highlights on its flagship football programme, 'Match of the Day'.

Sky Television continues to grow with three of its channels dedicated to sport, while another channel, Eurosport, continues to be freely available to those with satellite receivers. Following the latest contract with satellite companies all-England rugby international matches played at Twickenham are now shown on satellite; for the time being, games played at the home grounds of the other five nations in the Six Nations Championship (Wales, Scotland, Ireland, France and Italy) are shown on terrestrial television. As we move into an era of having to pay to watch sport on television, will there be fewer young people able to see the best in sport?

CABLE TELEVISION

Cable television is very popular in the USA, and is now developing in this country. The principle of paying a subscription in order to view is the same as for satellite. This will make further sports channels available to the paying public. Even more sports channels may be introduced since digital television became available at the end of the twentieth century.

FUTURE

As the number of channels continues to increase, some soccer clubs are investigating the possibility of setting up their own television stations. Popular clubs such as Manchester United and Newcastle who have full capacity for their home games, could make coverage of their games available for a payment to those fans who are either unable to obtain tickets or live many miles from the grounds.

Video

Video has enabled elements of sports to be recorded and viewed on future occasions. Teams analyse videos of their future opponents in order to assist in their pre-match preparations. Sports-governing bodies and even individual sportsmen and women have realised that there is a market for sports-coaching videos. Most governing bodies produce videos for coaching purposes; sometimes these might be very technical and designed for use by experienced coaches. Other videos of top performers in basketball, for example, are designed to show off their special abilities. Golf videos will help the beginner to master that perfect swing by copying the top professionals. Many videos are about teams, allowing fans to see their favourite players in action, scoring that winning cup-final goal over and over again!

Cinema

Occasionally films about sporting events or individuals are made. Many are fictional, some based on true stories. Below is a list of films and the related sports subject:

- *Cool Running* – Jamaican bobsleigh team
- *Field of Dreams* – baseball
- *White Men Can't Jump* – basketball
- *The Mighty Ducks* – ice hockey
- *Fever Pitch* – soccer
- *Tin Cup* – golf.

Internet

If possible, look at the internet pages of some Premier League clubs. Which club has the best site and why?

Many sporting associations now have internet sites. This allows up-to-date information to be available, which can be easily and quickly changed. All Premier League football clubs have their own internet addresses. Fans can stay in touch with each other using electronic mail (e-mail).

Relationship between media and sport

Sport needs media coverage and the finance it brings; the media needs sport to attract customers; people need the media to bring them information about their favourite sport. Media and sport are now dependent on each other.

Television companies who have paid millions of pounds for the right to screen sporting events can sometimes influence when those events take place. The US television companies who gain contracts to screen Olympic Games have the power to ensure that the events happen during prime television time in North America. The Soccer World Cup held in the USA in 1994 was controlled by European television – matches were played at midday to coincide with European prime television time.

Tables 17.1 and 17.2 show the advantages and disadvantages of the relationship between the media and sport.

Positive aspects	Examples
minority sports popularised	basketball and American football on Channel 4
new events	indoor windsurfing
new technology	glass-sided squash courts and special, treated squash balls
miniature cameras giving good action shots	cameras in cricket stumps or on racing cars
television replays help with umpiring	third 'umpire' in cricket and rugby
sports development	huge sums paid by television companies can be used by sports-governing bodies to fund junior development programmes
raising awareness and promoting the image of sport	could encourage young people to take up a sport, leading to new sporting talent and healthy lifestyles
expense and access	some sporting events are expensive to attend, because of admission fees and travelling distance. Tickets are often in short supply for top matches. Television allows fans to watch their favourite team on large screens
better coverage, as more can be seen on television; the viewer at home is enabled to see much more of the whole match than a spectator at the event can see	golf on television gives the viewer at home, coverage of the whole course

Table 17.1   Positive aspects of the media and sport

This equipment allows a unique view of cricket – from the batsman/woman's middle stump!

Disadvantages	Examples
negative effects on individuals and teams	media coverage can give individuals and teams bad publicity, which might affect performances and ruin careers
rules and timing of events	events may be arranged at a time to suit television companies. Often large-scale events such as the Olympics are scheduled to coincide with best viewing times for US television companies. In games such as American football 'times out' is determined by television advertising
television equipment	the placing of television cameras and bright lights may interfere with play. Bright overhead lights in badminton can hinder players' performances
contradiction of decisions	the replay of an event may show that the referee has missed something, or made a wrong decision. A referee in soccer may award a goal after, in his opinion, the ball has crossed the line. Video evidence may refute this, and the referee could find his authority undermined
excessive coverage	if teams are regularly televised then spectators may stop attending matches and therefore the gate money will be reduced
media influence	the media may only promote certain sports, making other sports less popular

Table 17.2   Disadvantages of the media and sport

Questions on the media

1 Which of the following is a newspaper devoted to sport?
  a *Le Monde*
  b the *Daily Telegraph*
  c the *Sun*
  d *L'Equipe.*

2 Which of the following is a minority sport which has been featured on Channel 4?
  a soccer
  b wheelchair basketball
  c rugby union
  d athletics.

3 Give two examples of 'media'.

4 Name four facts which might be in a match report in cricket.

5 Name two specialist sports magazines.

6 How is the timing of a sports event affected by the television company which has the contract to screen it?

7 Give three advantages for a sport to be televised.

8 What two disadvantages might there be for Sky TV to win the contract for all soccer matches, league and cup?

9 Name two technological innovations which are beneficial to umpiring in two sporting activities.

10 Give one advantage and one disadvantage in using a video tape for coaching in a sport.

Exam-style questions

1 Give five facts which might be reported on in a newspaper report on a rugby match. (5 marks)

2 a Television coverage of a sport can raise public awareness about it. Give two examples where sports have been popularised by television. (4 marks)
  b How has technology helped to promote and develop sport? (6 marks)

3 Newspaper articles can be positive and negative about a player or a team.
  a Give a recent example where an article has been positive. (3 marks)
  b Give a recent example where an article has been negative. (3 marks)
  c Give an example of a specialist sports magazine. (2 marks)
  d Who are the people most likely to buy such a magazine? (2 marks)
  e What kind of information is there in this type of magazine? (5 marks)

4 Different types of media might be more suited to one sport than another. Select two types of media and compare their advantages and disadvantages in two chosen sports. (15 marks)

Quality of written communication. (5 marks)

18

Sponsorship

Individuals and teams often need large sums of money for equipment, training facilities, health and medical care and for travel to competitions. Sponsorship is now an important aspect of sport at all levels from school teams to national ones, from amateur teams to professional ones.

LEARNING OBJECTIVES

- individual sponsorship
- team sponsorship
- governing bodies and sponsorship
- sponsors

Individual sponsorship

Can you find out which other sportspeople are sponsored by a company for wearing an article of clothing?

World champions and other top performers are usually heavily sponsored, as successful companies want to be associated with successful sportsmen and women. Sometimes a top performer will be sponsored by only one company; at other times you will see a number of logos and company names on a player's shirt.

Whilst sportsmen are the major receivers of sponsorship, top sportswomen can receive high levels of sponsorship. Venus Williams is reported to have a deal worth £27 million over the next five years from Reebok for wearing their sports clothes.

Good young players who might be still at school may receive equipment at reduced rate, subsidised training facilities or assistance with travel. A junior county badminton player can sometimes get a racket at a special price from a manufacturer.

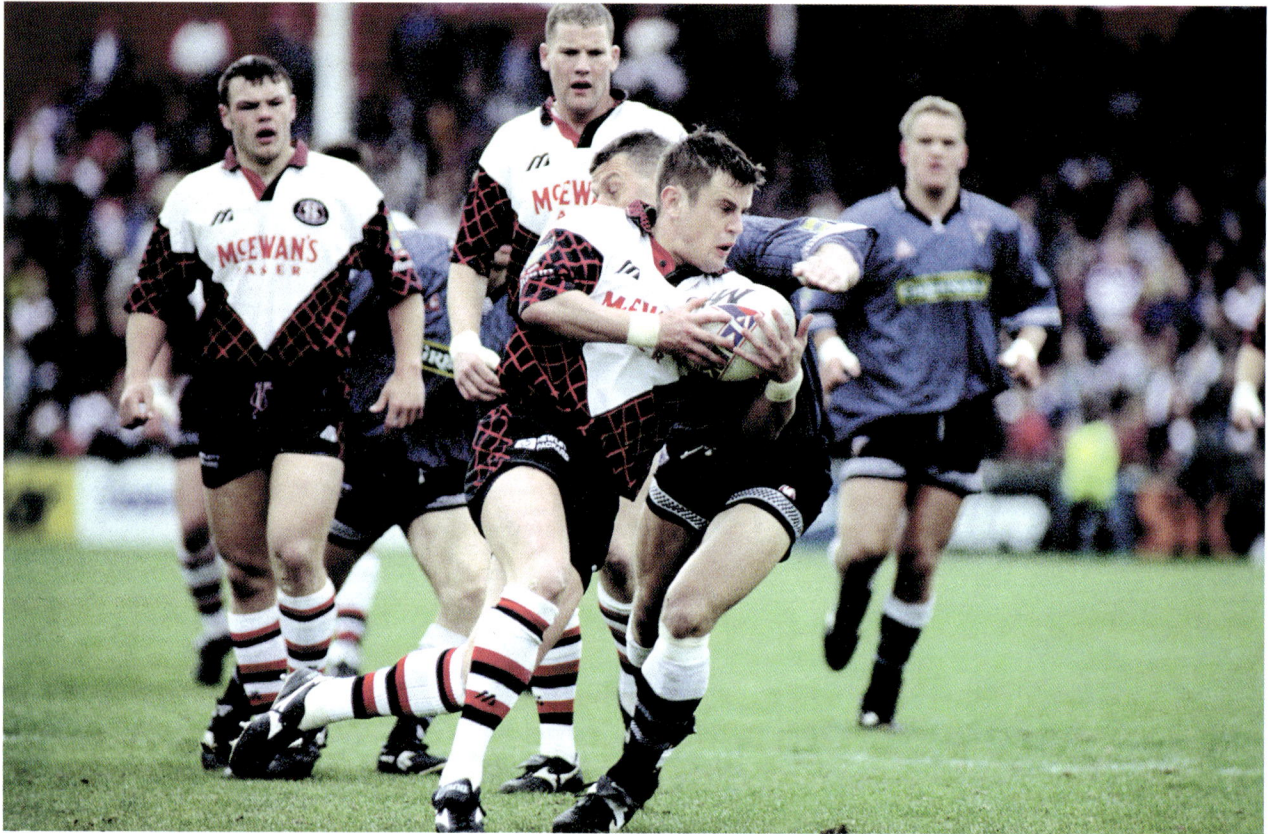

Sponsorship is big business

Team sponsorship

How many schools in your area have team strips with sponsors' names? Make a list of them and their sponsors.

Almost all League soccer clubs have some form of sponsorship. This can easily be seen by the badges, logos or even the colour of the team shirts. Premiership football is expensive to sponsor and only very large companies can afford this. Non-league teams, junior teams and school teams often have local business sponsors. The cost to these sponsors may only be a set of strips each year, but it will help to promote their name.

Imagine you are a head of PE. Write a letter to a potential local sponsor explaining how they might benefit from sponsoring your school strip. You will need to find out the cost of the strip and decide which are the best teams to wear it.

Many school and junior teams have sponsors.

Governing bodies and sponsorship

What sports in your school have badges or certificates with sponsors' names? Do you think sponsoring a badge scheme is a good idea? What might a company gain from such sponsorship?

Design a poster for a competition, sponsored by a company of your choice. Why would the company you have selected wish to sponsor the competition?

National governing bodies who control their sport (see Chapter 15) raise sponsorship money and use it in many different ways. For example, the Amateur Swimming Association are sponsored by Kelloggs. This provides extra funding for top competitors, and also helps to develop the sport with performance badges for beginners.

Leagues, prize money, special events and trophies are often provided by a sponsor. The sponsor's name then becomes associated with that event. For example:

- Nationwide Division 1 Soccer
- the Stella Artois Tennis Championships.
- Tetleys Bitter Cup – Rugby Union

Millions of people watch special sporting events such as the Olympic Games, Wimbledon Tennis Championships and the FA Cup Final. Sponsors are prepared to pay large amounts of money because of the publicity they will receive. Sometimes companies cannot afford to pay increasing amounts every year, and eventually may withdraw from the sponsorship of an event.

The amount of sponsorship for sport continues to grow: in 1963, Gillette's total sponsorship in cricket was £6,500 which was to be shared between the 17 county teams; Coca Cola's sponsorship of the Atlanta Olympic Games in 1996 was the biggest sponsorship of any single event.

In a small group, plan a presentation to the chairperson, treasurer and public relations officer of a company to persuade them to sponsor an event. Act out the presentation.

Subtle sponsorship? The Coca Cola Company makes itself known at the 2000 Sydney Olympics.

Sponsors

Sponsorship of sport has a long history. Athletes in the ancient Greek Games were often supported in their training with free weapons, food and other equipment. In the eighteenth and nineteenth centuries, prize fighters (early professional boxers) and pedestrians (professional runners) were backed by wealthy patrons, who supported them in their training. The first England cricket team to tour Australia in 1861 was sponsored by a catering company, Spiers and Pond.

There are many large and small businesses providing sponsorship. In 1987 the Confederation of British Industry (CBI) realised that sponsorship was very important to the future of sport, and they encouraged 118 new companies to enter sports sponsorship deals.

In 1997 the Labour government banned tobacco advertising at sporting events in the UK (apart from Formula One motor racing, to be phased out gradually), but there is still sponsorship in some European countries.

As you can see, not all sponsors are linked directly with sports or sporting activity. Banks, building societies and food companies can be sponsors for many different sporting events, purely as an advertising vehicle. Sports goods manufacturers, however, are often major sponsors for teams and individuals.

GEORGE WILSON.

Pedestrians were professional runners who were sponsored by a patron, often their employer

Non-sport companies often sponsor large events

Watch an event on EuroSport. Can you identify the names of any tobacco products? Why do you think that the Labour government has banned sponsorship of sport by tobacco companies?

Advantages	Disadvantages
young and new rising sports stars will be able to train and compete in their sport without having to worry about money and equipment	young players may have their sponsorship withdrawn if their performance does not show improvement
it can increase the income of a top athlete	players in less well-known games may not be able to get sponsorship
sport can be promoted by sponsors through the staging of special events	sponsors may want more control over a sport. They may want to schedule events to coincide with peak television viewing time to get maximum publicity, or even alter the time of year when competitions are held (such as rugby league which is now played in the summer)
money can be paid to a sport to improve facilities, provide more coaching and encourage participation	governing bodies of sport may come to rely on sponsorship money
new sports can be promoted	

Table 18.1 Advantages and disadvantages of sponsorship for a sport and its players

Look through the sports pages of a newspaper. How many sports companies are sponsoring individuals, teams or events?

Advantages	Disadvantages
sponsorship is powerful advertising	sponsoring unsuccessful events or teams will not be beneficial to the sponsor, particularly if a team loses a lot of matches or an individual is injured and unable to compete
popular and televised sponsored events make brand names well known	sponsorship deals over longer periods of time may not be valuable if media coverage is reduced
successful individuals and teams are well supported and sponsors' names are linked with these	the company or product associated with a sport may not be appropriate
for certain sponsors, the image of healthy lifestyles and high level performances is important for their product	the money paid in sponsorship may be very high compared with the amount the company gets back in increased sales
sponsors can pay less tax by giving money to sports	

Table 18.2   Advantages and disadvantages of sponsorship for the sponsors

Questions on sponsorship

1 Large companies are keen to sponsor
   a a world champion in a sport
   b a local soccer team
   c a school team
   d a county tennis player.

2 One of the following types of company has been banned from sponsoring sporting activities:
   a drinks
   b banks
   c tobacco
   d sports clothing.

3 Give two ways a sportsman or woman can receive sponsorship.

4 Name one sportsman and one sportswoman who are heavily sponsored.

5 What are the disadvantages to a team being sponsored?

6 Give two ways in which sponsorship can help a young athlete.

7 Give examples of two companies which sponsor sport, but are not sports goods companies.

8 Name two sports teams and their sponsors.

9 Name two cup competitions and their sponsors.

10 Name a governing body which is sponsored by a company.

Exam-style questions

1 a Name one sport and its sponsor. (2 marks)

  b Give three ways in which a sponsor can support a young player. (3 marks)

2 a Name a drinks company and the sport they sponsor. (2 marks)

  b Name a food company and the sport they sponsor. (2 marks)

  c How does sponsorship help an experienced player in a named sport? (3 marks)

  d Name one type of company which you think should not be a sports sponsor and give your reasons. (3 marks)

3 a Explain what is meant by sponsorship in sport. (3 marks)

  b Give three advantages to a company for sports sponsorship. (6 marks)

  c Give three disadvantages to a company for sports sponsorship. (6 marks)

4 Venus Williams is receiving £27 million in a sponsorship deal. Many world-class individual and team players receive very large sums of sponsorship money. They also earn large amounts of money from their employers if they are in a team, or win very large cash prizes in competitions. Many young sportsmen and women receive no sponsorship. Discuss these issues about sponsorship and decide who you think should be sponsored and how it will benefit them. (15 marks)

Quality of written communication. (5 marks)

19

Amateur and Professional

In the past few years there has been a growth in the number of professional sportsmen and women. Rugby union and athletics are just two sports which have made significant changes in their rules to allow competitors not just to be paid expenses, but to earn a living from these sports.

> **LEARNING OBJECTIVES**
>
> - ⚽ brief history of amateurism and professionalism
> - ⚽ receiving support
> - ⚽ present-day sport

Brief history of amateurism and professionalism

EARLY PROFESSIONALS?

The athletes in the ancient Greek Olympics received no reward for winning, other than a laurel wreath. However, to be good enough to win, they had to be able to train, have the best equipment and have the right diet. These things would have cost a considerable amount of money at the time, probably much more than the athlete earned from their normal work (they were usually soldiers). They would have been supported and sponsored by wealthy individuals, or would have been provided for by their employers. These athletes were amateurs by the definition given above, as they were not directly paid for taking part in their chosen sport, although they did receive some financial support.

A laurel wreath

PRIZES AND REWARDS

During the late 1700s and early 1800s, there were substantial rewards in prize fighting (early professional boxing with few rules) and in pedestrianism (professional running). Cricket competitors could earn considerable sums of money.

Wealthy landowners and businessmen paid employees to train for events, particularly for pedestrian races. The competitors in this and in boxing not only received prize money, but they also placed bets on themselves to win.

GENTLEMAN AMATEURS

During the 1800s, the distinction between amateur and professional was not so much centred on payment but on social class. Gentlemen who did not have to work because they were wealthy, had time to pursue their sport, and did not need to win prize money. People from lower classes either had to work at their job and compete in sport for no prize, or had to work at the sport itself to earn a living.

The old-fashioned image of sport

In the later part of the nineteenth century, sport became more organised. People from the middle classes were taking control of sport, writing the rules and organising competitions. They felt disadvantaged against the few professional sportsmen and also against manual workers who were generally stronger and fitter. Having a job such as a waterman on the rivers would be an advantage in rowing competitions. Because of this, a distinction was made on which sports were amateur and which were professional. This had nothing to do with winning prize money.

In 1866, the Amateur Athletic Association declared that all manual workers were professional and could no longer compete in amateur events. They changed the rule in 1890 to allow manual workers to compete. The Amateur Rowing Association had a similar rule, but did not change it until 1936!

Can you find the names of three sporting organisations which have the word 'amateur' in their title?

Professionals by trade

TRUE PROFESSIONALS

Cricket became one of the first truly professional games. Between 1750 and 1850, there were a number of professional touring sides taking the game to all parts of the country. Apart from playing in the matches, these professionals would also coach amateur players. Many cricket clubs today even in local leagues have a professional player.

Can you find which major sports have amateur and professional players and competitions?

Football and rugby continued to develop in the latter part of the nineteenth century, attracting more and more spectators. These sports were particularly popular in the north of England and the Midlands. Money was offered to the best players to join a club, thereby improving the club's results and drawing in more spectators. The Football Association brought in rules about wages and transfer of players between clubs.

What is the name of the nearest local cricket team with a 'professional'? Can you find out his/her name and nationality? Apart from playing, what other responsibilities does s/he have?

In rugby, however, a split occurred between clubs in the north and south of England. In 1895, 21 northern clubs suggested that players should be paid for the time they missed from work (broken time). The southern clubs did not agree with this, so the northern clubs set up their own organisation called the Northern Union, which became the rugby league in 1922. Rugby union and rugby league developed into different styles of games with different rules. Rugby league players became professional and semi-professional, whereas rugby union was regarded and defended as a totally amateur game. No professional sportsman from another sport would ever be allowed to take part in a rugby union match!

An early spectator sport

Find the names of three rugby players who have played rugby union in the winter and rugby league in the summer. What clubs do they play for?

A hundred years after the split, rugby union and rugby league players were able to play against each other and on the same teams, as rugby union became a professional sport. The first official matches between Bath and Wigan were played under union and league rules in 1995.

Many sports did not have professionals until fairly recently. However, to train and compete at a high level, these sportspeople needed funding. Even some professionals were restricted by their associations as to how much they could earn. In soccer the maximum wage of any player in England was £4 in 1900. In 1961, Newcastle player George Eastham went on strike over the minimum wage, which was then £10 per week. Johnny Haynes at Fulham became the first soccer player to earn £100 per week, and David Beckham the first Premiership player reported to earn £100,000 per week.

Trace the development of the two rugby games. Find out the differences between league and union: the rules, the organisation and in which parts of the country they are played.

Receiving support

Sportspeople can receive five main kinds of financial support:

- illegal and irregular payments
- state support
- scholarships
- trust funds
- sponsorship.

ILLEGAL AND IRREGULAR PAYMENTS

As far back as 1900, there were recorded cases of illegal payments to soccer players to supplement the maximum wage. Amateur soccer players and rugby union players often received illegal payments known as 'boot money'. Players in many sports received generous expenses perhaps for overnight accommodation, when they could easily travel to and from a match on the same day. Athletes might win goods as prizes, and then sell them for a profit.

STATE SUPPORT

In some Eastern European countries such as the former USSR and East Germany, sportspeople were often in the armed forces, police or civil service. Although they did not receive cash payments, they were provided with training facilities, coaching, extra food and travel to competitions. Some well-known UK sportspeople have been in the armed forces and competed at a high level. The rugby player, Rory Underwood, was a pilot in the RAF; the runner, Kelly Holmes, was in the Army.

SCHOLARSHIPS

In the USA, top athletes and games players are often offered places at universities and have their fees paid. This enables the students to participate in their special events with high-level coaching and training facilities. The universities then gain a reputation for having excellent teams, and encourage other students to attend. In the UK, a number of universities now offer similar types of scholarships, and it is even possible to get scholarships to specialist sporting schools such as Millfield School in Somerset.

TRUST FUNDS

In 1981 the Amateur Athletics Association set up trust funds which allowed athletes to place sponsorship money and prize money in a

Can you find any local competition (athletics or a road race might be a good example) where there are prizes to be won? Are these prizes worth a lot of money?

Loughborough is one of the most pre-eminent sporting universities in the United Kingdom. Our Sports Scholars are exceptional women and men and the University is delighted to support the next generation of sporting superstars.

Jim Saker
Chair of Loughborough Students' Sports Foundation

sports

LOUGHBOROUGH
SPORT

Loughborough
University

Sports Scholarship Information from Loughborough University

fund. The fund could then be used to help the athlete pay for training, equipment and travel. When the athlete finished competing at the end of their career, they would be entitled to any money remaining in the fund. Other sports followed this example, particularly rugby union, but now many sportspeople are paid directly.

Present-day sport

Few players will earn as much in the early part of their career, as Tiger Woods

Most people who play sport at the present time are amateurs. They play for fun and enjoyment without any interest in prizes or money. However, in every sport, there is a group of professionals who earn their living from their sport in some way: playing, coaching or in the administration of events. Since the relaxation of rules (particularly in rugby union), there are many more semi-professionals.

At one time there was little opportunity for amateurs to either play against or even on the same team as professionals. However, in recent years many sports have allowed professionals and amateurs to compete against each other, such as in the 'Open' Championship in golf. Cricket, tennis, badminton and horse-racing have been open sports for many years, and every year more and more sports become open to all players.

BECOMING A PROFESSIONAL

Top professionals can earn huge sums of money. With a win in a 'big' event they can become millionaires. However, there are advantages, and disadvantages to being a professional rather than amateur sportsperson: see Table 19.1.

AMATEURS AND THE MODERN OLYMPIC GAMES

The modern Olympic Games began in 1896, with the intention that amateurs would compete. There would be medals only and no prize money. In 1920, tennis was dropped from the games as there was a suspicion of infringement of the amateur status. By 1988 in Seoul, tennis had returned, with professional players winning the first medals, but no money. In 1992 in Barcelona, the US basketball team (known as the 'dream team') was composed entirely of professional players, and dominated the competition to take the gold medal.

Can you find the name of a player who has had to retire because of injury? What was the injury and how did it occur? What do they do now?

Professional basketball players are able to play in the Olympic Games for honour, but not for money

Advantages	Disadvantages
professional sportspeople can become celebrities, and live a lavish lifestyle	injury can ruin a sporting career, thereby cutting off the person's source of income
they can perfect their game	a stable lifestyle is difficult, as international competitions require competitors to travel for weeks or months at a time
they can travel the world to compete at the highest level	there are always new young competitors challenging for a top place, which can impose increasing stress levels on individuals to keep their place at the top
they are paid to do something they enjoy	the ability to maintain fitness and performance usually decreases with age; the sportsperson's career may not be very long
they can normally afford to retire early	once their sporting career is over, they may have few qualifications to do another job

Table 19.1 Advantages and disadvantages in becoming a professional sportsperson

Questions on amateur and professional

1 A semi-professional sportsman or woman
  a play their sport to earn a living
  b play their sport for health reasons
  c accept no money to play their sport
  d only play for recreation.

2 State support means a sportsman or woman is
  a assisted by the government
  b paid by a club
  c paid to play
  d given money from a fund.

3 What did the winners receive in the ancient games?

4 What was pedestrianism?

5 What was known as boot money?

6 What is meant by a scholarship and how might this benefit a sportsperson?

7 What is the purpose of a trust fund?

8 Give two advantages of being a professional in a sport.

9 Name two sports which have amateur and professional competitions.

10 How might being in the armed forces help a sportsperson?

Exam-style questions

1 Give five types of financial support a sportsperson might receive.   (5 marks)

2 a What is a professional sportsperson?   (1 mark)
  b Name two sporting events in which amateurs and professionals can compete against each other.   (2 marks)
  c Give three reasons why professional sport should be of a high standard.   (3 marks)
  d How have the Olympic Games changed with regard to amateur competitors?   (5 marks)

3 a State what is meant by
    i an amateur sportsperson.   (2 marks)
    ii a semi-professional sportsperson.   (2 marks)
  b State three ways in which an amateur could receive financial assistance without becoming a professional.   (6 marks)
  c Should all sports be open sports? Discuss this in terms of the standards of performance in a named sport.   (5 marks)

4 Many young soccer players are aware of the considerable amounts of money being paid to world-class players. However, many do not understand the advantages and disadvantages of being a full-time professional. In a chosen sport argue the case for becoming a professional in that sport.

Quality of written communication.   (5 marks)

20

Funding in Sport

Sport can generate considerable sums of money, but many sports need large amounts of money to exist. Professional sportsmen and women demand higher salaries, spectators want new and better facilities. However, many sports are dependent on grants and fund raising.

LEARNING OBJECTIVES

- paying spectators
- merchandising
- clubs
- government funding
- National Lottery
- governing bodies
- sponsorship
- Foundation for the Sports and Arts (FSA)
- Football Trust
- private funding
- stock market

Paying spectators

Professional sport usually has spectators who pay to watch events. This is often referred to as 'gate money', and even today entrance to soccer matches is through a turnstile or gate. For special events such as major cup finals in the National Basketball Association, Super Bowl American Football, the FA, and in world championships, the gate money can be considerable.

Taking the gate money

Semi-professional soccer clubs often forfeit their right to play at home when drawn against Premier League opposition, because of the safety of many more spectators than usual attracted to their ground. Also, by transferring their game to a club which has a large capacity for spectators, they are guaranteed more income than they would receive if they played on their own ground. There are exceptions of course. Stevenage Town played on their own ground against Newcastle United in the FA Cup in 1998. They received a substantial sum of money from Sky TV, and earned a considerable amount in their replay against Newcastle at St James' Park.

Merchandising

Can you find out the name of a non-league club who had been drawn at home in the FA Cup, and gave up their home advantage to play at a bigger ground? What was the attendance at the match?

Spectators of course spend more money at their club than their entrance fee to the games. They buy programmes, refreshments and other items such as flags and team strips. The income from the club shop can exceed the gate money. The biggest growth in the market has been with replica strips; as many teams now have at least three strips this boosts the sale of replica strips.

However many spectators there might be at a world-class event, the revenue they bring will never be sufficient to cover the players' wages and the staging of the event, and therefore there have to be other means of funding.

Send for a merchandise catalogue from a Premier/First Division club. What are the three most unusual items available?

Clubs depend on the money spectators spend on merchandising

Clubs

At the centre of all amateur sport is the club system. Groups of players come together to form clubs and teams. They may be entirely recreational, or formed to enter a league. Clubs may have their own facilities, or may hire pitches and sports halls for their practices and matches.

Clubs are supported by their members in a number of ways:

- they may have to pay an annual subscription to their club treasurer
- they may pay a match fee every time they play, or even practise
- they might have special fund-raising events such as sponsored activities, jumble sales, raffles and car boot sales to bring in extra funding for, say, a special piece of equipment, or to help fund a tour
- members may work for their club free of charge in some way. They may cut the grass at a tennis club, coach a junior section of the club, or offer professional services such as accountancy by taking care of the club's finances.

Professional clubs with considerably more income and expenditure need to have full-time administrators to deal with all aspects of finances. As many rugby union clubs have in recent years moved from being amateur to professional, they have had to employ more staff to run their clubs. All clubs need to receive income from other sources, as members and spectators can never provide sufficient finance.

Can you find the name of a local club which has had some kind of event such as a raffle or sponsored run for club funds? Was there a particular reason for this fund raising?

Government funding

Both national and local government provide funding for sports and sporting events. This is rarely direct funding, but finance and support is made available through national and regional sports councils and other organisations.

NATIONAL GOVERNMENT

The national government decide how much tax people have to pay from their wages. Businesses also pay tax; even sporting businesses who get money from the government pay tax. Most of the things we buy have tax added to them (Value Added Tax – VAT). The government also receives money from gambling on horse and dog racing and various other sporting events. For every £1 gambled, the government receives six pence.

Each year the government decides how much money each of its departments should receive. The Department of Culture is

The government always wins when money is gambled

responsible for sport as well as other things. When the amount available for sport has been worked out, the Minister for Sport decides how this will be allocated. The funding is then made available to the Sports England and to local government.

LOCAL GOVERNMENT

Local councils collect money in a number of different ways:

- council tax, which is paid by all households and businesses, is the main source of revenue
- councils also run sports centres, swimming pools, golf courses and playing fields, and receive income from these. These facilities, along with school and other community sports facilities, have to be maintained; in addition, councils give grants to support sports clubs
- councils also receive money from central government and grants from the Sports Council
- many local councils working with other agencies such as sports councils have received grants from the National Lottery.

If you were the sports minister, which three major policies would you introduce to develop sport in the UK?

National Lottery

The National Lottery began in 1994. Plans for dividing the money raised by the lottery were put into place. Sport was one of the beneficiaries. For every £1 spent on the National Lottery (including scratch cards), sport receives 5.6 pence. This may not seem much, but over £17 million is awarded each month.

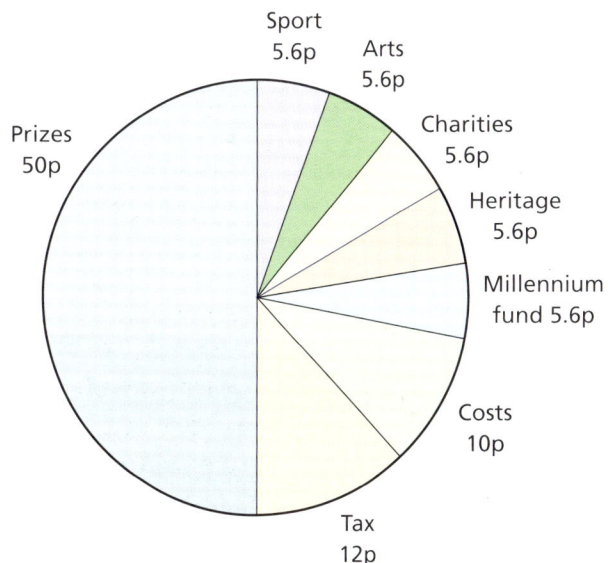

Can you find any local sport or club that has benefited from the National Lottery in your area in the last year? What was the money used for?

Find the total amount of money spent on the National Lottery this week (excluding scratch cards). Can you work out how much money sport will receive this week?

Sport 5.6p
Arts 5.6p
Charities 5.6p
Heritage 5.6p
Millennium fund 5.6p
Costs 10p
Tax 12p
Prizes 50p

National Lottery distribution – where the £1 goes

Governing bodies

Sports are controlled by their governing bodies (see Chapter 15). Many of these governing bodies receive finance from the national government through grants.

Money from national government $\rightarrow$ Sports Council $\rightarrow$ CCPR $\rightarrow$ national governing bodies

Can you think of large-scale sporting events where the finance might be used to help develop that sport?

The bigger governing bodies can also earn money with sponsorship deals or with television coverage of large events such as international matches or cup finals. This money can then be distributed to the clubs which form that sport. A good example is in rugby union, where the proceeds from the Six Nations Championship are used also to develop the game at a national level. Rugby clubs throughout the country receive financial support, particularly in the development of new facilities.

Sponsorship

Large sums of money are made available to sport through sponsorship deals (see Chapter 18).

Foundation for the Sports and Arts (FSA)

This was created in 1991 with money from the football pools. The original intention was that about £40 million per year would be donated to sport. However, since the National Lottery began, the organisers of the football pools claim that there has been a reduction in the amount of money people are spending on the pools; there is therefore less money available from the FSA.

Football Trust

The Football Trust was started in 1975 and is organised to support football only. Money is provided by the football pools companies, and the trust gives grants to clubs and teams. A considerable amount of trust money has been used in recent years to improve the safety at football grounds after the Hillsborough tragedy in 1989 when 95 football supporters were killed due to overcrowding at the stadium. This expenditure was a result of the Taylor Report on ground safety.

Private funding

Elton John is a major shareholder in Watford football club

Wealthy individuals or groups of businessmen might provide funding for a sport or sportsperson. Often, an individual millionaire may have a passion for a sport or perhaps a link to a club since childhood; it can often be an ambition to own a club. Becoming a millionaire through business interests enables them to buy or take control of a club.

In 1982 Tottenham Hotspur football club were £5.25 million in debt. Irving Scholar, a lifelong supporter of the club and shrewd millionaire businessman, and his friend Paul Bobroff, took control of the club by buying shares, and in 1983 the club was launched on the stock market. Scholar and his friends bought slightly more than 50 per cent of the shares to keep control of the club. Their financial investment was enormous: Scholar bought 2,659,000 shares at £1 per share.

Richard Branson of the Virgin business empire has bought a rugby league team, London Broncos. The singer Elton John has bought his way back into Watford Association Football Club after several years' absence. He used to be a major shareholder of the club.

In the USA, many teams are owned by individuals and in some cases they may even move 'their' team to a different part of the country. The new owner of Los Angeles Raiders moved his team to San Francisco, 500 miles away.

Are any of your local sports clubs owned or controlled by one person? If you were able to own a sports team, which one would it be and why?

Stock market

Using a broadsheet newspaper such as *The Times, the Telegraph* or *the Guardian,* can you find which sports clubs are listed under the main market (main listings for shares) and which under the AIM market (alternative investment market)?

A number of professional soccer clubs have become public limited companies (plcs). This means that shareholders invest money in the company and expect to have a share of the profits. The first club to become a plc was Tottenham Hotspur in 1983. Since then more clubs have become plcs, but very few have increased their share price; indeed the prices of shares of Premiership teams have dropped, and there have been no profits. The performance of a club on the field affects the performance of its shares, and when the first is unpredictable the second follows the same pattern.

Questions on funding in sport

1 For every £1 of lottery money sport receives
   a 5.6p
   b 6.5p
   c 10p
   d 50p.

2 Gate money is
   a the money given to players in a professional team
   b expenses paid to players in an amateur team
   c money paid by spectators to watch a match
   d the main income of a professional club.

3 What is a match fee?

4 Name two items which a professional club might sell in their shop?

5 Give two ways in which an amateur club might raise funds.

6 How can a club member help their club by offering their time to the club?

7 How does the National Government raise money for sport?

8 What is the Football Trust?

9 How can a National Governing Body of a sport raise funds for their organisation?

10 Name the owner of a well know sports team?

11 Which organisation allocates National Lottery money to sport?

Exam-style questions

1 List five ways in which sport can be funded (5 marks)

2 Amateur and semi-professional clubs rely very much on their members. These clubs may also receive financial support from Sports Councils both national and locally.
   a How can club members support their club? (5 marks)
   b How can a local sports council help a club? (5 marks)

3 a What is meant by the term 'gate money'? (2 marks)
   b What is meant by merchandising and why is it important? (5 marks)
   c How did the Taylor Report have a major effect on professional soccer club finances? (5 marks)
   c How might a professional sports club raise finance without involving spectators? (3 marks)

4 The national lottery has provided millionsof pounds for sports and sporting facilities. Manyu of the people who spend money on the national lottery have no interest in sport. Argue the case for sport receiving these large amounts of money. Consider whether the money should be spent on developing school sporting facilities, amateur club facioities or given to individual sportsmen and women. (15 marks)

Quality of written communication (5 marks)

21

Technology and Sport

Technology has had a significant impact on sport. New materials, equipment and designs have ensured safer sport for performers, improved performances in many sports and better opportunities for spectators.

LEARNING OBJECTIVES

- clothing and footwear
- sports surfaces
- facilities
- sports equipment

Clothing and footwear

There has been a considerable development in sports clothing with the use of new materials. In some speed events such as sprinting in athletics, speed ice skating, cycling and swimming one-piece suits made out of 'slippery' materials might have helped improve performance times in these events. Man-made breathable fibres are used for outdoor activity clothing where weight, wind and waterproofing are important factors. Protective clothing for events such as cricket and hockey have been improved with the use of material such as Kevlar which was developed as body armour in the armed forces.

Sports companies continue to develop footwear specific to sports. Companies spend considerable sums of money on research and development, and make many claims about the quality of their sports shoes. Air cushioning and the use of shock absorbent materials make

Speed skaters require specialist clothing to be successful.

sports shoes more comfortable and can reduce the risk of injury. The growth of road running such as marathons has been matched by improvements in sports shoes for these events. However, sports shoes are now as much a fashion item and sports companies continue to make huge amounts of money from this market.

Sports surfaces

The playing of hockey on artificial pitches such as plastic grass has revolutionised the game. Teams in national hockey league must now play matches on this type of surface. Even the quality of these surfaces has been improved in recent years and now international matches are played on 'water based' synthetic pitches. New facilities for the English Institute of Sport include the installation of ten water-based pitches at different centres throughout the country. More and more schools and sports colleges are installing artificial pitches which are used for many sports.

However, after a brief experiment with this type of pitch over ten years ago the FA decided that they were unsuitable for the game, and the few clubs which had them installed had to re-lay their grass pitches.

Many US football teams play on artificial surfaces, but there has been an increase in injuries with this type of surface. However, as many games are played indoors this is the only surface possible.

Artificial cricket wickets are popular in schools because of low maintenance levels, but are not used for club cricket matches.

In tennis a variety of playing surfaces are used. Many clubs now have plastic grass surfaces, which can be used throughout the year. However, international matches are played on two main types of surface outside: grass and shale or clay. Players adapt their game for these surfaces which require different techniques because of the speed and bounce of the ball of the surface.

Tennis can be played on many different surfaces

There is a wide variety of indoor sports surfaces, from traditional wooden floors found in most school gymnasiums, to carpeted, vinyl and block-type of flooring mainly used in large sports halls. Again the quality of the surface has an impact on the sport. In games such as volleyball there is a need for a 'softer surface' than for basketball. In gymnastics special floors allow the gymnast to get some spring from the surface.

In athletics the introduction of a rubberised track and jumping run-ups instead of shale or cinder led to improved performances in all track and in many field events. In high jump and pole vault the development of soft landing areas was essential for the safety of jumpers as their performances improved.

Facilities

The quality and provision of facilities for sport affect both performers and spectators. (See Chapter 10 for more details of facilities). A number of new stadia have been built with retractable roofs. The Australian tennis stadium can be covered to reduce the heat levels making playing and spectating more comfortable when temperatures can rise high during the Australian summer.

The Millennium Stadium in Cardiff has a retractable roof to keep out bad weather. The advantage to players is that the conditions can be perfect, with no wind or rain. This should produce a better game, particularly rugby where place kicks are not affected by wind and handling the ball should be better.

One of the problems of an enclosed stadium with a roof is that natural grass does not grow well. The unique way of providing a quality grass surface in the Millennium Stadium is to grow the grass elsewhere in trays, and then lay these trays to form a pitch when required.

The Millennium Stadium in Cardiff

Some stadia are constructed for a different range of sports and activities. The Newcastle Arena is used for National League basketball but can be converted to an ice hockey rink for recreation and league fixtures.

Better facilities also benefit spectators. Many stadia have large screens for replays of important moments of a match, or screens which give an analysis of performance such as an athletics heptathlon competition.

Sports equipment

New design, new materials and new technology have an impact on a wide range of sporting equipment. These can be considered in a number of different ways.

PERFORMANCE

The playing surface mentioned above is an important factor affecting performance. In hockey the trueness of an artificial surface means there is less chance of errors because of the pitch. This has led to more accurate passing and better control of the ball and a faster game. Some sports equipment has had a much greater impact on performance. The introduction of the fibreglass pole in pole vaulting led to a significant improvement in performance. In javelin throwing the development of javelins became more effective, with the result that top throwers were launching the javelin over 100 metres, sometimes far beyond safe limits. By adjusting the design of the javelin by altering its centre of gravity distances thrown were reduced.

Streamlining

In all racket games the use of graphite enabled designers to produce better rackets allowing them to be strung far tighter than was possible with wooden and aluminium rackets. Also the shape of racket heads was altered to provide a large hitting area. The result of this was to increase the power and resulting speed of a tennis ball, so much so that the design of the tennis ball itself has undergone change to make it go slower. There are some advantages to this type of development; very slow tennis balls are particularly useful in teaching tennis to beginners.

New materials for equipment such as cycles, skis and toboggans bring about improved performances. At present scientists are developing a golf ball which will travel further distances, but have yet to design clubs which always hit golf balls.

TEACHING AND COACHING

Video recording of a sport can be particularly useful in teaching and coaching. Underwater video of swimming can be useful in showing the correct stroke technique which is often difficult to see from the pool side. The video recording of a performer is particularly useful for picking out faults in technique, and this type of analysis is an essential part of the GCSE physical education examination. The use of digital cameras and interactive white boards continues to grow as pupils learn more and more about their sport. Using hand-held devices or wristwatch-type heart monitors, pupils learn more about heart rate and exercise.

In higher-level coaching more sophisticated techniques of analysis are used. Computer-generated movement shows the match of the perfect model against that of an athlete. Athletes are connected to machines which record their performance in cardiovascular fitness tests. Results of performances in a sport can be analysed with computers. Diets and training can be accurately planned with the use of data.

REFEREEING AND UMPIRING

A number of sports now use 'video replay' to help officials make the correct decision where there is some doubt. In cricket the 'third umpire' is able to analyse video and make decisions about run-outs and stumpings, but not yet LBW. New technology is at present being developed for this. In rugby league and union the referee can call on a video replay to help make a decision; the first use of a 'video referee' in the Six Nations Championship was in the France v Scotland match early in 2001, which resulted in France not being awarded a try for not grounding the ball. In soccer no use is made of video refereeing during a match, but more use is being made of video evidence of matches to resolve disputes involving foul play.

In athletics and swimming electronic starting, timing and photo finishing allow officials to judge finishes accurately and give athletes exact times for their events. In tennis 'electronic eyes' can detect a ball out of court, and other electronic devices attached to the net can indicate a 'netcord', although these have not replaced line and net judges.

SPECTATORS

Spectators often want to see in more detail what is happening during a sporting event. Being high up and at the back of a large stadium is not the best place to see action on the pitch below. Large stadia often have large screens for replay of events; in some sports, however; it is difficult for a spectator to see anything at all. The use of miniature TV cameras has brought onto the screen what the performer sees. In motor racing, cameras are placed on the car; in sky diving cameras are sometimes placed on helmets. Not quite the same view as a batsman or woman, but cameras installed in cricket stumps give an indication of the flight and direction of a cricket ball being bowled. In golf, television coverage lets spectators follow a player round a course. Being at the event, it is likely that the spectators would probably spend most of the time at one tee or green.

Questions on technology

1 'Kevlar' is used in sport for making
 a protective clothing
 b cricket bats
 c video recordings
 d netballs.

2 Which of the following sports do not have 'video' to help officials with refereeing?
 a rugby league
 b cricket
 c hockey
 d rugby union.

3 Name two types of protective clothing worn by sportsmen and women.

4 What is meant by an artificial surface, and give one example?

5 What is the advantage to a school to have an artificial cricket wicket?

6 What are the disadvantages of having an artificial pitch for games like soccer and American football?

7 What two advantages are there for having a stadium with a retractable roof?

8 Name two events where the development of equipment has led to improved performance.

9 Why is a video recording of a GCSE pupil useful to that pupil?

10 Give two ways in which technology has helped spectators to get a better view of a sporting event.

Exam-style questions

1 Name five types of sports surfaces.   (5 marks)

2 a What type of material has been developed for competitors
   in speed events?   (2 marks)

   b What advantage might it give to these competitors?   (2 marks)

   c How have popular sporting events influenced sports footwear
   manufacturers, and what has been the impact of this?   (6 marks)

3 a Name one game and how the development of an artificial
   surface has influenced the performance in that game.   (5 marks)

   b A number of new stadia have retractable roofs.
      i Name one of these.   (1 mark)
      ii Give two advantages of having a retractable roof.   (2 marks)
      iii Give two disadvantages of having a retractable roof.   (2 marks)

   c In sports such as soccer and rugby, the governing bodies
   have decided that a grass surface is best for the game.
   Explain why they think this.   (5 marks)

4 Equipment has been improved with new technology. Describe
   with examples
   a how this affects performance in named sports.   (5 marks)
   b how it affects coaching of a sport.   (5 marks)
   c how it affects refereeing and umpiring in named sports.   (5 marks)
   Quality of written communication.   (5 marks)

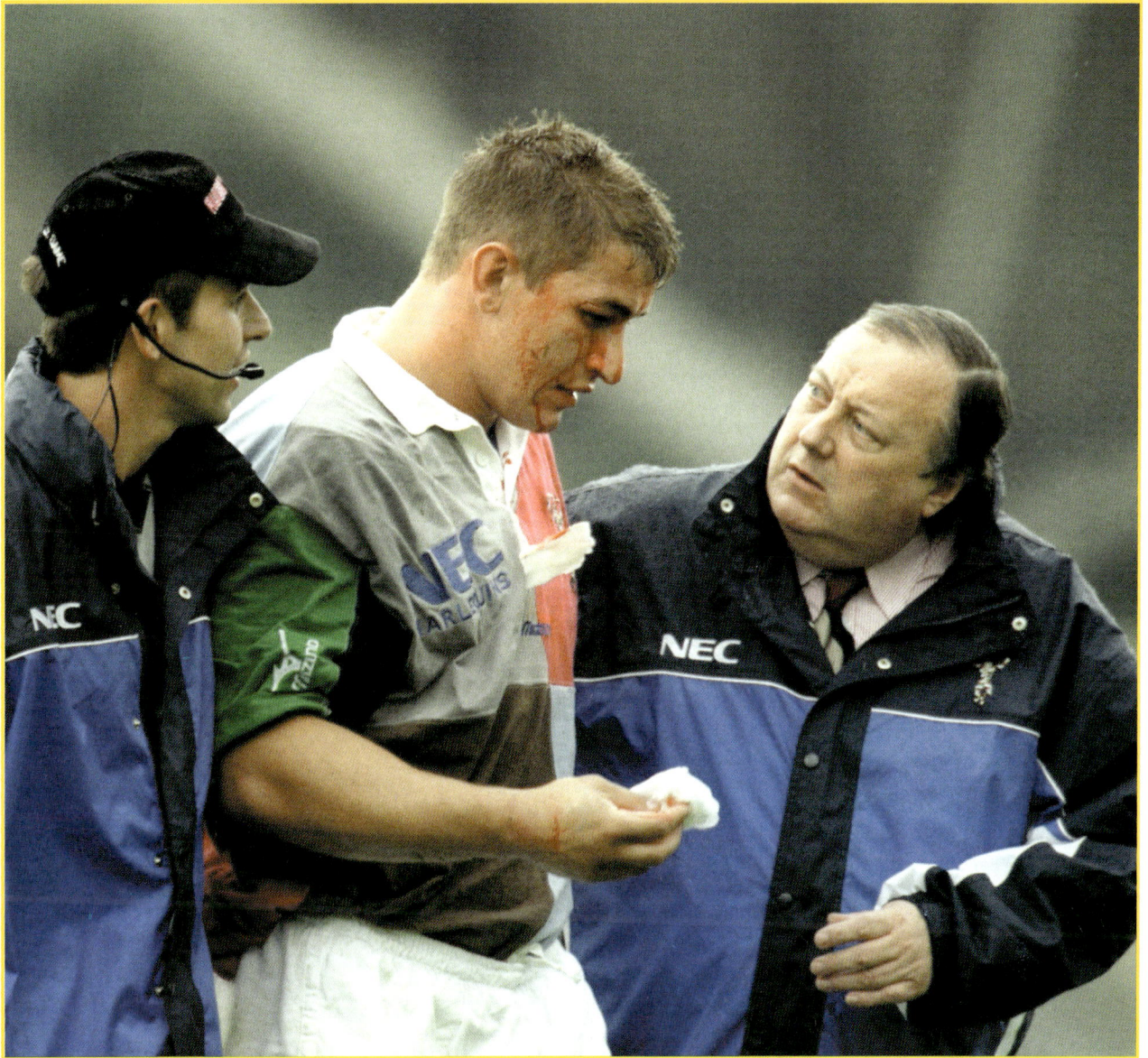

F

22

Health and Safety

In any physical activity there is a risk of being injured. Some activities are more dangerous than others, and sportsmen and women, and spectators, need to assess this risk and take the necessary precautions. However well this is done, injuries and accidents do occur, and it is important to know what to do when this happens.

LEARNING OBJECTIVES

- risk assessment
- preventing injury
- causes of injury
- injury and treatment
- emergency treatment
- health and hygiene

Risk assessment

There are very high risks in some sporting activities; in others such as green bowling they are low. In athletics, javelin and discus, what were once weapons are now thrown in competitions. In rugby there is considerable physical contact, which is part of the game; in cricket and baseball a hard ball is thrown with considerable force. A walk in the hills in good weather in the summer has considerably less risk than the same walk in winter weather. Spectators at events such as cycle racing are at risk of being hit by competitors. People taking part in sport assess the risk and make decisions when and when not to take part. In physical education in schools there are high- and low-risk areas and activities. Throwing events in athletics are high-risk events for other pupils, swimming might be a high risk to oneself depending on ability in the water. Most outdoor and adventurous activities are high risk, but dance could be classed as low risk. Some games have a higher risk than others; gymnastics and trampolining could be high risk depending on the level of the performer.

Preventing injury

PHYSICAL AND MENTAL PREPARATION AND RECOVERY

Warm-up and cool down are essential parts of physical activities. See pages 91–2 for more details.

The level of activity is also an important factor. Playing at the correct level for age or ability can prevent injury. In sports such as boxing and judo there are levels associated with both age and weight, which ensure that contests are fair. In team sports playing in the correct age group is important as this often, but not always, is a factor in size. Taking part within your capabilities is particularly important in outdoor activities, attempting climbs of the right level, canoeing, sailing or surfing in conditions in which you can cope.

PLAYING TO THE RULES

The rules of activities are designed to enable play to take place and to reduce the risk to competitors and spectators. Waiting for an umpire before bowling in cricket and rounders ensures the batsmen and women are ready. In athletics it is important to wait for a signal to jump or throw for the safety of officials and other competitors. Playing to the rules of correct tackling in hockey, soccer and rugby ensures the safety of the person being tackled and the tackler themselves.

CORRECT EQUIPMENT

Most activities with high risk of injury require the competitors to wear the correct equipment. In cricket in schools safety helmets must now be worn by batsmen and women when hard cricket balls are being used. In soccer, players are required to wear shin pads and there are regulations about the length of studs in boots. Wearing of jewellery can be a danger to oneself and others. Earrings, rings and watches should not be worn when taking part in sporting activities, particularly in contact sports. In these sports many players of all ages wear mouthguards. Having the correct clothing and footwear, and tying back long hair are all important preparations for being safe in sporting activities.

In outdoor activities it is essential to have the correct equipment, not just footwear and waterproofs for hill walking and lifejackets for water sports, but also safety and survival equipment.

Personal equipment must also be checked for safety: ski-bindings, cycles, climbing equipment and similar items which can become worn and ineffective.

The playing area itself needs to be checked that it is clear of hazards, perhaps glass on a pitch, or a slippery netball court due to ice. In gymnastics it is usually up to the organisers to check that gym equipment, particularly parallel and asymmetric bars, are firmly attached to the floor

Causes of injury

Injuries can occur through

- accidents
- contact sports
- foul play
- overuse of particular muscles by repeated actions
- poor or damaged equipment.

ACCIDENTS

Most injuries are caused through accidents:

- tripping up in the crowded start of a long-distance race
- slipping because of poor footwear in soccer
- being hit with a hockey ball
- bumping into someone on the same team.

Usually accidents happen because of external factors such as these. Sometimes the player may damage themselves by moving or twisting too quickly – in tennis or squash, the sudden movement to reach a ball might result in a torn Achilles tendon; a twist in soccer could cause damage to the knee.

CONTACT SPORTS

Making contact in certain sports is part of the game:

- in combat sports such as boxing and wrestling, contact is the essential element
- in rugby, contact is an integral part of the game during scrummaging and tackling

Boxing is essentially a contact sport

⬡ in soccer, fair contact can be made by players challenging for the ball, although this does not often happen

⬡ in some invasion games such as basketball and hockey, there is no contact (officially), but it often occurs.

FOUL PLAY

Players can be injured in games when the rules are broken. Many rules are devised to keep players safe from injury, as well as providing a pattern to the game. Tackling around the neck in rugby and lifting the ball near a player in hockey can cause injury to other players; such actions are against the rules of these games.

OVERUSE OF BODY PARTS

Repeating actions in sports can cause damage to muscles, tendons, ligaments and bone. High-level performers need to practise individual skills over and over again, and then repeat them in a match situation. A cricketer may spend many hours in bowling practice; s/he may play most days of the week, and so bowl thousands of balls during a season. Professional players may even have to play when injured, causing further damage to their bodies.

There are different types of contact sports. Name three which involve low-, medium- and high-level contact. Describe what type of contact occurs.

Think of two sports where there is repeated action in a specific part of the body. Name the sport and describe the action. How does this affect a particular part of the body?

A bowler will use repeated actions

EQUIPMENT

Incorrect or ill-fitting equipment may cause injury. Marathon runners need to run considerable distances most days, so running shoes must be suitable for running on hard surfaces and must fit well. Bindings on skis must be at the right tension both to keep the ski attached to the boot and release it on impact to prevent damage to the skier's legs. Equipment may break during use; in pole vaulting this can be extremely dangerous.

Injury and treatment

There are many types of sporting injury, and often these can be treated quickly and effectively on the spot. Fast action can prevent the injury from becoming worse. A common treatment for many soft tissue injuries is the RICE method:

- **R – Rest**; continued use of the damaged muscle will cause even more damage and make the recovery time longer
- **I – Ice** applied will reduce swelling and pain
- **C – Compressing** the area will provide support
- **E – Elevating** the part of the body injured will decrease the circulation, and enable blood and other fluids which cause swelling to be removed from the injured area.

Where injuries look more serious then medical help must be found as quickly as possible. Injuries can occur to the following:

- skin
- muscle
- ligaments
- tendons
- joints
- bones
- head.

SKIN INJURIES

Usually the result of a sliding fall on a rough surface, such as a shale hockey pitch or a hard tennis court, layers of skin are scraped off. This is known as an **abrasion** which may be painful but not serious. Sharper objects catching the skin can tear or puncture and cause more severe bleeding where the wound is deeper, and an artery might be severed. Being 'spiked' in athletics is a common but not serious injury.

When the skin is broken, it is often necessary to have a tetanus injection. Most people have these injections when they are younger, but often need a booster when they are adults.

Treatment

Abrasions and cuts need to be examined to decide how much damage has occurred. In most cases, the wound can be cleaned and dressed. Larger and deeper cuts usually need hospital treatment, where a wound may have to be closed by stitching. If blood is strongly pumping out of a cut, then it is important to stop blood flow and get medical help. To stop serious bleeding, a clean pad needs to be applied firmly and held in place. Extra pads may need to be used over the top in addition. Applying pressure to an artery can prevent further bleeding, but it is important that the blood flow is not restricted too long as permanent damage may occur.

BLISTERS

Repeated action with friction can cause blisters. Often these occur on the feet with poor-fitting shoes, but holding a tennis or badminton racket might cause blisters on the hand. A blister is the body's way of protecting the skin from further damage.

Treatment

Small blisters can often be left, or covered with tape. Larger blisters may have to be punctured to release fluid and enable the skin to rebuild. Blisters which are punctured become more susceptible to infection, and therefore care must be taken to see that they are kept sterile.

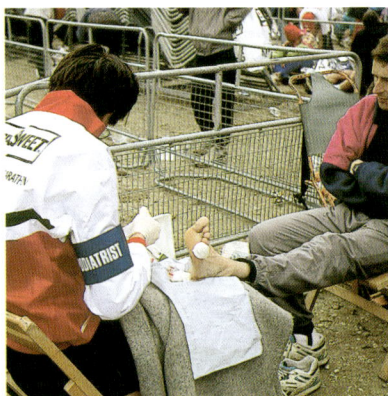
Treating blistered feet

MUSCLE BRUISING

Muscles can be damaged by external forces or by internal stresses. Bruising of muscles is a common injury in contact sports such as rugby and soccer. A hard impact on the surface of the muscle results in a bruise. The blood vessels just below the skin and deeper (depending on the strength of impact) are ruptured (burst). The area may swell and the skin may become discoloured, from the blood being released under its surface. Bruises change from purple to yellow over a period of time.

Treatment

Ice applied to the bruise reduces the swelling and blood flow, and reduces the level of pain.

MUSCLE TEARS AND PULLS

Athletes can often damage muscles internally by applying too much force in moving their own bodies or an external object. In a sprint start, a runner tries to accelerate as quickly as possible to maximum speed. This means considerable internal forces are being applied to the body mainly through the legs. Under this extreme pressure, some of the muscle fibres are torn or ruptured, causing localised pain.

Treatment

Carry out RICE treatment. Damaged muscle repairs itself; depending on the extent of the damage, it could be working near full strength within seven days.

MUSCLE CRAMP

A muscle or group of muscles go into an involuntary spasm. This can happen at any time and last from under a minute to a few hours. Cramp can occur during swimming when the muscles are chilled, or because of a lack of salt and minerals.

Treatment

As the muscles are in a state of tension, they need to be mechanically stretched. Cramp can often occur in the calf muscle, which can be stretched by pulling the foot towards the knee.

Suffering from cramp

STITCH

Cramp can occur in the diaphragm, the sheet of muscle below the chest. The blood supply to the diaphragm is reduced, causing a sharp pain in the abdomen. Increasing the strength of the diaphragm can help prevent cramp occurring. Exercising after meals can cause cramp, as blood is diverted to the digestive system. Delaying exercise for a few hours after a meal is beneficial.

Treatment

Sitting and resting is an effective way of reducing the pain. In more severe cases, gently stretching will help.

LIGAMENTS

The ligaments hold joints together, and excessive force on a joint can result in a sprain. Depending on the severity of the damage, a sprain may be minor or quite serious. Where extreme pressure is put on a joint the ligament may be ruptured, requiring extensive medical treatment. One of the most common injuries in soccer players is to the cruciate ligaments in the knee. Sudden turning during the game can cause these ligaments to be damaged. In some cases, artificial ligaments are fitted inside the knee which allow people to continue participating in sport.

Treatment

RICE treatment can be used for a minor sprain, but in more serious cases medical treatment is needed, as bones may be broken as well.

TENDONS

A tendon attaches a muscle to a bone. Movement takes place when the muscle contracts with force, which is transmitted through a tendon. These forces are powerful: jumping into the air requires a considerable force from the legs to be transmitted to the feet. As with muscles, parts of a tendon may become torn or ruptured. In very extreme cases, the whole tendon might rupture. The most common tendon injury is in the lower leg, at the Achilles tendon. Badminton, tennis and squash players are susceptible to this injury which may occur because of poor warm-up, decreased flexibility or overuse of body part.

Treatment

RICE can be used in less severe cases, and often considerable rest. Where a rupture of the tendon occurs, surgery is required to join the tendon together again.

TENDONITIS

Tendons can become inflamed with constant use, causing tendonitis. The most common is tennis elbow as a result of repeated arm movements. Golfers experience tendonitis in a different part of the elbow.

Treatment

Physiotherapy and stretching exercises can help relieve pain and encourage healing. In extreme cases, cortisone injections may be necessary when tendonitis becomes **chronic**.

JOINTS

During sporting activities a heavy stress can be placed on joints: eg, turning quickly in soccer, dislocating the shoulders on the rings in Olympic gymnastics and throwing javelins. Often the ligaments in the joints and the surrounding tissue can be damaged. Sometimes the internal structure of the joint can be damaged.

Joints (Chapter 1) are designed to move in a particular way. Pressure to move the joint in the wrong direction can cause internal damage.

The cartilage in a joint enables smooth movement. However, cartilage can be torn with excessive and incorrect movement. In soccer, many players suffer damage to the cartilage in the knee because of the twisting and turning of the leg during the game.

Treatment

In severe cases, cartilage may be badly torn, causing the knee joint to be locked. Medical help will be needed. In less severe cases, the sportsperson may be able to walk but ultimately surgery will be required.

DISLOCATION

This occurs at the joints and involves the bones. Extreme pressure on the joint, such as landing awkwardly in a fall, can cause the joint to break apart. One bone is moved from its normal position in the joint. In a ball and socket joint in the shoulder or hip, the ball comes out of the socket. When this occurs, there is often damage to the surrounding tissues, ligaments and tendons. Dislocation of the shoulder joint is common in rugby where there can often be a large impact on the shoulder during tackling.

Treatment

Medical treatment is needed for this injury. Joints are often relocated under anaesthetic at a hospital. Because the ligaments and tendons are stretched during a dislocation, the joint can become much weaker and be prone to dislocation. Surgery may be needed to prevent this from happening in the future.

Humerus

Radius

Ulna

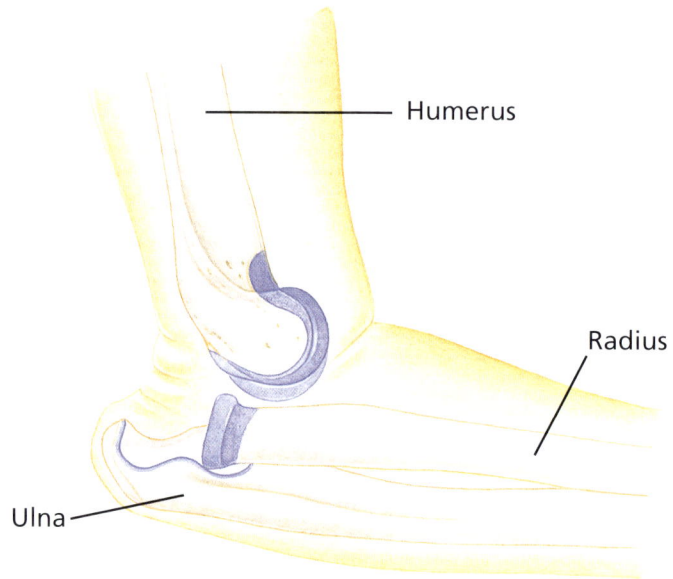

A dislocated joint

Name three different sports where the following bones may be broken:

1 collar bone
2 bones in the arm
3 bones in the leg.

The knee joint can often be damaged in many different sports. Draw a detailed diagram of the joint and indicate where damage could occur. Detail the sport and circumstances in which these knee injuries occur, and what medical procedures might be carried out to treat or repair the damage.

BONES

Because bones are rigid, they can be broken. Direct blows and awkward falls can result in broken bones. Some breaks such as toes and fingers may be inconvenient rather than serious, but breaks to the larger bones of the arms and legs, and to vertebrae, are more serious. There are different types of fracture:

- simple fractures – the bone is broken cleanly and does not pierce the skin
- compound fractures – parts of the broken bone come through the surface of the skin
- greenstick fractures – this often occurs in young children where the bones are soft and do not break cleanly.

Bones heal themselves over time.

Treatment

If a fracture is suspected, the person should be kept warm and comfortable until medical help arrives.

HEAD INJURIES

These can range from cuts and bruises to more serious skull fractures. The person may suffer from **concussion**, or in some cases be unconscious. Concussion occurs when the brain is shaken around in the cranium as the result of a blow, accidentally in some sports, or deliberately as in boxing. The person may become dizzy, feel sick or become confused, staring and with loss of memory; s/he may also lose consciousness.

Bone   Blood clot

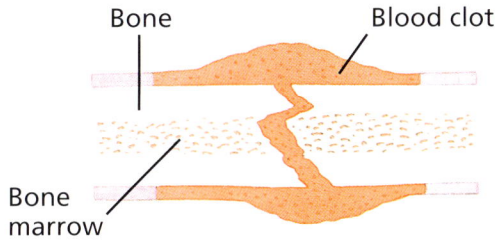

After a bone injury, blood oozes out of broken blood vessels, and forms a clot around the jagged edge of bone.

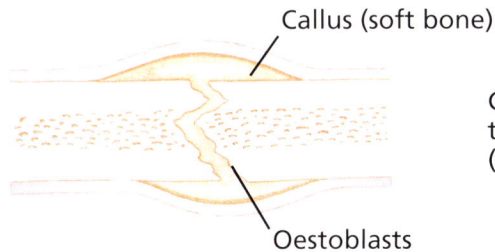

Bone marrow

Callus (soft bone)

Connective tissue forms a callus (soft bone) to hold broken ends together. Oestoblasts (special cells) strengthen the bone ends.

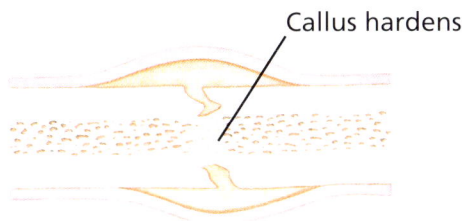

Oestoblasts

Callus hardens

After some time, the callus hardens, bridging the gap between bone ends.

Bone healing

Treatment

Medical help must be sought for all head injuries. Signs of concussion may not occur immediately, but some time later. Place the person in the recovery position and keep under medical observation for a further 24 hours.

OTHER CONDITIONS

In sports, certain conditions can occur which are not classified as injuries but still need to be attended to:

- hyperventilation
- shock
- hypothermia
- hyperthermia and heat stroke
- exhaustion
- asthma attack.

HYPERVENTILATION

After heavy exercise (such as a cross-country run) or when a person is very anxious, hyperventilation can occur. Breathing is speeded up as a response to the high level of acid in the blood, exhaling large amounts of CO_2 from the lungs.

Treatment

To reduce the rate of breathing, the person must be calmed down. Breathing into a paper bag helps the breathing rate to be restored to its normal level (because as you breathe in air which has already been expired, it is made up of carbon dioxide, not oxygen, and this calms the breathing down).

SHOCK

Being involved in an accident, even if not injured, can bring about shock in a person. They may look pale, have a rapid pulse or shallow breathing, yawn excessively or seem at the point of collapse.

Treatment

Remove the cause of shock if possible. Keep the person warm, lie them down with their head low, check breathing and pulse, and send for medical help.

HYPOTHERMIA

The body temperature falls below 35°C (normally 37°C). This can be brought on by a person being outside in cold and windy conditions, or in very cold water. Although this may often occur during outward bound activities, pupils can suffer from hypothermia on the playing fields if weather conditions are poor. The person may shiver, look pale and slightly blue, with slow shallow breathing and a weak pulse.

Treatment

Move the person out of the adverse conditions and insulate them with extra clothing, including the head. Give hot drinks if they are conscious. Call for medical help under extreme conditions.

HYPERTHERMIA

The temperature of the body is raised above 39°C. There are a number of factors which cause this rise in temperature; excessive physical exercise in hot and sunny conditions has an effect on how quickly the body can remove heat generated by muscular activity.

Sweating occurs naturally to remove the body's heat. When this becomes excessive, too much salt and water is lost with sweating, giving rise to **heat exhaustion**. As a result, **dehydration** occurs. In extreme temperatures **heat stroke** occurs, when the body loses the ability to sweat, and the body temperature rises rapidly.

Hypothermia can often occur in these conditions, but walkers are usually well prepared

Treatment

The person should be moved to a cool and breezy place. In the case of heat exhaustion, a weak solution of salt and water needs to be given. Dehydration should be treated with water to restore body fluids. In instances of heat stroke, the body temperature needs to be reduced by covering with cold wet sheets.

EXHAUSTION

Many sportspeople make considerable physical effort in their sport. Either during or when they have finished their event, they can become exhausted and be at the point of collapse.

Treatment

The person should be moved to a cool, quiet place, where the body can be allowed to recover naturally to normal levels of heart rate and breathing.

ASTHMA ATTACK

Many people taking part in sport suffer from asthma. Most of them can control their asthma with a range of drugs. However, adverse conditions, exercise and forgetting to take the correct amount of drug are all factors which could contribute to an asthmatic attack. Breathing becomes difficult; there is a shortness of breath and wheezing.

Treatment

The activity should be stopped and an inhaler used where possible. In severe cases, the person should be put in the recovery position and medical help sent for.

Emergency treatment

Although it is always best to get medical help immediately when an injury is serious, this is sometimes not possible. The injured person may be on a sports field, in a forest or on a mountain, and it may be hours before qualified medical help arrives. Being able to give treatment in such an emergency may well save the person's life. One system is to follow the DRABC routine on the next page.

MOUTH-TO-MOUTH RESUSCITATION

If breathing is stopped, the brain is starved of oxygen. It is therefore essential that every attempt should be made to restart breathing, and

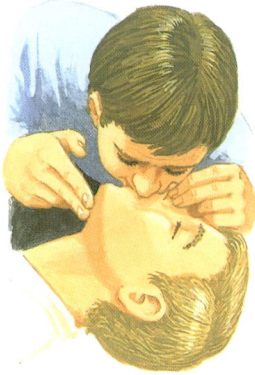

Mouth-to-mouth resuscitation

With a partner, practise the steps for mouth-to-mouth resuscitation, but do not actually breathe into each other's mouths. It is dangerous to do this to someone who is able to breathe.

the most effective method is mouth-to-mouth resuscitation. This is where air is blown into the person's lungs.

It is not easy, and there are a number of steps which must be followed to make it effective. While the person is being resuscitated, someone should urgently get medical help through the emergency services.

It is essential to restart the heart and lungs as soon as possible, otherwise brain damage could occur.

Steps to take

①   Check that the airway is clear and open. It is possible for debris to be lodged in the back of the throat, and this must be pulled out. The head should be tilted back so that the airway through the trachea to the lungs is clear.
②   The person's nose should be pinched shut, using the index finger and thumb of your right hand. Take a large breath, and breathe into the person's lungs from mouth to mouth. This should make their chest rise as the lungs are filled with air.
③   Take your mouth away. The person will exhale due to the lungs contracting, and at the same time you take a further breath.
④   The action should be repeated at the rate of one breath every six seconds. This should be continued until the person breathes normally, or medical help arrives.
⑤   Check the pulse at the end of each minute and if there is no pulse, coordinate mouth-to-mouth resuscitation with cardiac massage.

CARDIAC MASSAGE

If there is no pulse then the heart has stopped beating. This is known as **cardiac arrest**, and the heart must be restarted. External pressure applied to the chest above the heart is a method of restarting the heart.

Steps to take

①   The person is laid on their back.
②   The point to apply pressure is found about 1 inch above the lowest rib where it joins the sternum (breast bone).
③   Press the heel of the hand at this point, with your other hand on top.
④   Lean over and apply weight to depress the sternum by about 4/5 cm.
⑤   Apply pressure at the rate of 80 times/minute.
⑥   Check the pulse every minute. When it returns, massage can be stopped.

Danger

↓

* Assess the danger to the casualty and to yourself
* Danger could include fast running water, electricity, gas, fire, fumes, damaged machinery or buildings
* Do not endanger yourself
* Send for help
* Approach the casualty and clear the area of other people if necessary

↓

Response

↓

* Check if the casualty is conscious, ask name and gently shake
* If conscious find out where they are injured and use first aid if possible
* Continue to talk to casualty to reassure them
* If unconscious then move to **resuscitation**

↓

Airway

↓

* Loosen tight clothing
* Put casualty in recovery position
* Clear mouth of debris including gum shield, dentures
* Lie casualty on back, raise chin and tilt head back fully to open airway
* Check for any further obstructions

↓

Breathing

↓

* Check: is casualty breathing? Is the chest rising and falling? Are there breathing sounds?
* If breathing, put into recovery position
* If not breathing commence mouth to mouth resuscitation (MMR)

↓

Circulation

↓

* Check for pulse at carotid artery in neck
* If pulse is present continue MMR if necessary
* If no pulse then start cardiac massage and continue MMR

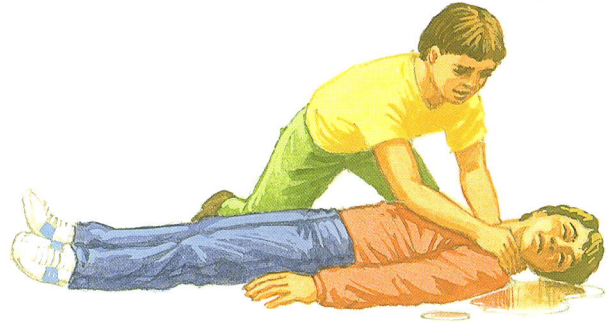

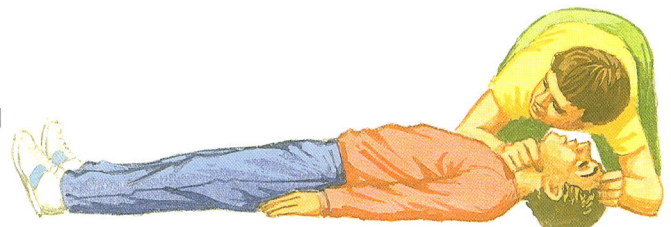

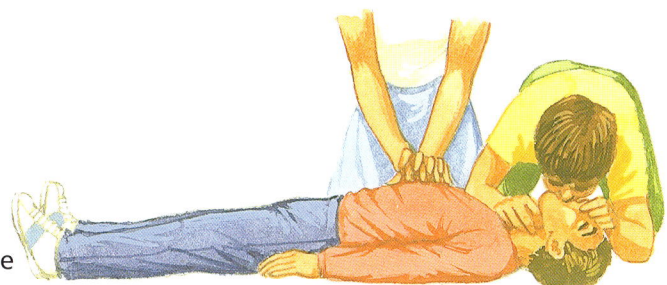

Immediate first aid – the DRABC routine

With a partner practise the steps for heart massage, but do *not* apply pressure. It is very dangerous to do this to someone whose heart is beating normally. Put your partner in the recovery position (see next page).

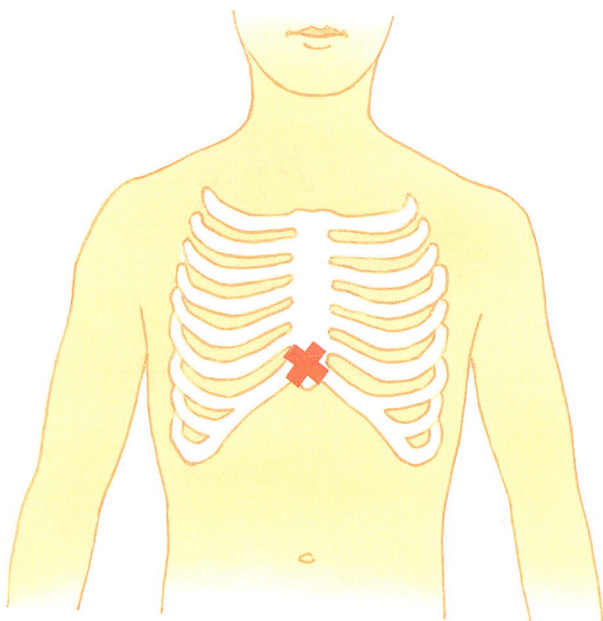

Cardiac massage procedure

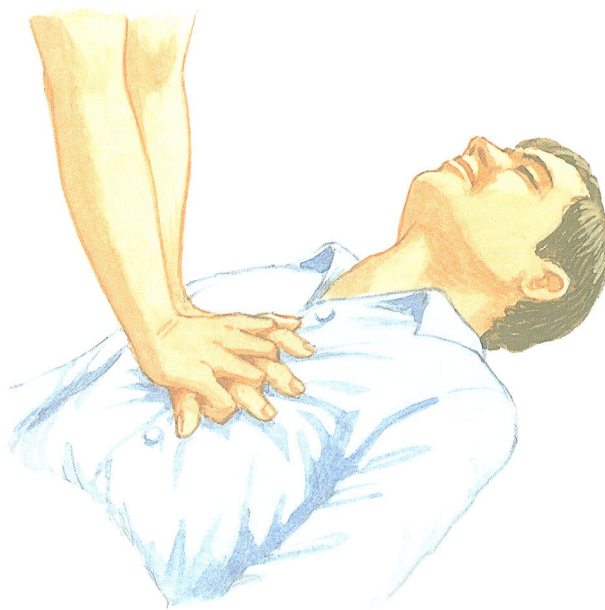

RECOVERY POSITION

A person who is unconscious or suffering an asthmatic attack should be put in the recovery position. This enables easier breathing, and stops vomit from blocking the airways of an unconscious person.

The recovery position

Health and hygiene

Hygiene is an important part of maintaining good health. There are a number of factors which are important to everyone, and particularly to people who take part in sport:

- keeping the body clean
- keeping clothes and equipment clean
- taking care in food preparation and the diet
- preventing disease
- having sufficient rest, relaxation and recreation.

KEEPING THE BODY CLEAN

Skin

Keeping the skin clean is not only an important way of resisting infection but also in preventing body odour. During sporting activity the body sweats, and in many activities such as hockey and rugby, dirt from the fields covers body and clothing. Showering and washing with soap and water is a simple and effective way of cleaning the body.

Deodorants used after washing give the body a nicer smell, but do not normally cover the smell of sweat. Anti-perspirants prevent perspiration, but as perspiration is the way the body remains cool it is not sensible to use anti-perspirants before sport or exercise.

Hair

Hair should be washed regularly. Long hair should be tied back so as not to restrict vision, or be pulled (accidentally or deliberately) during play.

Nails

Nails should be kept clean and short. Long nails can accidentally scratch other people and also easily be damaged if caught in clothing.

Teeth

Teeth should be brushed regularly after eating. Dental care is important, and regular check ups will ensure that teeth and gums are kept healthy. Sugary food and drink causes decay and should be taken in moderation. It is often dangerous to play sport wearing a plate or false teeth, in case it is swallowed. In many sports teeth are now protected with gum shields.

Feet

Feet must be kept healthy. Correctly fitting footwear for sport and activity is essential. Corns, bunions and blisters are caused by poor

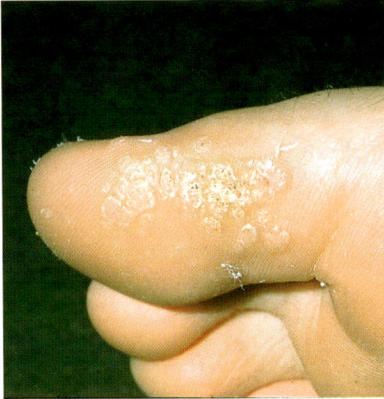

quality and ill-fitting shoes. Special sports shoes are used in activities such as javelin throwing and triple jumping, where there are high forces exerted on the feet.

There are two common infections of the feet:

① **athlete's foot** is a fungal growth between the toes. Usually occurring next to the little toes, this fungal growth develops in warm moist places. The skin cracks, peels and becomes itchy. It is easily spread to other people by contact from floors and shared towels

② **verrucas** are warts on the feet. They spread easily through a virus, are difficult to get rid of and are often painful.

Keeping feet clean and drying them well helps to minimise the chance of these diseases. If either of these are contracted, treatment is necessary.

A verruca

CLOTHING AND EQUIPMENT

Clothing should be washed regularly as it absorbs body sweat and bacteria from the skin. Underclothes and socks are of particular importance. A complete change of clothing for sport is best, and materials such as cotton are preferable to nylon. In outdoor activities such as walking and climbing, waterproof clothing which is breathable is essential for comfort.

Equipment should be cleaned and maintained:

- sports shoes should be regularly cleaned, particularly the insoles
- walking and climbing boots should be cleaned and waterproofed where necessary
- soccer and rugby boots should be cleaned and studs checked for wear to prevent injury to yourself and others.

Check on the quality of a range of trainers by seeing what special features are described on the box.

How should you maintain this sports equipment?

FOOD PREPARATION

Good food preparation is essential for health and therefore participation in sport. Food should be prepared on clean surfaces, and care should be taken not to use the same chopping boards and knives for raw meat and vegetables. Meat should be cooked at the correct temperature, and for a sufficient length of time; eg chicken can contain **salmonella**, but correct cooking destroys this.

PREVENTING DISEASE

Although disease can be prevented by good hygiene, some diseases are transmitted through the air and by contact. Usually a series of injections or vaccinations are given in early childhood to prevent some diseases being caught. An important protection for people who play sports and often get cuts and grazes is an antitetanus injection. This bacteria is often found in soil and can be picked up as a result of breaking the skin when falling on a playing field.

REST, RELAXATION AND RECREATION

Everyone needs rest and sleep. Most people require seven to nine hours sleep each night to allow the body to recover both physically and mentally. Before sports competitions, sleep may be difficult because of stress. Rest is often taken between training and competitions, and is needed where high levels of physical and mental abilities are used. Recreation is important to reduce stress and help with mental health.

Can you find out what injections and immunisations you have had, and when they were done?

Questions on health and safety

1 Which of the following activities is not a high risk one?
   a   skiing
   b   rugby
   c   green bowling
   d   swimming.

2 A sprain is damage to a
   a   bone
   b   muscle
   c   tendon
   d   ligament.

3 Name two items of sports equipment which are designed for protection.

4 Name four ways in which injury can occur in sport.

5 Give two instances of equipment failure which might cause injury to a sportsperson.

6 What is meant by RICE treatment?

7 Badminton and squash players can often suffer injury to the lower leg. Describe the type of injury.

8 What is tendonitis and why does it occur?

9 What is hyperventilation and how might it be treated easily?

10 Name two common infections of the foot.

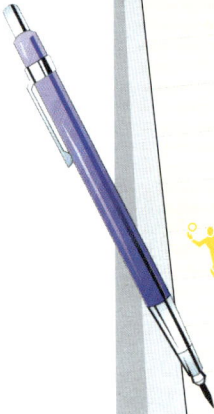

Exam-style questions

1 Name five ways in which injuries occur in sport. (5 marks)

2 a Extreme heat and cold can affect an athlete. Give the technical term used for each of these, and describe how an athlete might be affected and the treatment necessary. (6 marks)

 b What is muscle cramp? (2 marks)

 c What is the effect of exercise soon after having a large meal? (2 marks)

3 Describe and give the cause and location of

 a a sprain (3 marks)

 b tendonitis (3 marks)

 c a simple fracture (3 marks)

 d a dislocation (3 marks)

 e a bruise. (3 marks)

4 Some sports have high risk of injury, others have low risk.

 a Name a low-risk sport. (1 mark)

 b Name a high-risk sport. (1 mark)

 c For the high-risk sport you have named.

  i Describe two specific risks. (2 marks)

  ii Describe how to minimise these risks. (2 marks)

 d Describe the procedures in mouth-to-mouth resuscitation. (9 marks)

Quality of written communication. (5 marks)

23

Practical Activities

All GCSE physical education courses are consistent with the National Curriculum 2000. They are designed to enable progression from Key Stage 3, building on the knowledge, skills and understanding acquired during this Key Stage, and previous Key Stages 1 and 2.

LEARNING OBJECTIVES

- acquiring and developing skills
- selecting and applying skills, tactics and compositional ideas
- evaluating and improving performance
- knowledge and understanding of fitness and health

Acquiring and developing skills

In all practical activities new skills are learned, and with practice are improved, often over a period of time. Sometimes learning the skills of a new sport happens very quickly, but as skills become harder, learning slows down. Learners can often reach a plateau, from which they find it hard to make significant improvements in their performances. A good example of this is in trampolining, where performers can practise skills such as tuck jumps, seat drops and similar basic skills with consistently high quality, but find difficulty in higher level skills such as somersaults. As sports skills are developed performers are able to show higher levels of control and consistency in their performances.

- Control – in many activities performers have to show control, particularly in striking and net games. In tennis, higher level players show good control by playing the ball with the correct speed, spin and flight into a chosen area of their opponent's court.
- Consistency – this is a distinguishing feature of high level performers in all sports. In cricket, bowlers need to be able to bowl a good length consistently. In golf the better player has a consistent swing and striking of the ball.

Selecting and applying skills

There are a number of ways in which a performer makes use of their learned skills in competitive situations

STRATEGY AND TACTICS

- Strategy – before taking part in an activity performers often plan what they will do in a particular event. Sometimes the planning may involve the organisation of training so that the performer is at their peak for a particular event. Strategic planning can be used in individual events such as athletics, or in team events. A tennis player might analyse the strengths and weaknesses of their opponent before the match and plan their game accordingly. In team games coaches may have video of opponents' previous games and plan how to organise their teams.
- Tactics – strategies may be thinking, whereas tactics can be considered as the action required. Tactics in individual events such as long-distance running might be to take a lead early in the race, or stay just behind the front runner until the final lap. Higher level performers, particularly in individual games, change their tactics during the game, in response to their opponent's actions. In team games planned substitutions, or those necessary because of injury, often require the coach to make changes in tactics, or team formation.
- Team formation – teams usually have some form of organisation and pattern of play. Even when there are only two players on a team, such as badminton, tennis and table tennis, various formations are used when serving and receiving serve; when attacking and defending.

In invasion games such as basketball, hockey, netball, soccer and rugby there are many specialist positions and formations. Goalkeepers, sweepers, defenders, midfield, wing backs, point guards and strikers are some of the technical terms used for player's positions.

In badminton or tennis doubles, experiment with different formations when serving and receiving service.

Find the usual team formation of two Premier League football teams. Do either of these teams use the same formation for both home and away matches, or do they change it? Give reasons why they might change their formation.

In your favourite game, list four special playing positions and say what roles the positions have.

Team formation at the start

List three set plays in an invasion game. When might they occur?

The way that players work together, and methods of moving the ball from defence to attack, is determined by team formation. Defending in invasion games can be done by either marking another player (man to man), marking an area of the pitch or court (zone), or a combination of these.

For games on large areas, such as hockey, rugby and soccer, full man to man marking is rarely used, although sometimes a very skilled striker may be marked man to man. Where areas of play are smaller, man to man might be more effective, but often in games such as basketball, the type of defending can often be changed during the game depending on the effectiveness of the defence. In many games there are set plays, where particular routines are practised before the game. Line outs in rugby, free kicks in soccer, centre pass in netball and corners in hockey are examples of these.

RULES

All sports and games have rules. The governing bodies of sport, national and international have devised rules and regulations, which are sometimes called laws. There may be local rules because of the conditions. In small village halls the rules for badminton might be adapted to take into account size of the court and the height of the roof.

Rules are important as they:

- give structure to the sport
- determine the playing area, number of players
- ensure the safety of the competitors.

CONVENTIONS

These are unwritten rules and concern expected behaviour in a game. Sometimes this is referred to as **etiquette** and is about sporting behaviour and attitude. There are many examples of this in all levels of sport. Playing individual and team games without a referee or umpire requires the competitors to call 'ball out' or foul play themselves. In more organised situations examples of etiquette exist in professional soccer, by returning the ball to a team after injury to a player, applauding a team off the pitch, or perhaps shaking hands with opponents after a game of tennis or badminton.

Evaluating and improving performance

ANALYSIS OF ACTIVITIES

In order to improve performances in sporting activities, it is necessary to evaluate strengths and weaknesses. Once this analysis has been done then performances can be improved through specific practices, to eliminate faults and build on performers' strengths. One's role in a sporting activity has an important bearing on analysis of performance and consequent improvement of that performance. Different roles are.

Performer

When taking part in a sporting activity it is often difficult for a person to analyse why they are losing both in individual and team activities. The person may well be aware of the strengths of the opposition, but may lack both the knowledge and skill to overcome this. Self-assessment is often difficult, but in some activities it is easier. A long-jumper can see the distance they have jumped, but this may not give the athlete any indication of how they might improve. In games involving shooting at a goal with a goal keeper, does the scorer know that he or she has performed a good shot, or is the goalkeeper weak? Where there are fewer scoring opportunities, perhaps in netball, how does the centre know how she or he has played? A gymnast may perform a complex floor routine but may be unaware of the quality of their movement. It is often difficult for a performer to make an accurate evaluation of their own performance. It is easier to watch someone else's performance and make an analysis, than assess yourself.

Teacher

The role of the teacher is important in introducing children and students to new sporting activities. In lessons there are often few opportunities for a teacher to spend a lot of time with an individual student because of the length of the lesson and the number of students in the class. However, physical education teachers often have high level skills and interests in specific sports. They are able to use these skills when running school clubs and school teams.

Sports coordinator

The first sports coordinators were appointed in September 2000 with key roles to include:

- establishing and developing physical education and sport support programmes for local primary schools
- developing links between schools and local sports clubs
- establishing and supporting after-school and inter-school sports programmes
- developing leadership and coaching programmes for senior students.

These people are funded through Sport England Lottery funding.

Coach

A coach is often a specialist in a sporting activity. He or she may have been a player before becoming a coach, or a parent who has worked with their child from a young age and learned about a particular sport and eventually taken coaching examinations and awards. Coaches are supported by the National Coaching Foundation, who provide the appropriate training. However, most large governing bodies have national and regional coaches, who work with clubs, schools and also in centres of excellence.

Coaches are very knowledgeable about their sports, and often work with high level performers. At international level some sportsmen and women have their own coach, who travels with them to competitions. This is often the case with sports such as athletics and tennis. Professional teams have coaches, who might work with the whole team or with specific areas of the team. In rugby union there may be a coach who has responsibility for forward play, whilst another may work specifically with a goal kicker. In cricket there may be an overall coach in charge of a team, but other coaches who have responsibility for batting and bowling. Not all coaching is in physical preparation; some high level performers have coaches who help them to prepare mentally for an important competition.

Trainer

Larger sporting clubs may have a trainer who is responsible for the physical preparation of players. They will have a good knowledge of the sport or game and will be able to work closely with a performer so that he or she is in the best physical condition for an event. Sometimes the coach may also be the trainer, particularly in individual events such as athletics.

An official

All sports need officials when competition and rewards are high. A friendly recreational game of tennis or badminton does not need an umpire, as players control the game themselves. However in games where there are high rewards, or where physical contact is part of the game, or where there are complex rules, it is essential to have an **official**.

Officials have different names in different sports, but their job is to ensure that the game or sport takes place according to the correct rules. In some sports such as tennis or athletics there are many officials who each have special responsibilities, but there is usually a chief official who is in charge of part or the whole event. An umpire sitting high above the court takes charge of a tennis game, and he is assisted by officials who take charge of lines or the net. If there is a dispute between players then sometimes the umpire has to refer this to the referee who is in charge of the tournament.

In most invasion games there is a need for more than one official because of the number of players and the size of the pitch. Increasing use is being made of an additional official who is able to use video evidence, and this is common to rugby league and union, and cricket, but not yet in other games. In events such as athletics, swimming and cycling where differences in distances between competitors is marginal, photographic evidence is essential. Officials need to have a good knowledge of the rules of the sport and be able to control games fairly and without bias. In sports such as golf, officials need to be able to interpret complex rules about hazards on the course fairly and when players may or may not move their ball without penalty.

Many officials are unpaid, and may often be older players who want to put something back into their sport. However, in many games officials receive far less money than the competitors.

Basketball needs special officials to referee, score and keep time

Using an official scoresheet, can you keep score for your school or college in a competitive game?

Knowledge and understanding of fitness and health

Performers and coaches need to have a good knowledge about the relationships between exercise and sporting activity and how this relates to a performer's physical, social and mental health. There is more detailed information about health related fitness in Chapter 6 and risk assessment in sport in Chapter 22.

Glossary

abrasion   the scraping off of layers of skin due to a sliding fall on a rough surface

adrenaline   a hormone which produces fast responses in other body systems

aerobic   with oxygen

aerobic capacity   the ability to sustain prolonged activity

aesthetic quality   looking good while performing, eg in dance, diving

agonist   prime mover

alveoli   small air sacs in the lungs

anaerobic   without oxygen

anaerobic activities   fast, powerful action

angina   a sharp pain warning that the heart is not getting sufficient oxygen

antagonistic muscle action   two or more muscles working opposite each other

antibodies   proteins which help fight against germs and infections

apartheid   policy of racial segregation in South Africa

ATP   adenosine triphosphate – chemical energy provider

atria   the upper chambers of the heart

balance   maintaining equilibrium when still or moving

blood pooling   lactic acid remaining in the muscles longer, causing pain

BMR   basic metabolic rate

bolus   pellet into which food is formed, in the mouth

BSAD   British Sports Association for the Disabled

carbohydrates   a compound of carbon, hydrogen and oxygen, forming an important part of the structure of plant material and of human food

cardiac arrest   the heart stops beating

cardiac output   amount of blood pumped out of the heart from one ventricle per minute

cardiorespiratory endurance   the systems of pumping blood and delivering oxygen

cartilage   a tough layer of tissue found at the end of bones in joints

CCT   compulsory competitive tendering

cholesterol   a sterol found in the blood; too much can lead to clogging of the arteries

chronic   term to describe severe illness lasting a long time

closed skills   skills where the performer has nearly complete control of his/her performance

colon   the large intestine

complex skills   skills which involve more movement and finer control

concentric contraction   the muscle shortens

concussion   a head injury which could cause unconsciousness

dehydration   loss of water from the body due to excess sweating

dendrites   pick up and receive messages or impulses

diazepam   type of tranquilliser

doping   using drugs to alter performance

duodenum   the first of the small intestine

dynamic balance   balance while moving

eccentric contraction   the muscle lengthens

ectomorph   thin shape, little body fat

endomorph   pear shaped and fat body type

epimysium   strong connective tissue enclosing the muscle fibres

ethanol   chemical found in alcohol

etiquette   unofficial rules, not enforced but usually followed, eg shaking hands with opponent

expiration   breathing out

exteroceptors nerves which pick up information outside the body, eg eyes, ears, nose

extroverts people who are outgoing, lively and sociable

faeces waste material, excreted from the body

fartlek a Swedish word meaning speed play; a method of training

fast twitch muscle fibres which respond powerfully and quickly during anaerobic work

flexibility the range of movements of limbs at the joints

governing bodies the organisations which control sport

glycogen the form in which glucose is stored

haemoglobin a chemical compound of iron and protein

hippodrome a stadium in which chariot racing was held

homeostasis the way the body temperature is regulated

hormones chemicals produced by endocrine glands

inspiration breathing in

introverts people who are quiet, shy and retiring

invasion games where two sides share the same court or pitch, eg soccer, netball, basketball

jejunum part of the small intestine where digestive juices are released

JSLA Junior Sports Leaders Award

lactic acid colourless acid produced in the body

merchandising the spending of money by fans on items connected to their team, eg strips, scarves

mesomorph wedge shaped and muscular

minute volume amount of air breathed in a minute

modified game rules, formation etc may be altered to enable specific skills to be used

motor skills physical skills

myofibrils small, thread-like structures which make up muscle fibre

myosin microscopic protein molecule

NCF National Coaching Foundation

neurons the basic cells of the nervous system

nucleus the main cell body

oesophagus canal through which food travels from mouth to stomach

oestrogen a hormone produced by women

officials people who control the game and ensure that the rules are obeyed

open skills skills which are affected by the environment or others taking part

orienteering navigating courses through forests and mountains using map-reading skills

ossification turning to bone

oxygen debt a state where the body has used more oxygen than it can supply

oxy-haemoglobin iron and protein combined with oxygen in the lungs

parasympathetic nerve decreases the activity level of an organ

pentathlon five-event competition in athletics

peristalsis muscular movement which forces the food down to the stomach

phagocytes white cells which produce germ-destroying enzymes

pleural membrane the lining of the thoracic cavity

polyunsaturates fatty acids found in fish oils and products made from vegetable seeds

protease enzyme which helps break down proteins

ptyalin enzyme which starts the process of turning starch into sugar

public limited companies (plc) shareholders invest money in the club and expect to share in the profits

racism   discrimination against people because of their race

reaction time   the time taken when reacting to a stimulus

residual volume   amount of air left in the lungs, as they cannot be completely emptied

respiratory rate   number of breaths taken per minute

role model   an individual who sets standards of behaviour and achievement for young people

saliva   a digestive juice found in the mouth

saturates   fats found in animal products

set plays   where particular routines are practised

skill   the ability to perform a correct technique with maximum efficiency and certainty

slow twitch   muscle fibres which work for long periods during aerobic exercise

somatotyping   classifying people into types

sphincter muscles   rings of muscle which keep the food in the stomach

Sportsmark   an award to schools for good physical education

static balance   a position is held without movement

STM   short term memory

strategies   game plans

striated muscle   (striped or voluntary muscle) skeletal muscle

sympathetic nerve   increases the activity level of an organ

synapse   a junction between the dendrite of one neuron and the axon of another

synchronised swimming   swimming in formation to music

synergists   muscles working together, enabling other muscles to work

synovial fluid   fluid surrounding a synovial joint

synovial joint   a joint which has a large range of mobility

technique   movements needed for a sport or activity

tendons   fibrous tissues which join a muscle to a bone

testosterone   a hormone produced by men

thyroxine   a hormone important in the control of energy production

tidal volume   amount of air taken in or out with each breath

transfer   the effect an old skill has on the learning and performance of a new one

urethra   duct through which urine is discharged from the bladder

ventricles   the lower chambers of the heart

verrucae   elevations of the skin (warts)

villi   minute projections on the inside walls of the small intestine

vital capacity   the maximum amount of air that can be breathed out in one breath

$\dot{V}O_2$ max   the maximum amount of oxygen the body can transport and use in the muscles

whole-part-whole   a method of teaching or coaching

WSF   Women's Sports Foundation

YST   Youth Sports Trust

Index